American Football
The Records

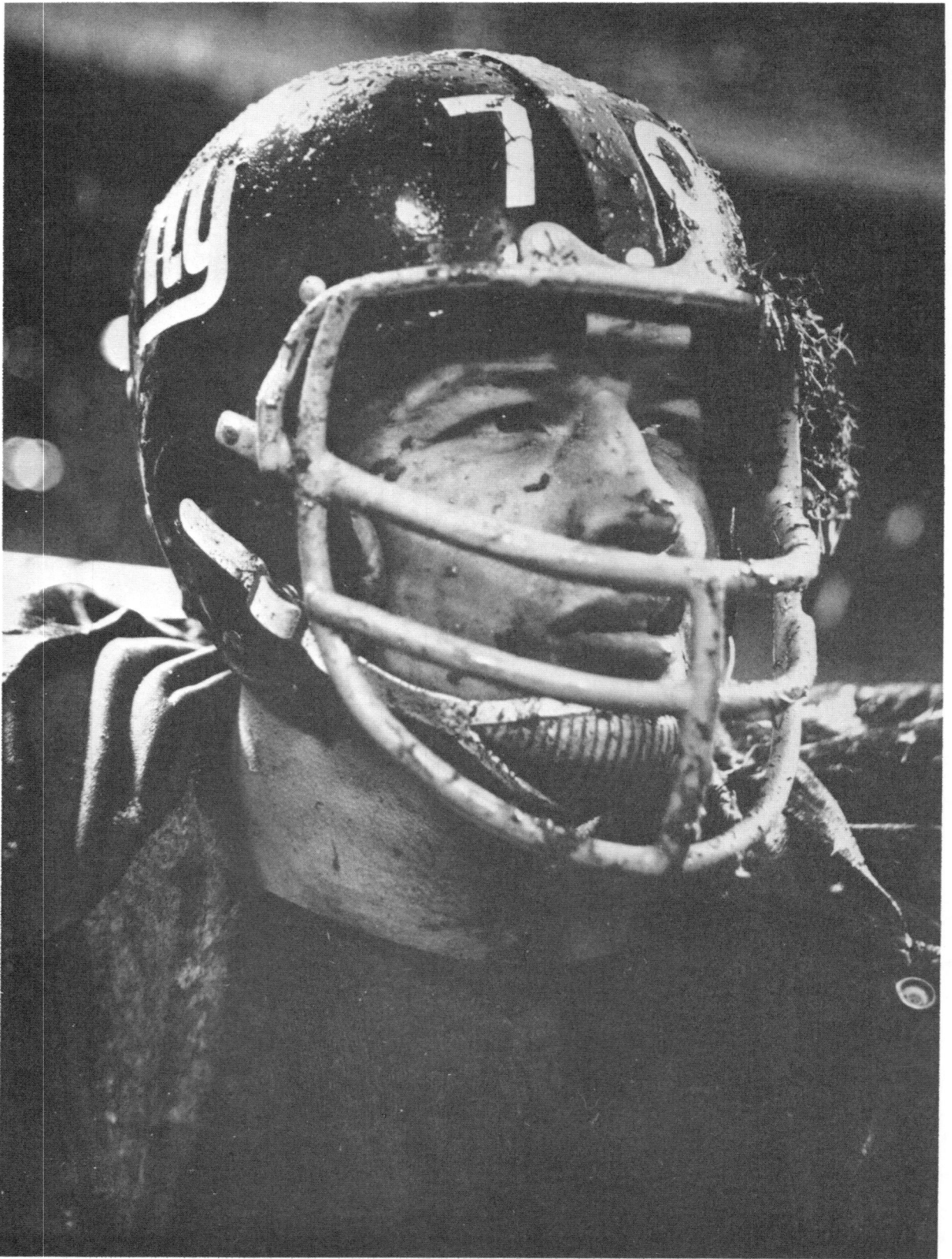

'Rugby is a beastly game played by Gentlemen. Soccer is a Gentleman's game played by beasts, and football is a beastly game played by beasts'. Anon.

American Football

The Records

Miles Aiken & Peter Rowe

GUINNESS BOOKS

EDITOR: Beatrice Frei
DESIGN AND LAYOUT: Michael Morey

© Miles Aiken
and Guinness Superlatives Ltd, 1985
All colour illustrations by Allsport

Published in Great Britain by Guinness Superlatives Ltd,
2 Cecil Court, London Road, Enfield, Middlesex

Phototypeset in Palatino and Univers
by Input Typesetting Ltd., London, SW19 8DR

Printed and bound in Great Britain by
Hazell Watson & Viney Ltd., Member of the BPCC Group,
Aylesbury, Buckinghamshire.

British Library Cataloguing in Publication Data

Aiken, Miles
    Guinness American football: the records.
    1. Football—History
    I. Title
    796.332'09   GV950

    ISBN 0–85112–445–3 Pbk

Contents

We the authors sincerely hope that the reader enjoys the book as much as we enjoyed writing it.

Naturally, whenever tight deadlines are to be met, numerous "thank yous" are in order. Thank you to Mike Niblock, *Touchdown Magazine*, UK, *Gridiron UK*, The National Collegiate Athletic Association, The Canadian Football League, Mr. Bruce Carnahan, all sports information officers of the professional and college teams, and the office staff of Guinness Books.

CHAPTER ONE

History of American Football

The roots of American football, as all football games, can be traced back over 2000 years to 206 BC when the Chinese were known to have played a game called Tsu Chu. Although nothing like the ball games of today, Tsu Chu and its ancient equivalents, Harpastun from Rome, Episkylos from Greece, Kemari from Japan and the 11th century Norman game of La Soule were evidence of our ancestors' basic inclination to kick around an object for pleasure and perhaps sport.

During the next few centuries various types of unorganized games involving a ball that was kicked were developed and played all over Europe. There is evidence that a rudimentary game of football was played in the American colonies as early as 1700.

Naturally when the European settlers flooded into the New World in the 19th century they brought their ball games with them.

As in England, at the turn of the century the sport had a school tie image and the north eastern colleges of Princeton, Rutgers, Columbia, Yale and Harvard all played a game more akin to soccer than rugby.

The very first rules giving a semblance of order to the game were set down in 1867 and were known as the 'Princeton Rules'. Two years later on 6 November 1869 the first intercollegiate game took place in New Brunswick, New Jersey where Rutgers defeated Princeton 6–4. In a return match the following week Princeton won 8–0. Whilst the majority were playing a largely kicking game Harvard had decided to allow a certain amount of running with the ball as in rugby. No one else in the north eastern

Ivy League was interested in playing this style of game which is known to historians as 'The Boston Game', so a Canadian rugby team from McGill University in Montreal was invited to travel the 250 miles south to play in Cambridge, Massachussets.

Unfortunately, four members of the McGill team fell ill before leaving and only 11 of the 15 playing members made the journey across the border on 15 May 1874. As a result the game went ahead with 11 instead of the normal 15 men per side. Had those four men been fit, American football might well be played with 15 men today.

The game was an enormous success and slowly the other schools in the Ivy League took up the same style of play. On 13 November 1875 Yale met Harvard in the first game between two American Universities under the new rules. A year later, on 23 November 1876 at Springfield, Massachusetts the five Ivy League colleges met and drew up the rules for the first intercollegiate league based largely on the rugby code and proclaiming itself the Intercollegiate Football Association.

The rugby style of heeling back the ball was played until 1880 when Walter Camp, the father of the modern game, introduced the scrimmage which allowed for more orderly possession of the ball. It was also Camp who brought the word 'gridiron' to the lips of the nation when in 1882 he marked chalk stripes every five yards across the field, parallel to the goal line.

Another founding father of the game was a gentleman with the unlikely name of Amos Alonzo Stagg. Stagg was a great innovator, designing and introducing the huddle in

1894, as well as the center snap, man-in-motion, reverses, diagrammed playbooks, backfield shifts, tackling dummies and various other refinements such as numbers on uniforms. Stagg was not only an inventor, he was also a brilliant coach. His 314 career victories was a record until Paul 'Bear' Bryant of Alabama University surpassed it in 1981.

Whilst Camp and Stagg were steadily moving the game away from its European roots other States in the nation were taken an interest in what they were doing.

In 1887 the Virginia Military Institute at Lexington introduced the game to the southern States. But it wasn't until 1898 that the north eastern stranglehold was broken when Chicago University's halfback Clarence Herschberger was elected to an All-American team.

During this same period professional football had begun to take root. In 1892 Pudge Heffelfinger was paid the princely sum of $500 to play for the Allegheny Athletic Association. Travelling with three companions, who only received their return rail fare, Heffelfinger proved himself to be worth every penny of his fee. He won the game in one fell swoop by jarring the ball loose from an opposing half back with a crunching tackle, then returning it and running across the goal line for the only score of the game in a 6–0 victory.

By 1895 professionalism had made rapid progress. During these stone age days of football, however, players received on average only $10 apiece for their efforts. Most of the teams in the new 'Professional' leagues operated in the steel belts of Pennsylvania and Ohio and were sponsored by local steel companies. Of necessity games were played on Sundays and local busi-

The University of Chicago, first team to use the T-formation. (*Touchdown Magazine*).

nessmen found them worth backing in order to give their workers some recreation over the weekends. The better players in the teams were more often than not college men 'moonlighting' in the pro ranks, and the majority of colleges played their games on Saturdays. The game continued to grow and the very first night game was played in 1902 with makeshift floodlights set along the sidelines of a field in Elmira, New York.

Many of the teams were operated by baseball clubs who found it a useful occupation for their players during the winter months. One such player was the legendary turn-of-the-century pitcher Rube Waddell. Waddell however could not use his potent throwing arm since the forward pass was not to be legalized until 1906.

There were at this time no leagues, schedules, or league offices, and there was no Commissioner and very little money. As a

First Rules
The first rules were set down in 1867 and were known as the Princeton Rules.

result colourful episodes of ingenuity and rivalry were commonplace. Among the teams that flourished briefly during this period were the Duquesne Country and Athletic Club, the Homestead Library and Athletic Club and a team from Beloit, Wisconsin whose players had the nickname of the 'Fairies' because they were sponsored by the Fairbanks-Morse Company.

Since there was no overall governing body eligibility rules were only conspicuous by their absence. Players would move from club to club and many used more than six aliases in one season. In 1902 Philadelphia Athletics claimed to be National Champions. A Pittsburg team made the same claim and guaranteed the Phillies $3000 if they would settle the matter with a game. When the Athletics showed up at the football round no money was forthcoming, so coach Connie Mack loaded his players into hansom cabs and headed back to the railway station. Fortunately for the fans who had turned up for the game a prosperous looking gentleman stopped them on the way. Mack explained to this gentleman that without the guarantee there would be no game, so the gentleman, who turned out to be William Lovey, the President of Carnegie Steel, saved the situation by signing one of his own personal

First Game between two American Universities
Rutgers met Princeton on 6 November 1869.

First League
The five Ivy League colleges of Yale, Princeton, Harvard, Rutgers and Columbia formed the first football conference, the Intercollegiate Football Association, on 23 November 1876, at a meeting in Springfield, Massachusetts.

cheques, whereupon the Athletics returned to win the game.

In 1905 the first major scandal in the history of professional football occurred. It centred on the fever-pitched inter-city rivalry of the Canton Bulldogs and the Massillon Tigers, both of the State of Ohio. In 1904 the Tigers, so called because of their striped jerseys, met the Bulldogs for the local championship.

The Tigers are to this day the only team in recorded history to be owned by a city editor, and it was he who thoughtfully provided a 10-ounce school ball for the game

The Massillon Tigers who were involved in the first gridiron betting scandal. (*Touchdown Magazine*).

9

instead of the regulation 16-ounce one used by the professionals.

Needless to say Massillon won the game 10–0. Blondy Wallace, the Canton coach protested vigorously, but to no avail, so he retaliated by recruiting the whole Massillon starting backfield for the next season. At this suffering its setbacks, college football was developing. Variations of the game were sprouting up in the far west and a version known as 'Kickball' was played as early as 1880. In this game a touchdown was worth only five points instead of the usual six.

The Universities of Stanford and Cali-

The Canton Bulldogs, considered to be the world's professional champions of 1922–23. (*Touchdown Magazine*).

stage in football's history there were no draft rules or restrictions against raiding other teams, so his action was perfectly legal.

The next year with his new backfield Wallace beat Massillon 10–5 in the first game of a two game series. The Bulldogs were naturally made favourites for the second, to be held in Massillon. They lost 12–6 and the day after the game the city editor of the *Massillon Independence* broke football's first betting scandal story. It is still the only substantiated story of a fix in pro football history.

Wallace, so the story went, had first tried to bribe several players in the Massillon team, with no success. So he then persuaded one of his own players to throw the game. The player was allegedly chased out of Canton by irate citizens, but Wallace protested his innocence and even sued the newspaper. He later dropped the lawsuit when he was shown proof of his guilt. The scandal almost stopped the growth of professional football for good. It was ten years before it began to thrive again.

Whilst the professional circuit was

fornia met in 1892 in what was the inaugural west coast collegiate game. Three years later the Western Athletic Conference (later to be called the Big Ten), was formed in the mid-west. On 1 January 1902, 8000 fans turned out to watch the very first bowl game—the Rose Bowl. The game was the brainchild of the organizing committee of the Pasadena flower pageant, who the previous year had decided that this exciting new ball game would add to the attraction of their annual festival.

In the first game Michigan travelled the 2000 miles west to defeat Stanford 49–0. For mainly financial reasons the game was then suspended for the next 14 years. College football was on the increase, but like its professional counterpart, the college game was heading for trouble. It experienced nothing as scandalous but there was still a serious enough problem to warrant the intervention of the President himself.

During the 1890s and early 1900s the game had become increasingly violent. In 1892 Harvard introduced their famous flying wedge, one of the most spectacular yet highly dangerous moves ever seen in football. It was employed at a kick-off when a great wedge of the team's biggest and meanest players would form a 'V' shape and thunder towards the opposition's goal protecting the ball-carrier and inflicting as much damage as possible. This violent style of play continued unchecked until it reached a peak in 1905 when 159 players were seriously injured and 18 actually died.

It was at this point that President Theodore Roosevelt stepped in and demanded to see the organizers of the Ivy League at the White House in Washington. He declared that if the league didn't make efforts to clean the game up he would ban it.

So it was that in 1906 the National Collegiate Athletic Association was set up to revise the rules, with the aim of ensuring safer, more open football without losing any of the game's character. Slugging, hurdling, mass turtleback attacking, and interlocked interference (which included the flying wedge) were all banned. The most important change, which broke the last major link with British rugby, was the introduction of the forward pass.

By 1912 American football had achieved its present form, which makes it quite distinct from any other kind of football.

The Indian Jim Thorpe was the biggest draw in the professional league until Red Grange came along in 1925, playing for Cleveland, Toledo, New York Giants as well as Canton during his ten-year career (see 'Gridiron Giants').

Whilst the Indian was helping to re-launch the professional game another Indian settlement in Indiana was giving the college game an enormous lift. The former Indian fur trading post of South Bend had on its doorstep a university founded by French priests in the late 1800s. Notre Dame first came to prominence in 1913 when it unexpectedly beat the all conquering Army team at West Point. After the First World War the university became part of football's folklore as its team was unbeaten for five seasons. A former chemistry graduate of Scandinavian parentage made the 'Fighting Irish' of Notre Dame into one of the country's most feared yet respected teams. Knute Rockne took over the reins at Notre Dame in 1918 and during his twelve-year tenure the Irish won 105 games and lost only 12. In 1920 running back

George Gipp set a record of 4833 yards on 2341 carries, before being struck down with pneumonia in his senior year. On his deathbed he reportedly told coach Rockne, 'When things look bad, tell the boys to go in there and win one for the Gipper', an historic battle cry that was to make the foot-

---

First Professional Player
Pudge Heffelfinger was paid $500 to play for the Allegheny Athletic Association in 1892

First Floodlit Game
Makeshift floodlights were set along the sidelines for a game in Elmira, New York in 1902.

First West Coast Collegiate Game
Stanford met California in 1892 in what was the first inter-collegiate game on the west coast of the USA.

First Marked Pitch
Walter Camp marked chalk stripes across a field, parallel to the goal lines in 1882—the word 'Gridiron' was born.

---

ball-crazy Irish the team of the thirties and forties. Rockne waited eight years to relay this parting request. On 10 November 1928, after losing two of its first four games, an injury riddled Notre Dame team travelled to Yankee stadium to face the unbeaten Army. At halftime, Rockne made a passionate speech to his team relaying Gipp's request of 1920. He concluded, 'This is the day and you are the team'. Notre Dame went out and beat Army 12–6 in what many to this day describe as the finest demonstration of inspired football. Rockne was killed in a plane crash in 1931, but he still ranks as one of the best college coaches ever with his 105–12–5 record.

Three months before Gipp's untimely death a meeting took place at the Ralph E. Hay Motor Company at 122–134 McKinley Avenue North in Canton, Ohio. It was a hot Friday evening in September and the men who had gathered to discuss the formation of a stable professional football league sat on the running boards of the eight cars in the showroom in their shirtsleeves. Twelve teams were represented: Akron, Canton, Cleveland,

Dayton, and Massillon, all from Ohio; Chicago, Decatur and Rock Island from Illinois; Hammond and Muncie from Indiana; Rochester from New York, and Wisconsin.

About the only thing the organizers decided on that day was the name—The American Professional Football Association. The fee to own a team (known as a franchise) was set at $100 and Jim Thorpe, who was representing Canton at the meeting, was elected as its first President. Thorpe is said to have known a great deal more about baseball than about running a football league and his tenure only lasted one year. In 1921 the new association was reorganized.

In that first season there was no official schedule of matches and the whole affair was rather haphazard, three teams eventually claiming the National Championship. The first season recorded officially in the NFL record books was that of 1921 when George Halas's Chicago Staleys won the championship. There was again no official schedule, teams played each other on a catch-as-catch-can basis from week to week. Halas's club compiled a 10–1–1 record and despite protests from Buffalo that many of the Staleys' games were against non-league opposition they became the first and only champions of the APFA. In 1922 under the guidance of Halas the league changed its name to the National Football League, which it has been ever since.

Despite the new name and some reorganization the league continued to operate on a rather casual basis for the first few years. There was no constitution until 1926 when Joe Carr, a former sports writer who had taken over the presidency from Thorpe, drew up the first rules.

The rules, were few and insubstantial. The number of players per team was established at 16, and the total payroll per game per team was limited to $1200 which was to include the coach or manager if either of them played. A team decimated by injury could, in an emergency borrow a player or two from its opponents but had to pay his wages for that game.

The prize for winning the championship was a small engraved gold football for each player, which was not to cost more than $10 and the team was given a pennant. The one significant clause in the rules that had much to do with the subsequent success of professional football concerned the recruitment of players.

College 'moonlighting' was ended by a ruling that stated that no player who had performed on a Saturday could turn out in the same city for a professional team, or any other for that matter, on a Sunday. More importantly, the signing of a college player before his class had graduated was forbidden. An infringement of this rule carried a $1000 fine, no mean amount in those days, and could even result in a loss of franchise.

This ruling was put in to counteract the storm of protest that had surrounded the signing of Red Grange by the Chicago Bears immediately after his final game for Illinois University in November 1925. The publicity that followed the signing of Grange was enormous and brought the professional ranks into the public eye at a national level for the first time.

Grange received a staggering $50 000 for playing 7 games in 11 days. Some thought it madness to pay such an amount but George Halas and the Chicago Bears were more than happy to hand it over. The Bears played before 36 000 fans in Chicago, 35 000 in Philadelphia and more than 65 000 in New York. Such huge crowds for professional football were unheard in the mid 1920s.

After he had finished his first tour with the Bears Grange departed on a hastily arranged trip to the South and West for which he earned another $75 000. No player, or owner, had ever earned $100 000 in a season before, and none would for many years to come. Grange, however, was a fine football player, and partly because of him professional football at last began to gain respectability on the sports pages of the national press.

The prosperity Grange brought to the Bears, though, was short-lived. Halas spent much of his time on street corners hawking tickets for the games and getting his share from an away gate was an even more hazardous affair. The Chicago boss would collect his percentage at half-time in a brown paper bag. He then assigned the task of escaping with the money to George Trafton, an All-American center from Notre Dame who he later described as 'meaner than a junkyard dog'. By the time the game was coming to an end most of the home fans were baying for Trafton's blood, since one of his favourite ploys was the use of the 'Notre Dame drop kick', a particularly nasty knee to a sensitive part of an opponent's anatomy. Halas would take Trafton out of the game with a minute or two left, give him the brown paper bag and despatch him to the railway station at top speed. Such was 'Mean' Trafton's reputation that no one dared interrupt his flight and he was always at the station with the paper bag waiting for the arrival of his team mates.

Professional football struggled through the 1920s. Twenty-two teams started the 1926 season, but by July 1927 ten of them had folded. In the late 1920s most of the franchises held by small towns died. The Depression that followed also had a damaging effect on pro football's status. Towns such as Providence Rhode Island, Dayton Ohio, Hammond and Muncie of Indiana all lost teams. Providence actually won the championship in 1928, hit the Depression in 1929 and went out of business in 1932. Only eight teams survived the Depression and only six of them are still in business today: Chicago Bears, Chicago-St Louis Cardinals, the Detroit Lions (formerly the Portsmouth Spartans), the Green Bay Packers, the New York Giants and the Philadelphia Eagles, who began life as the Frankford Yellowjackets. It wasn't until 1932, that a new breed of owner enabled professional football to expand again.

College football, like its professional brother, was in difficulties but was beginning to attract growing crowds and during this period witnessed one of the greatest college games of all time.

In 1922 Notre Dame's genius of a coach Knute Rockne had devised a line-up of backfield players that for four seasons ran rampant through their opponents' defenses. The Four Horsemen (see College Nick-

names, Chapter 3) were quarterback Harry Stuhldreher, left halfback Jim Crowley, right halfback Don Miller and fullback Elmer Layden.In four seasons together Notre Dame only lost twice, both times to Nebraska. Their nickname, now one of the most famous in American sports history, arose after the Irish had defeated the Army 13–7 on 18 October, 1924. A reporter wrote, 'Outlined against a blue-grey sky the four horsemen rode again'. A legend was born.

The four played their last game for the Indiana college in the 1925 Rosebowl against Pop Warner's mighty Stanford. A crowd of 53 000 packed the Pasadena stadium that day in sweltering temperatures to witness a show of pure magic as Notre Dame's Elmer Layden scored three touchdowns to win the game 27–10. Included in Layden's tally was an interception of an Ernie Nevers pass when he ran 78 yards to give the Irish a 13–3 half-time lead. Stuhldreher broke an ankle early on in the game yet still returned to lead Rockne's team to a perfect 10–0 season and the national championship.

The Rosebowl game was reinstated in 1916 after a 14-year absence when Washington State beat Brown University 14–0. Many cities tried to copy the success of the Rose but mainly for financial reasons none succeeded and it wasn't until 1935 that a serious contender in Miami, the Orange Bowl, was founded. Over the years the Rosebowl had not been without its lighter moments. In the 1928 California's center Roy Riegels picked up a fumble and ran 68 yards the wrong way with the ball before being tackled by his own quarterback!

Notre Dame, along with Stanford and Pittsburgh continued to dominate college

(Cont. p. 16)

First Football Betting Scandal
This occurred during a match between the Canton Bulldogs and the Massillon Tigers in 1905.

First Tackling Dummy
Amos Alonzo Stagg is widely credited with this first. It is said that he sewed together an old gymnasium mat to make the first dummy whilst coach at Yale in 1889.

Jim Thorpe

It is fitting that the man regarded by most as America's greatest athlete was a 'true' American in every sense of the word. Jim Thorpe was born in Prague, Oklahoma in 1883, and was a descendant of the Sac and Fox Indian tribes. In his prime as an athlete he was 6ft 1in in height, weighed 185lbs, and excelled at almost every sport he played.

Described by many as the most complete football player ever, he began his football career at Carlisle University, where he helped his team to win the then mythical collegiate championship. The man whose Indian name of Wa-Tho-Huck meant 'Bright Path' certainly trail-blazed a path in the athletics department at Carlisle, playing not only football but baseball and lacrosse as well. He also excelled in track and field events, and was chosen to represent the USA at the Stockholm Olympics in 1912.

Not surprisingly he won gold medals for both the pentathlon and the decathlon. According to many sources, when he was congratulated by King Gustav V of Sweden with the words, 'You sir, are the greatest athlete in the world', he replied, 'Thanks, King!'

But the glory of his success was short-lived, for when the ruling Olympic committee discovered that Thorpe had played professional baseball the previous year they stripped him of his awards, and he had to return his medals. Nowadays this seems a rather harsh decision, since athletes in modern-day Olympics are professional in all but name, but at the turn of the century rules were strictly enforced.

The crime for which Jim Thorpe was so harshly treated was in fact for accepting $2 a game playing minor league baseball. After many years in which repeated requests were made, however, the medals were eventually returned to his family in 1982, and perhaps the accolade was restored to this great man in the 1984 Los Angeles Olympics when his great granddaughter carried the Olympic torch into the arena at the opening ceremony.

After being thus insulted, Thorpe did turn professional and played baseball for a year before joining the Canton Bulldogs in 1915. The signing of Thorpe was a great draw apart from anything else. Crowds flocked to games to see this elusive runner with the enormous power and strength in action. As a fullback he was almost unstoppable, and wore shoulder pads that many thought were made from sheet iron. They were in fact made from cured sole leather. George Halas was to comment years later that, 'when he hit you it was like being hit by a piece of four-by-four'.

Jim Thorpe was not only a powerful runner, he could also kick a football. It was said that on a good day with the wind in the right direction he could kick a ball all of 50 yards, and often scored drop goals with deadly accuracy from this distance.

Because of his fame football at last began to drag itself out of the doldrums and became both popular and respectable again.

In 1920 when the American Professional Football Association was formed in a garage in Canton, Ohio, Thorpe was naturally proposed as the new league's first president. Thorpe was still playing baseball at the time, and had in fact played a game with Akron on the day of the meeting. Jim Thorpe was a great player, but unfortunately he was not a good organizer, and his tenure only lasted a year, by which time the league had changed its name to the National Football League.

Despite being then nearly forty years of

The great Jim Thorpe during his happy days playing gridiron. (*Touchdown Magazine*).

age, Thorpe continued his playing career first at Canton and later with the Cleveland Indians, Oorang Indians, Rock Island Independants, New York Giants and finally with the Chicago Cardinals.

It was while he was still playing for Canton, in 1920 that rumours began to circulate about his gambling and the fixing of games. He was never actually accused of any misdemeanours, but neither was he beyond suspicion. One story, typical of the kind surrounding legendary figures of Thorpe's stature, was that after being injured in a game between Canton and Massilon, which ended in a 0–0 draw, he feigned further injury and let it be known that he would not be playing in the re-match. Through a third party he apparently managed to get good odds on a Canton victory.

Canton then won the game 23–0 and Thorpe scored all the points in what many described as one of the best games of his career.

But gambling and alcohol were beginning to take their toll and he retired from football in 1928 at the age of 46. An unhappy and broken man, he drifted from job to job, earning a few dollars wherever he could, and even appearing as a film extra in some early day Hollywood movies.

In 1950, he was voted the best athlete of the half century, but even this honour could not prevent his death at the age of 61 in 1953. Most legends begin after a person's death, and Jim Thorpe was no exception to this rule.

Bert Bell, first commisioner of the NFL. (*Touchdown Magazine*).

football until the early 1930s. But the untimely death of Rockne in 1931 created a vacuum at South Bend that was not to be filled until after the Second World War.

In 1932 two men entered the world of professional football and within a year their names were already imprinted in the pages of the game's history. George Preston Marshall was awarded a franchise for Boston on 9 July 1932. Bert Bell became a part-owner of the Philadelphia Eagles in 1933.

A year after joining the league Marshall suggested that it should be split into two divisions and that the two divisional champions should play for the World Title. In order to produce a believable championship for both the press and the public he insisted that each team should play the same number of games against the same opponents, an arrangement which, until then, had not been thought of.

At the spring 1935 owners' meeting, Bell, prompted by Marshall, made radical new proposals for a draft system. Until then it had been a dog-eat-dog affair with only a few of the top teams attracting the best of the graduating collegians. Bell's idea was simple: the last team in the league would get the first pick, and so on until the champions got the last selection in each round. The draft worked and some twenty years later Bell could say with justification, 'On any given Sunday, any team in this league can defeat any other'.

Coincidentally, the first draft in 1936 saw Bell's Philadelphia Eagles gain the first pick, as they had finished at/ the bottom of the league the previous season. The first player picked was Chicago University's tailback, Jay Berwanger. Berwanger could have become one of the greatest backs in professional football history, but because he wanted $1000 per game no team in the league could afford him, not even the rich Green Bay Packers or the Chicago Bears. So the very first draft pick in football history disappeared into oblivion.

In 1937 George Preston Marshall moved his Boston Redskins to Washington. Overnight the game of football took on a new perspective. Marshall introduced the first marching band and even had a team battle song specially written for the band to play. At half-time in all of his games he would have the band marching up and down the field and his showmanship gave football the broad appeal it has today.

The 1930s marked the coming of age of the National Football League. In 1934 the first Chicago All-Star Game took place between the Chicago Bears and an all-star college team. The collegians held the Bears to a 0–0 draw and the game marked a truce between the two factions. Until then many

First Uniform
The first full uniform was worn by Leonidas P. Smock, who turned out for Princeton in 1887 in a jersey on which was the letter P in orange, a canvas jacket and black knee breeches and socks.

First Uniform Numbers
Numbers were first sewn on to jerseys to help identify players in 1908. The University of Pittsburgh was the pioneer of this new idea. The game in question was against Washington and Jefferson and the numberless Washington and Jefferson team won 14–0.

college administrators had openly declared war on the fledgling professional league. Now, with the inauguration of the all-star event, the colleges had more or less given the NFL the recognition it badly needed. The league had thus achieved respectability and at last established itself as a major element in American sport.

Despite the draft system the New York Giants and the Chicago Bears continued to dominate the league. The Bears were fuelled by a fullback from Minnesota who was to become a living legend. Bronko Nagurski stood 6ft 2ins tall and weighed in at 230lbs – this being an extraordinary size for the 1930s. Nagurski played for the Bears from 1930 to 1937 and during that time was credited with 4031 yards in 872 carries, averaging a remarkable 4.6 yards per carry. Bronko Nagurski could also pass and completed 38 of 80 passes during his career. His reputation was awesome, so much so that the owner of the Detroit franchise once offered him $10 000 to retire early

Nagurski did retire in 1937 to concentrate on wrestling and farming back in his native Minnesota, but in 1943, when many of the top players were away fighting in the Second World War, he was persuaded to return to help the Bears to win the divisional title. In the championship game that year he scored a touchdown as Chicago defeated Washington 41–21.

In 1936 the only championship game to be played on a neutral field before the advent of the Superbowls was staged at the New York Polo Grounds, when the Green Bay

Bronko Nagurski. (*Touchdown Magazine*).

Packers met the Boston Redskins. The reason for the neutrality of the location was that Boston owner George Preston Marshall had become displeased with the lack of support afforded to his team, and in a final act of defiance to the city moved the game to New York. The Packers, with end Don Hutson dominant in their passing offense, won the game 21–6, but the remarkable thing about the game was that nearly 30 000 fans turned out in a neutral city to watch it. This gave a strong indication that professional football had at last arrived.

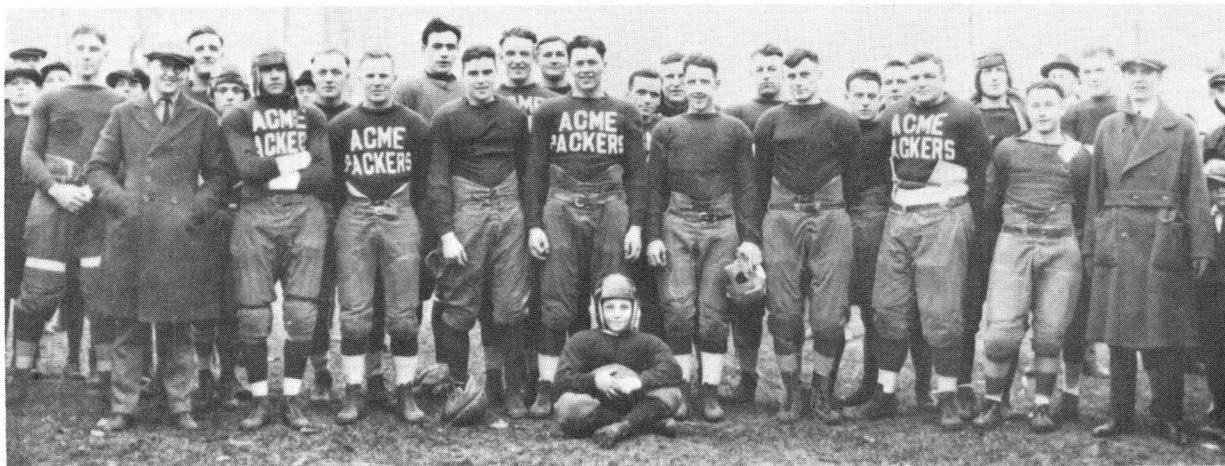

The Acme Packers, soon to be known as the Green Bay Packers. Note the player whose broken nose is being held in place by tape. (*Touchdown Magazine*).

First Radio Broadcast

A game between Texas University and Texas A & M was broadcast in November 1920. An experimental affair, the game attracted only a limited local audience.

First National Broadcast

Two years after the very first radio broadcast of a game, the first nationalized airing of a game took place in 1922 at Stagg Field, Chicago when the Princeton Tigers took on the Chicago University Maroons.

The 1940s began with what many experts reckoned to be one of the most influential games in the history of football: the championship final between the Washington Redskins and the Chicago Bears. The Bears completely swamped the Redskins to win the title 73–0. This became known as the game that changed the face of football.

The Chicago Bears used an updated version of the T-formation conceived by assistant coach Clark Shaughnessy, an eccentric genius who had previously coached at the Universities of Chicago and Stanford.

Before the advent of the T most teams had used a variety of formations, notably the single and double wing, the Notre Dame Box and the Punt.

The Chicago T-formation included a man-in-motion, and they had gone through the regular season with an 8–3 record. Before the championship game with the Redskins, who had won the Eastern division, the Washington coach Ray Flaherty devised a defense to stop the Bears' offensive moves. But George Halas and Shaughnessy came up with a simple counter measure that caught the overshifting defense unawares.

Before the game ended 10 Bears had scored 11 touchdowns and the T-formation had captured the imagination of the football world.

The T-formation also had its effect on the college game. Shaughnessy had been head coach at the University of Stanford, and in 1940, after only one season he had taken the Indians through the regular season unbeaten, ending the year as the nation's second best team with a Rosebowl victory.

The war years also saw the emergence in college football of the military academies. The Army team of the mid 1940s, led superbly by Glen 'Mr Outside' Davis and Felix 'Mr Inside' Blanchard, became as legendary in college circles as Halas's Bears had become in the pro ranks. In one season Army averaged a record high of 56 points per game.

In 1946 a new professional league was born. The All-America Football Conference started life as a second rate league but within two years it had established itself as a serious contender for the NFL's crown. At various times there were franchises in Los Angeles, San Francisco, Cleveland, Buffalo, Baltimore, Chicago, New York and Miami, but only the Cleveland Browns, the San Franciso 49ers and the Buffalo Bills were successful.

After four years in which Cleveland had won each of the AAFC championships, the NFL announced a merger between the two football leagues. Only three teams – Cleveland, San Francisco and Baltimore – entered the enlarged National American Football League. However, its new name lasted only three months and it soon became known again as the NFL.

The most successful of the new teams from the AAFC had been Cleveland. In 1946 the NFL champions, the Cleveland Rams, had been given permission to move to Los Angeles, as the Rams, while the new Cleveland Browns, trained by one of the greatest coaches in pro football history, Paul Brown, moved in to continue their success albeit in the rival league.

In 1950 the first championship game of the two merged leagues threw up one of football's greatest contests: the Cleveland Browns against the Los Angeles Rams. The game was eventually won by a Lou Groza field goal with only 28 seconds left as the Browns, in their first season of NFL play, won 30–28. The strict disciplinarian tactics of Brown worked wonders at his namesake club and throughout the 1950s Cleveland was one of the dominant forces in the NFL.

The club beaten in that 1950 final game, the Los Angeles Rams, was also about to make an impact on the league. Clark Shaughnessy's pioneering tactics that had

Elroy Hirsch.

a fearsome outfit. Leading the attack were quarterbacks Bob Waterfield and Norm Van Brocklin; Shaughnessy's air-orientated game with its variety of passing combinations to Hirsch, Tom Fears and Vitamin T. Smith broke almost every record in the book.

In the 1951 championship game an almost identical team met Cleveland in a replay of the 1950 game and this time reversed the result, winning 24–17.

Such was the ferocity of the Rams' offense that in one particular game against New York, Los Angeles gained a record breaking 735 yards, Van Brocklin throwing for 554 yards (still a record in the NFL today).

The 1950s saw the emergence of a new force that was to help football establish itself as the national game—television. Over a period of eight years or so television had built up a healthy interest in the game and the televising of one particular game in 1958 caused that interest quite literally to explode. The championship between the Baltimore Colts and the New York Giants was so dramatic that it changed the football-loving American's perspective of the game. The hero of the day was Johnny Unitas, the Baltimore quarterback. Unitas had recovered from an injury to lead the Colts from behind to one of the most famous overtime victories ever. With barely two minutes left on the clock he engineered the drive that secured Baltimore's equalizing field goal and then proceeded to march the Colts downfield in 14 plays to win the game with a delicate

(Cont. p. 22)

helped Chicago to the title in 1940 were now being used to change the face of football on the west coast.

In 1949, the Rams acquired Elroy Hirsch. Hirsch had only just recovered from a fractured skull that had ended his career with the Chicago Rockets, and Shaughnessy was reluctant to place his new back in the backfield where relentless tackling might cause another injury. So the genius of a coach took Hirsch out of the backfield and flanked him wide, outside the end. The new offense was so explosive that Elroy 'Crazylegs' Hirsch never returned to the backfield and the pro-set as it was called became the new offensive formation for practically every team in the league.

The Rams' team of the early 1950s was

First Televised Game
The year 1939 saw firsts for both the NFL and college football. On 30 September 1939 Fordham's 34–7 victory over Waynesburg College was televised in New York. A month or so later the National Broadcasting Company showed the game between Brooklyn Dodgers and the Philadelphia Eagles, again in the New York area only. Both broadcasts, because of the small area covered, and the fact that TV sets were very rare, were described as insignificant by local viewers.

19

Don Hutson

Every sport has its genius who is described in the media as being 'years ahead of his time'. In 1966 England's World Cup hero Martin Peters was branded as the genius of soccer. Football's man of the 1930s was a slim 6ft 1in receiver from Arkansas called Don Hutson.

Born in Pine Bluff on 31 January 1913, Hutson attended the University of Alabama where he quickly gained a reputation for being an excellent wide receiver.

His college record demanded that he turn professional, and in 1935 he joined the Green Bay Packers. The Wisconsin team got their man though, as they had been quicker off the mark. Hutson had been signed by both the Packers and the Brooklyn Dodgers. There was much argument over who owned the player and the NFL, in its wisdom, had to make a quick decision. Both contracts arrived by US Mail at their office on the same day, but because the Packers had posted theirs a mere 17 minutes earlier, they secured his registration.

In his very first programme, the Alabama Antelope, as he became known, caught his very first pass and ran it over for a touchdown.

The game in those early days was predominantly a rushing one, there was very little passing as Hutson's record for 1935 shows. In 10 games he made only 18 receptions, but totalled 420 yards at an average of over 23 yards per carry and scored 6 touchdowns.

Did You Know
That he is the record NFL scoring receiver with 99 touchdowns.
That he caught passes in 95 consecutive games.

Green Bay were quick to realize his potential and began to use him with greater efficiency. In 1936 he made 34 receptions and by 1942 his tally had gone up to 74.

Slowly but surely, and probably because of Hutson's influence, passing was becoming a respected part of football. There were critics, however, one of these being Jock Sutherland, the new head coach of the Brooklyn Dodgers. He did not believe in such things as double or triple coverage of pass receivers, and in one game against the Packers and Hutson, paid the penalty. Hutson caught two touchdown passes in a way which many writers of the day described as 'truly remarkable', and the great Jock Sutherland's mind was changed.

Not only was Don Hutson a great offensive receiver, he was also an outstanding safety on defense. In the 1930s teams did not have the huge squads that we see today, and nearly all the players had two positions—one on offense and the other on defense. Players would play for the whole 60 minute game, which makes the performances of the stars of this era even more remarkable.

As well as running both ways on the team, the genial Don Hutson developed into an excellent place kicker and during one particular game caught four touchdown passes and kicked five extra points, all in only one quarter of play! Like many of his contemporaries, Don Hutson was an inventor as well as an outstanding footballer. It was his idea to paint black polish on to the cheekbones to cut out the glare from the sun.

Don Hutson retired from football in 1945 after eleven years at Green Bay and was one of the inaugural members of the NFL Hall of Fame when it opened in 1963.

Don Hutson Firsts
First player to grease his cheekbones to cut out glare from the sun.
First receiver to run pass patterns.

The legendary Don Hutson with perfect concentration leaves a defender flat-flooted. (*Touchdown Magazine*).

hand-off to Alan Ameche from the one yard line.

Whilst pro football's dynasties of the 1950s were forming, college football also had its star teams. One of the greatest schools of this era was undoubtedly Oklahoma. Under coach Bud Wilkinson the Sooners had developed into a devastating outfit. Such names as Billy Vessels, Heisman Trophy winning halfback of 1952, and the giant tackle Jim Weatherall, were the outstanding players in a team that brimmed with confidence.

In 1957 a fullback of average ability was drafted by Cleveland. If Unitas was the yardstick for quarterbacks then Jim Brown was to become the same for running backs. A giant of a man, a fine performer in both track events and basketball, Brown was also an All-America lacrosse player, but above all he was to become the most devastating running back who ever carried a football. Standing 6ft 2ins and weighing 228lbs, Jim Brown was said to have run with the speed of a sprinter, and to have hit with the impact of an express train. During his nine-year career Brown broke almost every record in the book. He averaged an astounding 5.2 yards per carry against defenses whose sole purpose was to stop him, and was an awesome sight with his long low gliding stride, and his way of keeping both feet firmly planted on the ground when tackled.

It is quite a surprise to learn that in spite of his position and size he was only injured a couple of times in his career, a career that saw him gain 12 312 yards and carry the ball 2359 times.

Brown would glide down the line of scrimmage looking for a gap, and when finding it would blast his way clear of grasping arms, to set up record-breaking runs. When collison became inevitable, he would lower

Biggest Victory

Georgia Tech set a record that has never been beaten when in 1916 they defeated Cumberland 222–0. The Rambling Wrecks, as they were known, scored 32 touchdowns.

Although this stands as the record, the official NCAA record for the biggest victory goes to Wyoming who defeated Northern Colorado 103–0 in the 1949 season. Wyoming's points consisted of 15 touchdowns and 13 points after touchdowns. The NFL's record for the biggest win was achieved by Washington Redskins on 27 November 1966. The Redskins swamped New York Giants 72–41. This game also holds the record for the total points scored by both teams in a game (113).

his arm and shoulder and bring his thick muscular arm up into the tackler's head or chest with such ferocity that it would lift the defender off his feet.

Once when asked why Cleveland used Brown so much, coach Paul Brown replied, 'When you have the big gun, you pull the trigger'. Brown's influence on the growth in popularity of the league was probably greater than that of any player before him. At last the new breed of television fans had a figure to admire and attempt to copy.

The decade of the 1960s saw the beginnings of the game as we know it today, with the formation of the AFL and the appointment of Pete Rozelle as the league's third commissioner.

CHAPTER TWO

The National Football League

Although the history of the National Football League goes back to 1920, 1960 marks its coming of age. In that year Pete (Alvin) Rozelle was appointed as the league's new commissioner and the American Football League was born. This eventually merged with the NFL and took on its present day form.

In 1959 there were only 12 professional football teams in operation in the NFL. Football desperately needed a new spark of initiative and the two events of the following year certainly gave it that.

Pete Rozelle was given the Commissioner's job almost by accident. Since 1957 Rozelle had been general manager of the Los Angeles Rams, and when votes were cast at the NFL meeting in Miami on 26 January, his name was nowhere to be seen. The league's former commissioner Bert Bell had died suddenly the previous October of a heart attack whilst watching his beloved Philadelphia Eagles playing Pittsburgh. On Bell's death the NFL's treasurer Austin Gunsel had been appointed as interim commissioner, and it was Gunsel and Marshall Leahy, the attorney for the San Francisco 49ers who were the main contenders. After the first 22 ballots the voting was at a deadlock. The old guard favoured Gunsel whilst the new members were casting their votes for Leahy.

Leahy then made a calculated gamble that backfired. He proposed that if elected he would move the league's office from Philadelphia to his home town of San Francisco. Time was running out and a clear winner was yet to be found. As a compromise Cleveland's Paul Brown was suggested, but

Brown did not really want the job and, like Leahy before him, stated that he too, if elected, would move the office, this time to Cleveland. He in turn suggested Pete Rozelle, and on the 23rd ballot Rozelle became the third commissioner of the NFL.

In his first two years of office, Pete Rozelle became a powerful voice in American sport. He negotiated lucrative television contracts which eventually put the clubs on a sound financial footing; successfully lobbied congress to allow the NFL to negotiate TV contracts as a league rather than individually; upheld the league's name in the 1962 anti-trust suit brought before the courts by the ALF in which the NFL won the battle; and managed to get the US district court of New York to uphold the legality of the NFL's television blackout within 75 miles of a home game. Because of his work Rozelle was given a new five-year contract in 1962.

As well as the election of Pete Rozelle, 1960 saw the emergence of another league to challenge the NFL monopoly of professional football. The American Football League was the brainchild of one Lamar Hunt, the son of a Texas oil millionaire who had always harboured a great desire to own a football team.

In the summer of 1959, after months of flying thousands of miles, Hunt announced the formation of the league. To start with there were only six teams but within six months the number had increased to eight.

On 30 July 1960 the AFL was put to the test when the first pre-season game between the Boston Patriots and the Buffalo Bills was staged. The Patriots defeated the Bills 28–7 in front of 16 000 fans. The dream that Hunt had carried for many years was at last a reality. The first regular season game in the two conference league happened in Boston on 9 September. A crowd of 21 597 turned out in New England to see the Denver Broncos defeat their home team 13–10.

By the time the first championship game arrived the following January, football in AFL territory had begun to take hold. Houston Oilers won the first final game over the Los Angeles Chargers by a 24–16 score-line in Houston on New Year's day 1961. A pleasing crowd of 32 000 turned out for the event.

The 1962 Championship game, again held in Houston, turned out to be a real heart-stopper. Hunt's Dallas Texans eventually defeated the reigning champions, Houston, by 20 to 17 after 17 minutes and 54 seconds of overtime. A Tommy Brooker 25-yard field goal decided the outcome. This game was the longest game played in pro-football history at the time.

Despite their fine win, the Dallas Texans were in deep trouble. In 1960 the NFL had opened their own franchise in the city and it was their Cowboys who were getting the attendances.

It was said that Hunt was losing something in the region of over $1 million a year, and when his multi-millionaire father was informed of this he said, 'At that rate he will be out of business in about 150 years'.

But Hunt was a wise football club owner, and rather than stay and fight it out to the death, he decided in 1963 to cut his losses and move the team to Kansas City where they became the Chiefs.

Another team in deep trouble was the New York Titans. Owned by a news-paperman they had literally run out of money and couldn't even afford to heat their offices. Luckily, a month after Hunt's move the Titans were bought out by Sonny Werblin and renamed the Jets.

In the first two or three years of the AFL's existence, teams made do with NFL rejects or players who had extended their careers by moving into the new league. But slowly, with the help of television contracts, more money became available and they soon began to offer a serious challenge for the year's best college talent.

The battle between the two leagues proved to be a long and costly one. The

The 1973 Superbowl was the first for which the TV blackout was lifted and the game was screened locally. 90 182 tickets were sold, but because of the local coverage 8476 ticket holders didn't turn up.

war reached its peak in 1966 when the two leagues spent a combined total of $7 million signing their draft choices. It is arguable that if an agreement had not been found, and the open hostility had persisted, certainly one, and maybe both leagues would have gone out of business. Thankfully, commonsense prevailed and both leagues eventually got round a table in the spring of 1966 for merger talks. On 8 June the historic announcement of an agreement was made, and everyone breathed a huge sigh of relief. The two leagues agreed to play in separate schedules until 1970, but would meet from the following year in a World Championship game, and play each other in pre-season games. The World Championship game was the brainchild of two men: the then AFL Commissioner Al Davis thought of the idea and Lamar Hunt is credited with the title of 'Superbowl'.

Davis and Rozelle, who was named commissioner of the new league, never saw eye to eye. Their open dislike of each other is remembered to this day, but for the good of football, it seems, they agreed to bury their differences. Davis returned to Oakland and Rozelle carried on at the NFL.

1966 also saw the NFL expand. Atlanta and Miami were awarded franchises and in 1967 New Orleans became the sixteenth club in the league.

Football's long awaited battle of the giants came on 15 January 1967 when Vince Lombardi's Green Bay Packers proved their NFL supremacy over the AFL's Kansas City Chiefs in Superbowl I. The Packers won the game 35–10 in the Los Angeles Coliseum, and although the match brought together the two previously warring factions it did little to encourage the idea of equality.

The AFL did get their first taste of victory over the NFL, however, in a pre-season game on 5 August of that year when Denver beat Detroit 13–7, but it wasn't until

Superbowl III that people really began to take any serious notice of this young upstart.

1968 became the year of two teams — Green Bay and Cincinnati. Green Bay, because they won the Superbowl for a second successive year, beating Oakland 33–14 in Miami, and Cincinnati, because this was their first season in the AFL, although a disastrous 3–11 record did little to help their cause. By now the AFL had 10 members and the NFL had 16, a total of 26 teams playing professional football under one banner the length and breadth of the USA.

In 1969 the AFL came of age, for Superbowl III was the year of the Jets, and in particular their star quarterback Joe Namath. The Jets, the pre-game underdogs, defeated the favourites Baltimore 16–7 in a tense ground battle in Miami on 12 January.

The year 1970 saw not only the dawning of a new decade, but the dawning of a new NFL. The 1970 season was the first under the combined banner. Baltimore, Cleveland and Pittsburgh agreed to join the AFL teams to form a 13-team American Football Conference. The remaining NFL clubs formed the National Football Conference with both conferences adopting Eastern, Central and Western Divisions.

The season's Superbowl was played once again in Miami and Baltimore snatched a last minute victory over Dallas when Jim O'Brien kicked a 32-yard field goal with only five seconds left on the clock.

A week later the NFC gained their revenge as the first AFC-NFC ProBowl was held in Los Angeles, the National Football Conference winning 27–6.

The merging of the two leagues also brought about another change. At their meeting on 18 March 1970 the league agreed to print players' names on the backs of jerseys. The move was generally welcomed as it then became a lot easier not only for officials and commentators to identify players but for spectators as well.

Two months later the Boston Patriots changed their name to the New England Patriots, a decision which created some unrest in Boston itself, but after a while the locals got used to the name and it has become a proud symbol of professional football in America's north-east corner.

The 1971 season came and went with very little to talk about, except for the AFC

divisional play-off game between Miami and Kansas City on Christmas day. The Dolphins' kicker Gary Yepremian placed a 37-yard field goal for Miami after a record-breaking 22 minutes and 40 seconds of overtime. The game lasted 82 minutes and 40 seconds in all and still holds the record for the longest played game in the history of the NFL.

After all their work in the play-offs Miami stayed at home for Superbowl VI, but any home advantage they thought they might have had was quickly swept away by Dallas as the Cowboys ran up 24 points to the Dolphins' solitary field goal. It is interesting to note that the CBS coverage of the game was viewed in as many as 27 450 000 homes across the American continent.

The 1973 Superbowl just had to go one better, and of course it did. All 90 182 tickets were sold for the game to be held in Los Angeles. For the first time as well as being televised across the nation, the game was screened locally. Maybe because of this, 8476 ticket holders didn't turn up. The TV audience was huge as usual. A massive 75 000 000 people watched Superbowl VII, yet another record.

1973 was quite significant for the NFL for many reasons. A new system of jersey numbering was adopted, although players who had been in the league before 1972 were allowed to keep their old numbers. For a while the mixture of old and new numbers was a little confusing, but as a lot of these players gradually drifted from the league the problem decreased. There are literally only a handful of the old players still remaining in the NFL today, and one of the best known is San Francisco's linebacker Jack Reynolds whose number is 64, when linebackers under the new rules of 1973 should be between 50–59.

Jim Brown

If ever there was a poll to find the best running back of all time, the name of James Brown would figure high on the list. A prolific athlete who ran with the speed of a top class sprinter, Brown invented a new catch phrase in football—'Master Blaster'. Most backs need good linesmen to open up holes to run through, but Jim Brown made his own. With his deceptive speed and raw strength he could totally outfox a defense, and in a tackle he would lower his head, square up his opponent and blast his way past leaving the defender clawing the air.

Jim Brown began his football career at Syracuse University in 1953, and was a number 1 draft choice for Cleveland Browns in 1957. In nine years at the Browns, Brown the player broke almost every rushing record there was. Averaging 5.2 yards per carry, Brown gained a total of 12 312 yards and carried the ball over 2000 times. His achievement is all the more remarkable because the NFL season during his career lasted for only 12, later 14, games.

Unlike many of his modern counterparts, Jim Brown never missed a single game during his nine years at Cleveland and was voted NFL player of the year in 1958, 1963 and 1965. In seven of his nine years he rushed for more than 1000 yards and took the league's rushing title 8 times (from 1957 to 1961 and from 1963 to 1965).

Whilst Jim Brown was a coach's dream on the field, and sheer perfection as far as the watching masses were concerned, he was said to be at times moody and unapproachable. When things weren't going right Brown would often refuse press interviews and retreat from publicity.

With Jim Brown on the field, and coach Paul Brown on the sidelines, the Cleveland Browns were the best of their era—their record shows an NFL title in 1964 and two runners-up spots in 1957 and 1965. But for Vince Lombardi and his Green Bay Packers, they would undoubtably have won more, as it was they all had to be content with contributing to the 'Brown Bomber' legend.

In 1965, at the height of his career, Jim Brown announced his retirement from football and took his good looks off to Hollywood, where he has since become one of America's leading black actors, starring in, amongst other films, *The Dirty Dozen* with Lee Marvin.

What the screen had gained, football had sadly lost. Jim Brown could have carried on for two or three more seasons, but decided to go out at the top. 'I could have stayed around a little longer, slowed down and probably got hurt', he later recalled.

Today many try and adopt boxing's favourite pastime of comparing Ali with Marciano. Brown v Simpson, or Brown v Payton, it doesn't matter; to many Americans who lived through the fifties and sixties, Jim Brown was simply the best.

Did You Know

That NFL highlights are shown once a week in Thailand. The games are usually about six weeks in arrears but as there is no newspaper coverage of football in Thailand, the time-lag has little significance. The league just starts and finishes a bit later!

Jim Brown, perhaps the greatest running back ever. (*Touchdown Magazine*).

On 6 June 1973 another milestone in the NFL's history was reached. The NFL set up a charitable organization to derive income from money generated by the licensing of NFL trademarks, logos and names. The NFL Charity was set up to help other worthy charities across the country. Today this part of the vast NFL network gives millions and millions of dollars to charities each year.

The NFL has always been very aware of the product it puts in front of the spectators in the stadiums and the armchair fans. It is one of the only sports in the world which consistently updates its rules if it thinks that public support is waning. In 1974, for instance, sweeping rule changes were recommended by the Competition Committee to bring about a more offensive oriented game. There comes a time every now and then when the defense catches up tactically with the offense and the game itself becomes a defensive bore. The rule changes approved were designed to add action and quicken the tempo of the game. Sudden death overtime was introduced for pre-season games and one 15-minute period of extra time was added for regular season fixtures. The goalposts, which for a long time had been positioned on the goal line itself were moved back to the end lines. This was done mainly for safety reasons. Countless numbers of players had injured themselves running into the upright which is four inches in diameter. Kicking, like running, is something that an athlete can improve dramatically over the course of a number of seasons. The kick-off spot had been sited on the 40-yard line and nearly every week there would be an embarrassing occasion when a kicker would kick the ball straight out of the end-zone. To combat this, the kick-off spot was moved 5 yards back to the 35-yard line. Various other rules to open up the game were introduced; roll-blocking, or cutting out

Superbowl XVII was the first Superbowl to be televised live in Britain. John Riggins became a household name there when he led the Washington Redskins to a 27–17 victory over the Miami Dolphins.

wide receivers was made illegal; penalties for tripping within a certain distance were reduced and penalties were introduced for offensive holding and the illegal use of hands on the line of scrimmage. The results were immediate, the game once again became a feast of offensive play and the NFL's intention of keeping the game of football at the top of the sports listings was achieved.

The year 1974 also saw the formation of yet another new league, the World Football league. The original intention of the new league was to have franchises in cities all over the world, hence its name. But no sooner had it begun, that it was beset with all sorts of problems. Finance was the main cause of the fast decline of the WFL. The league only played one season, that of 1974, when the Birmingham Americans defeated the Florida Blazers in the only championship game of the 12-team league. The WLF folded on 22 September 1975.

The middle seventies belonged to Pittsburgh. The team won both Superbowls IX and X and continued its remarkable streak of success in 1979 winning Superbowl XIII to become the first team in NFL history to win three World Championships. In 1980, of course, the Steelers put their name firmly in the record books, having been led on the field by Terry Bradshaw and off it by coach Chuck Noll after chalking up their fourth victory in six years.

Every decade has it outstanding team. The sixties provided Green Bay, but the seventies gave football the Pittsburgh Steelers, one of the most efficient professional teams ever seen. With Bradshaw orchestrating the offense which included such stars as Lynn Swann and John Stallworth, and a defense known by all as the 'Steel Curtain', the Steelers swept all before them as they broke record after record.

Whilst the Steelers were notching up one victory after another, two new teams joined the NFL in 1976 bringing the league to its present day strength of 28 teams. The west coast city of Seattle, high up on the Washington border, was chosen, as was the fast growing area in central Florida known as Tampa Bay.

Seattle, with its home state, Washington, has had a long history of producing good footballers from its two main universities, so there was no surprise when its membership was announced. The inclusion of Tampa on the other hand was a strange decision, but under its president Hugh H. Culverhouse the 'Buccanneers' quickly found their feet, albeit getting them wet in the process. Tampa has consistently provided one of the league's hard-luck stories always finishing at or very near the bottom of their division.

On 16 August 1976 the NFL went oriental. The first NFL game to be played outside the USA was staged in the Korakuen Stadium in Tokyo, Japan. 38 000 Japanese fans turned out to see the St Louis Cardinals defeat San Diego 20–10.

The late 1970s saw many rule changes affecting almost every part of the game. Passing, receiving, rushing, kicking, punts and returns were all subjected to sweeping changes which even the hardest cynic would say were for the better.

A sports survey was conducted amongst America's fans in 1978 which threw up some startling results. According to the Harris Sports survey 70 per cent of the nation's sports fans followed football compared with only 54 per cent who had an interest in baseball.

After their success in Japan, two teams from the NFL, the New Orleans Saints and the Philadelphia Eagles travelled to Mexico City on 5 August 1978 to play an exhibition match 'South of the Border'. A capacity crowd greeted their arrival and the Saints went on to win 14–7. Due to its proximity to America it is no real surprise that in Mexico football is big business. Millions listen every week to ball-by-ball reports in Spanish on the radio. At the time of one Superbowl, which was televised live, only a handful of spectators turned up for the biggest bullfight of the year, and it had to be postponed. Soccer is still the Mexicans' national sport, but football is rapidly catching up.

Bolstered by the expansion of the regular season from 14 games to 16 in 1978, the league announced record attendances for the 1978 season. Over 12 million fans had paid to watch NFL football. The average attendance of 57 071 was the third highest in the NFL's history and the best since 1973. Football was indeed on a high.

The league under Rozelle's expert guidance had negotiated in 1977 what some sources considered to be the largest single TV package ever, and both the television

Did You Know

That the longest game in NFL history took place on Christmas Day 1971 between Miami and Kansas City. The game lasted 82 minutes and 42 seconds with the Dolphins winning 27–24.

companies and the league itself were highly delighted with the viewing figures.

According to CBS television the Superbowl XII game in Louisiana between Dallas and Denver attracted a record 102 010 000 viewers throughout the world, which meant that the game was watched by more people than any other show in the history of television. That record has since been broken by the *MASH* series.

The 1979 season began with the addition of a seventh official, a side judge, and ended with Pittsburgh defeating the Los Angeles Rams in Superbowl XIV on 20 January 1980. A record 103 985 fans packed into the Pasadena Rosebowl to witness the event, and the end of another era.

Until 1980 the rules covering the use of hands around the helmet were fairly lax, but this was to change. Several medical inquiries had produced evidence that players were suffering serious neck and head injuries as a result of unfair play. Under the heading of 'Personal Foul', players were now prohibited from directly striking, swinging, or clubbing around the head, neck or face of an opponent. If only for safety's sake, this new rule was badly needed, and almost overnight it cut down the number of serious head injuries.

In 1981 the Oakland Raiders became the first and only team in NFL history to go all the way as the wild card entry and actually win the Superbowl defeating Philadelphia in Louisiana's Superdome 27–10. The Raiders had finished second to San Diego in the AFC Western Division, widely regarded as the league's toughest. In the playoffs they beat Houston at Oakland and Cleveland and San Diego on the way to the championship game.

The following year, 1982, began on a bright note. The Superbowl game between San Francisco and Cincinnati in the freezing winds of Detroit attracted more than

Dan Marino

The 1984 season saw Miami's superstar quarterback Dan Marino set a new record for touchdown passes. The previous record was held jointly by Y. A. Tittle and George Blanda. Tittle, a former New York Giants star, passed for 36 touchdowns in 14 games, as did George Blanda in 1961 whilst leading Houston Oilers' attack.

Marino passed the mark after week 14 of the regular season with four touchdowns against the Los Angeles Raiders on 2 December 1984.

In week 15 of the season against Indianapolis Colts Marino threw four more to equalize with the then professional record of 44, and in week 16 the young man from Pittsburgh made the record his own with four touchdown passes as the Dolphins eclipsed the Dallas Cowboys 28–21.

The regular season record of 48 was further hoisted in the post season as Miami's magic man threw three against Seattle, and four against Pittsburgh in the AFC championship game to take his total for the whole season to 55. They then did battle in the Superbowl classic with the San Francisco 49ers. Unfortunately history records that Marino and his Dolphins did not have a very happy time being soundly beaten by another Pennsylvanian quarterback, Joe Montana. For Marino it was to be a sad day as he only completed one touchdown pass to end the season with 56 touchdown passes. Despite the inevitable disappointment, Dan Marino did set two new Superbowl records during the game: for pass attempts (50) and for pass completions (29).

Left 'Come on you guys' – Dan Marino urges on his Miami teammates.

The Miami Dolphins' record-breaking quarterback, Dan Marino. (Miami Dolphins).

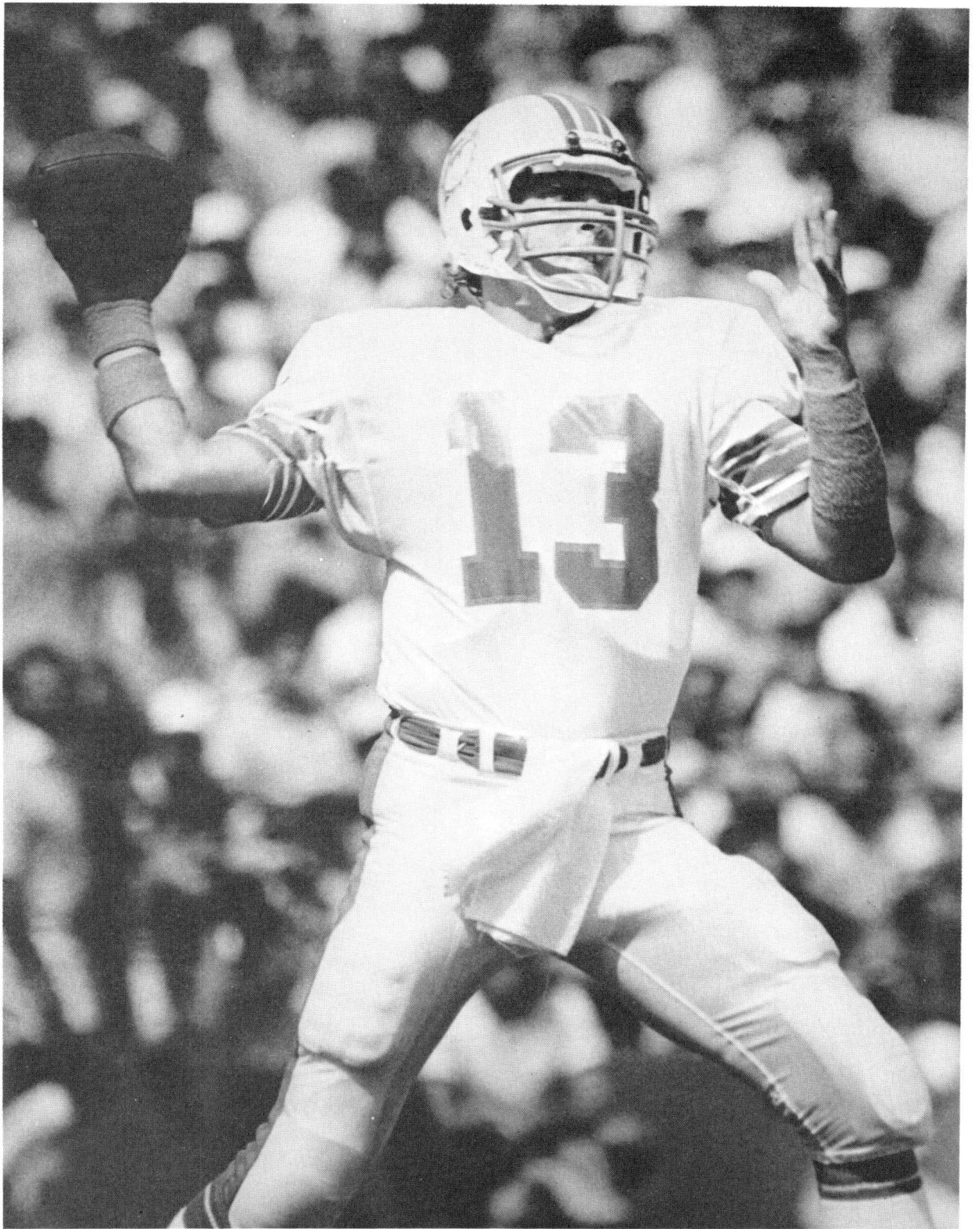

110 000 000 TV viewers. But within eight months the league and the sport were in turmoil.

After only two games of the regular season the players' association announced a players' strike on 20 September. The effect was catastrophic, and there are still repercussions today. The strike, which was about basic salaries and earnings deriving from the clubs' huge television receipts, lasted 57 days. It wasn't the first time that the players had exercised their right to withdraw their labour. In 1974 the veterans held out for most of the pre-season training period and many clubs were forced to play only rookies (new players) in their warm-up games. Luckily, a settlement was reached before the season began and the veterans returned to their clubs two weeks before the regular games were due to start.

Pete Rozelle's qualities as a negotiator were tested to the full, and the ever-smiling Commissioner eventually came through with flying colours. So did the players as their demands were met, or nearly, and the season began again on 16 November. Because of the stoppage a new schedule had to be hastily arranged. For the play-offs the league adopted a 16-team Superbowl Tournament which was operated on a sort of knock-out basis. The NFC's No 1 seed Washington eventually defeated the AFC's No 2 seed Miami in the Superbowl final itself, coming from behind to win 27–17 after a 'superman' performance in the second half.

The game marked the first Superbowl to be televised live in the homes of British fans. Some 4 million stayed up to the early hours glued to their sets with excitement. Their season had also suffered from the strike, since the new television Channel 4 had originally scheduled the start of their new sport's coverage for October. Despite its late arrival American football in Britain then took off.

The 1983 season gave British fans their first taste of live football action when the Minnesota Vikings played the St Louis Cardinals before some 35 000 fans at Wembley Stadium.

The new season also gave the sport its latest pretenders. The United States Football League was formed and began playing in the Spring of 1983. Despite a poor start, the league is still with us and attracts more and more top stars. Since it plans to move to an Autumn season in 1986, there are clear reminders of the old AFL of some 25 years ago. Whether the outcome is the same remains to be seen.

The 1984 season came to a climax in Stanford Stadium, California when the home team San Francisco 49ers whipped the Miami Dolphins 38–16. Again record TV attendances were announced and after the problems of the early 1980s, the National Football League is consolidating its position for another push in two or three years' time.

What the future holds for the NFL and its 28 member clubs, one can only guess. Many teams have admitted to problems, and two in recent times have moved lock stock and barrel, (Baltimore to Indianapolis, and Oakland to Los Angeles). The USFL, like its predecessor the AFL, has brought a case against the NFL, and if it wins, many observers think that the NFL could be bankrupted. It seems very doubtful that such a thing would be permitted to happen, but the worlds of American law and business are highly unpredictable. However, as it enters its 64th year of operation, one has a feeling that the National Football League is going to be around for many years yet.

Did You Know
That Cal Hubbard, who played on New York Giants' and Green Bay Packers' defense in the 1920s and 1930s, was the first really large football player. He was 6ft 5in tall and weighed 250lbs.

The Marching Band of the University of Southern California. George Preston Marshall introduced marching bands to American Football in 1934.

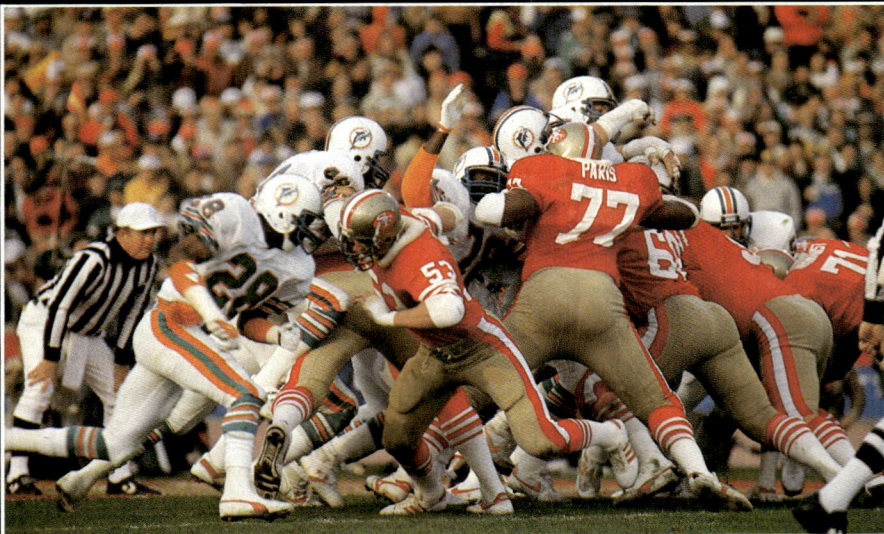

The "Rear" guard of the San Francisco 49ers holds the onslaught of the Miami Dolphins in Superbowl XIX.

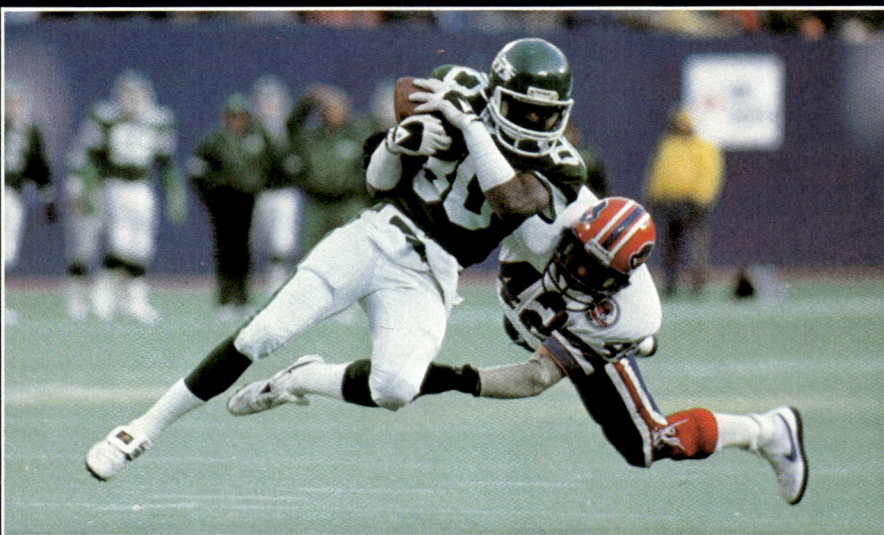

The aerial acrobatics of the wide receiver and corner back.

High fives are in order after a touchdown from the New Orleans Saints.

New York Giants linebacker Lawrance Taylor, ready for action.

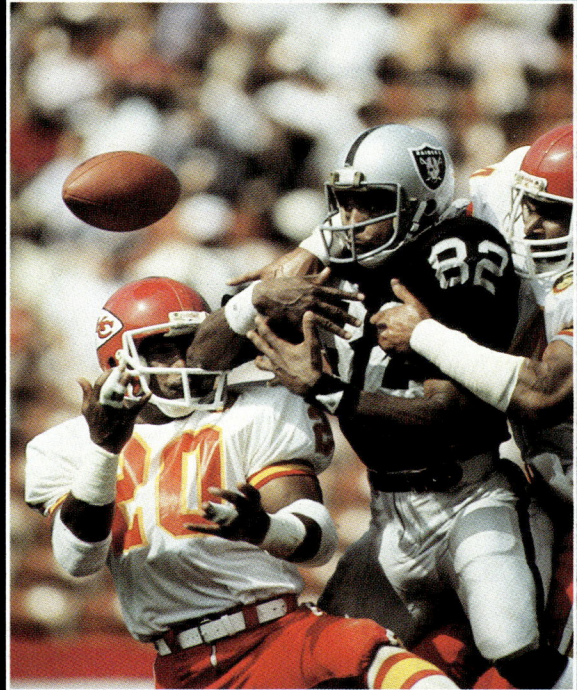

Strong tackling from the Kansas City Chiefs pops the ball loose from Los Angeles Raider Calvin Muhammad.

The Diamond Vision Board dazzles as dusk falls on Superbowl XIX.

Movie star James Garner is an avid fan of the Los Angeles Raiders.

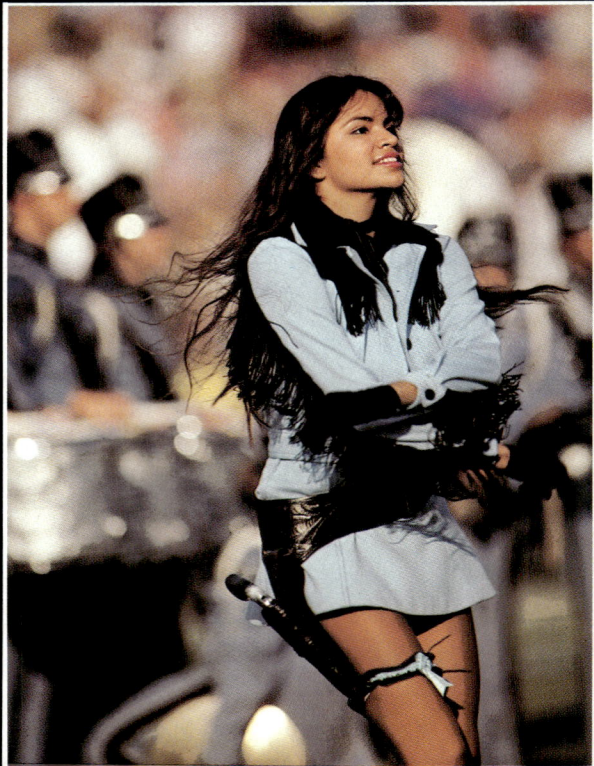
A pistol-packing Majorette struts with the band.

A lovely college cheerleader poses for the camera.

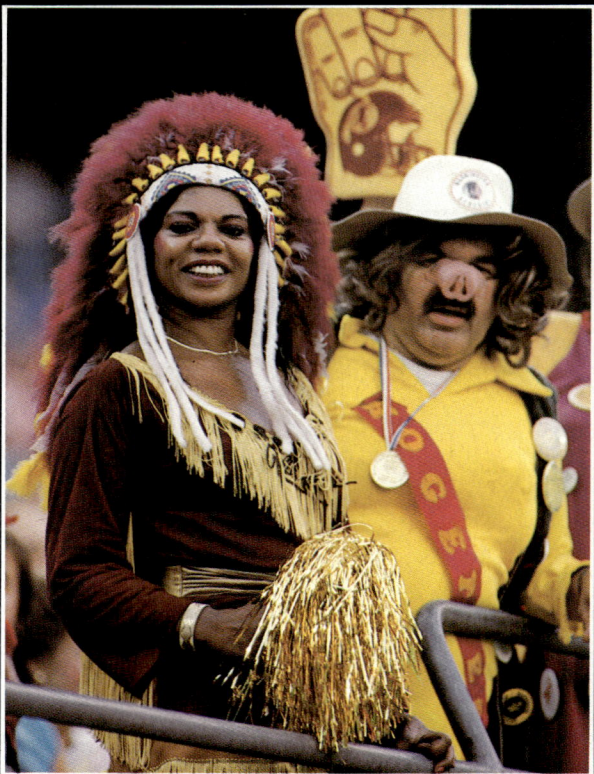
The fans of the Washington Redskins always go "Hog Wild".

The National Football League
Divisional Alignments

National Conference

Dallas Cowboys
Chicago Bears
Atlanta Falcons

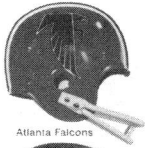

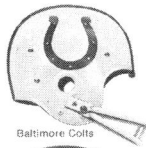

New York Giants
Detroit Lions
Los Angeles Rams

Philadelphia Eagles
Green Bay Packers
New Orleans Saints

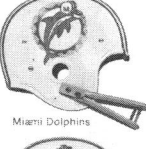

St. Louis Cardinals
Minnesota Vikings
San Francisco 49ers

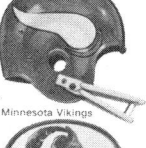

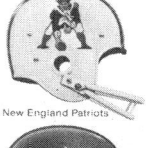

Washington Redskins
Tampa Bay Buccaneers

American Conference

Baltimore Colts
Cincinnati Bengals
Denver Broncos

Buffalo Bills
Cleveland Browns
Kansas City Chiefs

Miami Dolphins
Houston Oilers
Los Angeles Raiders

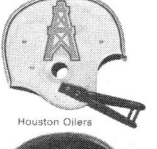

New England Patriots
Pittsburgh Steelers
San Diego Chargers

New York Jets
Seattle Seahawks

The Draft

Every spring the National Football League concludes its search for talented new stars from the college ranks with its annual draft. The draft was the brainchild of the league's second commissioner Bert Bell who, in 1935, was the co-owner of the Philadelphia Eagles. It was noticeable at this period in the league's history that only the teams with financial muscle were getting the best players. Chicago and the New York Giants, who had the most money, were able to sign the best players the colleges had to offer each year and thus continued to dominate the league.

Bell, with the help of George Preston Marshall, proposed that a draft system be inaugurated that would allow the worst team in the league to have first pick of the season's graduating collegians. The scheme was more advantageous to these two astute businessmen than to most, as their teams were suffering from a lack of success. On 19 May 1935 the draft proposal was adopted and put into effect the following year.

The first player selected in the first draft was Chicago University's talented halfback Jay Berwanger. Coincidentally it was Bell's Eagles who had finished last the previous year who selected him. But the very first player to be selected by this new process priced himself out of the market by apparently asking for $1000 per game, a figure which neither Philadelphia nor the rich Chicago or New York clubs could afford. But the system had been set in motion and over the years has developed almost into a piece of showbusiness. Today, the draft is normally held late in April at a hotel in New York City.

If a college player has graduated, that is to say, has completed four years of college education, he is eligible to be drafted. On draft day, an occasion which is covered by the news media in their thousands, each team has representatives at the draft headquarters. A telephone link is established

(Cont. p. 35)

Number One Draft Choices

Season	Team	Player	Position	College
1985	Buffalo	Bruce Smith	DT	Virginia Tech.
1984	New England	Irving Fryar	RB	Nebraska
1983	Baltimore (traded to Denver)	John Elway	QB	Stanford
1982	New England	Ken Sims	DT	Texas
1981	New Orleans	George Rogers	RB	S. Carolina
1980	Detroit	Billy Sims	RB	Oklahoma
1979	Buffalo	Tom Cousineau	LB	Ohio State
1978	Houston	Earl Campbell	RB	Texas
1977	Tampa Bay	Ricky Bell	RB	S. California
1976	Tampa Bay	Lee Roy Selmon	DE	Oklahoma
1975	Atlanta	Steve Bartkowski	QB	California
1974	Dallas	Ed Jones	DE	Tennessee St.
1973	Houston	John Matuszak	DE	Tampa
1972	Buffalo	Walt Patulski	DE	Notre Dame
1971	New England	Jim Plunkett	QB	Stanford
1970	Pittsburgh	Terry Bradshaw	QB	Louisiana Tech.
1969	Buffalo	O. J. Simpson	RB	S. California
1968	Minnesota	Ron Yary	T	S. California
1967	Baltimore	Bubba Smith	DT	Michigan St.
1966	Atlanta (NFL)	Tommy Nobis	LB	Texas
	Miami (AFL)	Jim Grabowski	RB	Illinois
1965	N. Y. Giants (NFL)	Tucker Frederickson	RB	Auburn
	Houston (AFL)	Lawrence Elkins	E	Baylor
1964	San Francisco (NFL)	Dave Parks	E	Texas Techn.
	Boston (AFL)	Jack Concannon	QB	Boston College
1963	Los Angeles (NFL)	Terry Baker	QB	Oregon State
	Kansas City (AFL)	Buck Buchanan	DT	Grambling
1962	Washington (NFL)	Ernie Davis	RB	Syracuse
	Oakland (AFL)	Roman Gabriel	QB	N. Carolina St.
1961	Minnesota (NFL)	Tommy Mason	RB	Tulane
	Buffalo (AFL)	Ken Rice	G	Auburn
1960	Los Angeles	Billy Cannon	RB	Louisiana State University
	(AFL had no formal pick in their first year of operation)			
1959	Green Bay	Randy Duncan	QB	Iowa
1958	Chicago Cardinals	King Hill	QB	Rice
1957	Green Bay	Paul Hornung	HB	Notre Dame
1956	Pittsburgh	Gary Glick	DB	Colorado A & M
1955	Baltimore	George Shaw	QB	Oregon
1954	Cleveland	Bobby Garrett	QB	Stanford
1953	San Francisco	Harry Babcock	E	Georgia
1952	Los Angeles	Bill Wade	QB	Vanderbilt
1951	N. Y. Giants	Kyle Rote	HB	Southern Methodist University
1950	Detroit	Leon Hart	E	Notre Dame
1949	Philadelphia	Chuck Bednarik	C	Pennsylvania
1948	Washington	Harry Gilmer	QB	Alabama
1947	Chicago Bears	Bob Fenimore	HB	Oklahoma A & M
1946	Boston	Frank Dancewicz	QB	Notre Dame
1945	Chicago Cardinals	Charley Trippi	HB	Georgia
1944	Boston	Angelo Bertelli	QB	Notre Dame
1943	Detroit	Frank Sinkwich	QB	Georgia
1942	Pittsburgh	Bill Dudley	HB	Virginia
1941	Chicago Bears	Tom Harmon	HB	Michigan
1940	Chicago Cardinals	George Cafego	HB	Tennessee
1939	Chicago Cardinals	Ki Aldrich	C	TCU
1938	Cleveland	Corbett Davis	FB	Indiana
1937	Philadelphia	Sam Francis	FB	Nebraska
1936	Philadelphia	Jay Berwanger	HB	Chicago

Did You Know

That New Orleans's Head Coach 'Bum' Phillips is, at 61, the oldest active coach in the National Football League.

Right Stanford University's John Elway was the no.1 draft choice in 1983. After sensationally turning down the Baltimore Colts, he signed for the Denver Broncos in a multi-million dollar deal. (Denver Broncos).

Did You Know

That in the 1966 draft when the AFL and the NFL were vying for the best college players, a University of Texas linebacker caught the imagination of the football world, and maybe beyond it.

Tommy Nobis was the cream of the crop in the 1966 draft and was the first player selected in the NFL draft, when the expanding Atlanta Falcons acquired rights to him.

He was also first to go in the AFL draft when the Houston Oilers staked their claim.

For weeks the two teams negotiated with Nobis. Houston owner Bud Adams seemed to be in an excellent position because he was prepared to offer the young Nobis a salary estimated to be worth $750 000. Houston also had the upper hand when it came to where Nobis would prefer to live for if he signed for the Oilers he could stay in his native state of Texas.

The whole of the sporting world were rivetted by the affair, and Astronaut Frank Borman radioed back from his spacecraft Gemini 7, 'Tell Nobis to sign with the Oilers'.

But, despite the plea from outer space, Nobis eventually signed for Atlanta, wishing to test himself against NFL opposition, rather than against the new league.

between each team's representatives and their coaches, staff and scouts in their home town.

The 28 clubs select their choices in reverse order to their positions at the end of the previous season. Hence the team with the worst record picks first and the Superbowl champions last. There are 12 rounds in the draft, and in every round each team makes a selection. Some teams might have more than one selection or none at all in certain rounds; this is because many teams will trade draft selections for current players either during the close season or during the pre-season. But in mathematical terms, since their are 12 rounds at which 28 selections being made, a total of 336 players are drafted.

There is a specific amount of time allowed for teams to make their selections. In rounds 1 and 2 each team is allowed a maximum of 15 minutes to make their choice. There will often be frantic telephone calls between representatives and their home bases, relying information about who has already been chosen and who is left. For rounds 3 to 12 only five minutes is allowed, so everybody must be on their toes. If a team hasn't made their choice in the allotted time, they must wait and try to jump into the order when they can—not an easy thing to do when everybody is frantically trying to snap up the best players.

Back home in the team's draft room huge boards are placed on the walls listing many hundred of players. As players are chosen, they are taken off the board and others are moved up, so when it is a particular team's turn to make a selection, the staff in the draft room can inform their representative over the telephone who they want, and the choice is then made. The selected players are then informed by the clubs that they have been selected, and, subject to agreements, they will turn up at the team's summer camp in July.

Those players not selected are called 'free agents,' and will often travel around trying to sell their talents to individual clubs. There is no limit to the number of free agents a club can sign. Once a player has agreed to sign with a certain club, the next item on the agenda is of course the size of his salary.

In 1984 the minimum allowed under an agreement between the NFL and the players' union was $40 000 a year. For the 1985 season this minimum has increased to $50 000. Depending on the round in which they were drafted, players can then negotiate a figure above this. The earlier the player is drafted then of course the more he is likely to get. Salaries are then augmented by substantial signing-on bonuses and other inducements that can earn a round one draft choice well over $250 000 per annum.

The Babysitters

The nickname of 'babysitters' was first given to scouts in the mid-1960s during the NFL-AFL war.

Such was the fierceness of the competition to sign top quality players, the clubs' scouts were employed to take their prized catches into hiding and to literally 'babysit' them.

Of course when the AFL and the NFL eventually forgot their differences and merged, the need for babysitters disappeared. With the emergence of the USFL in 1982 the babysitting ploy again came into use as the two rival leagues battled to get their hands on the best of the year's college graduates.

All professional teams employ a team of scouts and most of them also belong to a scouting consortium to which they pay fees for certain player information. A scout will attend practices and games and look at miles and miles of film, evaluating each player from all angles. Not only will his playing ability be taken into account but his academic qualifications and his general attitude to life and to other people will also be noted on his report file.

Scouts will then grade the player on a 1–10 scale and the player will be filed away with hundreds of others until draft day.

For obvious reasons the highest graded players will almost certainly be first round draft choices, and so on down the scale.

Human nature being what it is many scouts will mark a player as a certainty, where others might grade him as a reject, and another might report that he has scope for improvement, all of which makes the scout's job one of the hardest yet most crucial to any team's success.

Training Camp

The first weekend in July marks the start of the football season as far as the players are concerned, for this is the time when the pre-season training camps begin. Every team has either a small college or sports complex usually near their home town where they get down to some serious fitness and tactics training. A few, Dallas for instance, site their camps away from their local cities, for various reasons. Dallas hold their annual pre-season camp at Thousand Oaks in Southern California, because the temperature in Texas during the summer can go well over 100 degrees fahrenheit. Some of the northern clubs hold their camps in sunny Florida.

The first two-week period at a training camp is reserved for the newcomers, those who have been drafted, and the free agents who are dubiously nicknamed 'rookies'. The established players, known as 'veterans', will not return to camp until the middle of the month. The training camp provides a rigid month of gruelling training designed to make the players 100 per cent fit. It is also where the coaches will develop their playing tactics to a fine art. The rookies are expected to learn the club's playbook (the coach's tactics) from cover to cover in only a few days, and they are penalized for any slackness or mistakes by being made to do extra work or laps of the field in full equipment under a certain time.

At any time during training the coaches can decide to drop a player from the camp. The most feared man at a training camp is the official designated to tell players that they are not required. This man is known to all as 'the Turk'. The Turk is most active on certain days when teams have to cut their squads down to certain numbers. Most teams will have more than 100 players at their training camp, so the Turk could be a very busy man. Most players, however, instinctively know when their time is up, when they are asked to report to the head coach's office with their playbooks. Being dropped doesn't necessarily mean the end of a player's career. He is then technically a free agent and can display his wares to any of the other teams in the league. During the pre-season period a player's negotiated salary is waived. If he comes through the training camp and the pre-season games and is put on the team's official list of players, he will then begin to earn his wage. Whilst at the training camp the players will live in dormitories within the complex. Their bed and board is provided by the club.

They do, however, receive a little pay. In 1983 rookies received $375 per week, and veterans $425. By 1986 these rates will rise to $450 and $500 respectively. Veterans will also receive $200 for each pre-season game they participate in, but rookies will not get any extra pay. For the first few weeks the players will not even see a football. Physical fitness will be the main course of the day. Various forms of exercises, unique to Amerian football, are adopted to stretch and strengthen almost every part of the body.

One of the main tests they have to do on arrival is the 40-yard sprint. It is assumed that players will rarely run a distance of more than 40 yards, but sprints of 40 and less are very common. So players are wired up to electrical timers and have to run the 40-yard sprint within certain strict time limits. A time of 4.5 seconds for this distance is considered very good. Players will have every conceivable device available to them to help them to get fit. The camp will have its own

gymnasium, weight-training area, swimming pool, treatment rooms and sometimes its own running tracks where even the biggest and meanest of the squad are ruthlessly put through their paces. Everything the player does from getting up in the morning to going to bed at night will be carefully monitored. He will undergo an exhausting series of examinations at the hands of doctors, dentists, heart specialists

Players go through the most unusual exercises whilst at training camp. (All-Sport).

and many others. Every part of his body will be checked to make sure that he is in tip-top condition. If there is the slightest doubt, then he will be rejected. Competition, especially amongst the rookies, is very tough. There could be over 70 rookies trying to get into the team and maybe only 4 or 5 will eventually be selected.

One of the major tasks of the trainer and his staff at camp is to ensure that drinks are available to players at all times. One of the only reasons for which a player is permitted to take a quick break is to replace some of his lost body fluid; in fact, special breaks are taken each day to enable the player to take in sufficient liquids. If it is too hot, and checks show that the heat is causing too great a loss of fluids, then practice can be called off. Every day for over a month the players will go through the same ritual striving to get themselves into the squad.

Normally towards the end of July teams will arrange a scrimmage game with a near rival behind closed doors. Coaches will then have a close look at every player in an ideal match situation.

Hayes & Haynes

THE RAIDERS DOUBLE H DEFENSE

If there had been a special award for the Los Angeles Raiders' Superbowl victory over Washington in 1984 then it should have gone to the 'Texas Terrors', Lester Hayes and Mike Haynes.

For Hayes and Haynes, the all-star cornerback duo for the black and silver mean machine, stifled the league's leading passing offense so effectively that the Redskins' dream of consecutive championships was well and truly shattered.

It is said that owners will give kingdoms for cornerbacks of quality, and the acquisition in the winter of 1983 of Mike Haynes to partner Lester was one of the smartest moves in football history.

Haynes and Hayes, both from Texas, formed one of the best last lines of defense as the Raiders rolled on to the Superbowl and their showdown with the Redskins. Everybody pretending to know anything about football predicted a feast of a game

Double trouble: Raiders' cornerbacks Lester Hayes and Mike Haynes give wide receivers nightmares.

Left Lester Hayes

Right Mike Haynes

Opposite Lester Hayes takes up his defensive position.

with many touchdowns, but they didn't reckon on the dynamic duo's plan to stop Washington passing the pigskin.

When the lights had gone out on Superbowl XVIII, three names stood out above everybody else. For obvious reasons Marcus Allen's rushing enabled him to claim the MVP (Most Valuable Player) award, but connoisseurs of this great game were also enthusing about the talents of the two cornerbacks: Hayes and Haynes.

Hayes from Houston teamed up with the Oakland Raiders (as they were then named) in 1977 after four exciting years with Texas A&M. Whilst at Texas he was a key performer both as linebacker and cornerback and starred in the 1977 Sun Bowl where he was noted by many for his strong hitting.

Haynes's route to the Raiders was less straightforward. Born in Denison, Texas on 1 July 1953, Mike was actually brought up in Los Angeles and went on to play for Arizona State's Sundevils while he was at college. During his stay with the Sundevils Haynes was MVP in the 1973 Fiesta Bowl and MVP in the 1976 Japan Bowl, before becoming the first defensive back to be taken in the draft of 1976 by the New England Patriots. As the Patriots' top interceptor for three consecutive years (1976–78), Haynes quickly established a name for himself as a punt return specialist. As a rookie he scored two touchdowns on punt returns with runs of 89 and 62 yards.

After an injury riddled 1981 season Mike Haynes became a free agent at the end of the 1982 season and eventually joined the Raiders in November 1983, in return for two high round draft choices.

Teaming up with Lester Hayes has made Mike Haynes a better all round player, and few would disagree that the Raiders' Double H defense is one of the toughest in the NFL today.

The first weekend in August marks the beginning of the pre-season games in front of the public. Four games will be played against various teams, although traditions governing who plays who go back a long way. Dallas almost always play one of their games with the Houston Oilers.

Although not part of the regular season, these games are taken very seriously by players, coaches and supporters alike. They make up the first real test of their ability for the coming campaign, although they are not a definite indication of a team's forthcoming chances. The Los Angeles Raiders are notorious for their poor results in pre-season games, yet no one could deny their success once the season starts. Sadly for many an aspiring professional footballer, that success never comes. They are usually rejected somewhere along the trail. Yet masochistically most of them return each year to the training camps trying to fulfil their dream of instant stardom in the ranks of one of the most glamorous sports of the world.

Cuisine à la training camp

It is said that the food prepared at training camps for college and professional teams alike rivals that of many top restaurants.

The meals are planned by qualified nutritionists who spare neither quality nor quantity. To make sure that players have regular intakes of food a roll call is taken at every meal to make sure everyone is there.

Generally the rookies will sit together and the veterans when they arrive will have their own little areas, which they may possibly have occupied for many seasons. There are some special areas, notably one called the 'fat-man's table', where those players with too much body fat are given a special diet of low calorie food to bring their fat content down to a required standard. A lineman in the prime of life will average about 18 per cent body fat, whilst a linebacker will have approximately 14 per cent, a running back 10–12 per cent and a defensive back will only have about 8 per cent body fat. As a guideline, most people of average fitness and weight will carry 12–14 per cent fat on their bodies.

The variation on the camp menu is enormous and quite extravagant, but these are highly tuned, highly paid professional athletes who must be looked after. It is not

unknown for a player in a fit of hunger after a hard day of practice to eat one of each dish on the menu.

A typical menu at a football training camp would be as follows:

Breakfast

Fresh blueberries	OR	Fresh strawberries
Scrambled eggs with ham		Bacon and cheese omelette
French toast		Rolls and eggs (variations)
Bacon		
Eggs (variation to order)		

Lunch

Vegetable and beef soup	Fillet of sole
Hot turkey sandwich	Cream of potato soup
Mashed potatoes and gravy	Buttered noodles
Shrimp Chop Suey	Grilled steak sandwich
Buttered broccoli	

Dinner

Salmon fillet	Broiled lobster
New York steak	Baked chicken
Green beans	Corn on the cob
Cottage fried potatoes	Baked potatoes
Zucchini parmesan	Pecan pie
Chocolate cake	

Training Camp Schedule

A typical training camp schedule would look like this:

6.30–8.00	Breakfast and physical therapy Taping
8.00–8.30	Offense and defense meetings
8.30–9.00	Special teams meeting
8.50	Specialists leave meetings
9.00	Specialists on field
9.15–11.15	Field practise
11.45–12.30	Lunch
12.35	Report for treatment
12.35–1.15	Taping for rookies
12.35–2.15	Rest period
2.15–2.55	Taping for veterans
3.00–4.00	Offense and defense meetings
4.00–4.15	Specialists on field
4.15–6.15	Field practise
6.45–7.30	Dinner
7.30	Report for treatment
8.00	Evening offense and defense meetings and sometimes whole team talk
11.00	Bed

All in a Week's Work

Professional athletes follow rigid schedules during their in-season training and their off-season, and professional footballers are no different. Most games in the NFL are scheduled for Sundays, but some are played on a Monday or Thursday night. A few are played on Saturdays in certain areas and mainly towards the end of the season. Across the league most players follow a standard schedule, and when games are played on a day other than the normal Sunday, the day-off granted to players is normally re-scheduled.

Apart from this variation a normal working week for a professional footballer would look something like this:

Monday

Monday is the day that everyone is naturally tired from the previous day's endeavours.

following Thursday. Whilst the players can relax the coaches are at their busiest—there is no day off for them. They will spend the day in meetings, watching films and planning their strategy for the next game.

Wednesday and Thursday

After the Tuesday rest, the players return on the Wednesday for two days of intense work. Both days are a physical grind as both

---

National Football League—Least and Most

The Oldest Player in the NFL

The oldest player in the NFL at the moment is Green Bay's kicker, Jan Stenerud. Stenerud, who was born on 25 November 1943 has been kicking points in the National Football League for 19 seasons. The oldest outfield player in the league is Washington's veteran back-up quarterback Jim Hart. Hart was signed by the Redskins from St Louis in the spring of 1984 at the ripe old age of 40! Which proves that experience is sometimes more valued than youth.

The Tallest

Dallas Cowboys can boast two of the tallest players now playing in the NFL. Ed 'Too Tall' Jones and tackle Phil Poderac tower way above anyone else in professional football circles at 6ft 9in.

The Shortest

The award for the shortest player in the

NFL, belongs to Cincinnati's kicker Jim Breech. Breech measures 5 ft 6 in in his stocking feet, a full 15 inches shorter than the giant Ed Jones.

The Heaviest

Weight is an all important factor for lineman in professional football, and Angelo Fields takes the trophy for being the weightiest. Fields, a tackle for the New Orleans Saints weighs in at a massive 314lbs or 22st and 7lbs. Not far behind are Louie Kelcher (San Diego) at 310lbs and Washington's Joe Jacoby at 300lbs.

The Lightest

Two players tie for the lightest player award. Both Atlanta's wide receiver Ervin Sullivan and Houston's receiver Herkie Walls tip the scales at only 154lbs or 11st. A pound heavier at 155lbs is Green Bay's wide receiver Philip Epps.

The team meet on this day and begin their preparations for the next game. Videos are shown of the previous game and players are graded on their performances. Injured players report for treatment and the fit players often go through what is termed an easy workout, walking through some of the plays to be used in the next game.

Tuesday

Tuesday is the traditional day-off for players, unless the teams have played on the Monday evening or are due to play on the

the defense and the offense prepare to meet their next opponents. The greater part of these two days is spent on the practise fields perfecting new tactics. Mornings are used for both squads to study their opponents on film and then the afternoons are used to perfect the gameplan.

Friday

Friday is special plays day. The day is devoted to working on parts of the match strategy, not covered in the work done earlier in the week. Such things as short yardage defense, two-minute drills, kicking plays and formations are tried and tested to their full on this day.

Saturday

The Saturday routine depends upon whether the game is to be played at home or away.

If the game is at home, then the team will normally have a light practise in the stadium on the Saturday morning. Nothing physical will be done, plays will be walked through and maybe the special teams' assignments will be studied and gone through at a slow pace.

If the game is away, however, then Saturday is travelling day. A plane will deliver the team to their destination on Saturday afternoon or early evening. If there is time the team may have a short practise in the host stadium. Again this only consists of walking through plays, but it is especially important if the home team uses a different type of surface than the one the visiting team is used to playing on. Over the years crowd noise has also become a problem, and it has become increasingly difficult for visiting quarterbacks to make their play-calling heard. The Superbowl champions of 1984, San Francisco 49ers took with them on a visit to New Orleans a tape of crowd noise, which they played in the New Orleans Superdome whilst practising the night before the game, so as to get used to the accoustics of the stadium. Whether at home or away players have to attend the 9 pm meeting, which is the last full team meeting before the game. Even for home games the players are required to check into a hotel in their home city for the night. Coaches always like their players to be together, away from any family or outside distractions prior to a game. An 11 pm curfew is very strictly enforced and anybody who violates this usually incurs the wrath of the head coach and receives a very heavy fine.

Sunday

Sunday is traditionally match day in pro football circles. Four hours before the game the players will share their almost ritual pre-game meal, and travel by team bus to the stadium arriving some two hours before the kick-off.

Preparing for a game involves many things such as taping legs, ankles, wrists, etc;

putting on the various pieces of equipment and having a last minute review of what is expected of the players. In professional football the coach rarely makes a do-or-die speech to get the adrenalin flowing; only in college football is this part of the pre-game ritual still observed.

About 45 minutes before the game is due to begin the players take to the field for a warm up, before retiring to the seclusion of the dressing room. The game begins with the introductions of the teams, the national anthem and the coin-tossing ceremony.

At half time, back in the dressing rooms the coaches compare notes, and the spotters sitting high up in the press box of the stadium give their reports to the coaches. Fine tuning, or in some cases a complete change of plan will be made before the teams take the field for the second half.

At full time both teams return to their respective dressing rooms, where they face the barrage of the press. American sports have the self-inflicted ritual of a post-game press conference in their dressing rooms, where the victors are displayed in all their glory, whilst the vanquished are equally exposed drowning their sorrows.

After they have had showers, and stored their equipment the players will head for home, either by themselves, or in the team bus if they have been playing away from home.

The following day, Monday, sees the routine begin all over again, as the players forget the triumphs or failures of the previous day's work and start on the next week's game.

The National Football League's Hall of Fame

The National Football League decided on 27 April 1961 to set up a professional football

---

Did You Know

The most interesting nation in the world to which the Superbowl is beamed live is Brunei in South East Asia. The Sultan of Brunei is said to be an avid fan of football gridiron-style.

The NFL's professional football Hall of Fame in Canton, Ohio. Note the white football-shaped dome rising from the centre of the building. (NFL Hall of Fame).

Hall of Fame at Canton, Ohio. Canton was chosen because the original meeting to found the NFL had been held there way back in 1920.

Individuals, foundations and companies in and around the Canton area donated nearly $400 000 in cash and services to help fund the project and the Hall of Fame was opened on 7 September 1963.

The original complex was almost doubled in size in 1971 when a $620 000 expansion project was completed. A second expansion was finished in 1978, which included three extra exhibition areas and a theatre twice the size of the original one.

The Hall of Fame caters for every aspect of professional football. There are three large and colourful exhibition galleries built around two halls enshrining football greats, a theatre, a research library, and an NFL gift shop. In recent years the Hall of Fame has become an extremely popular tourist attraction. By the end of 1983 a total of three and a half million fans had visited the centre.

Members of the pro football Hall of Fame are elected annually by the 29 members of a national board of selectors, made up of media writers from every league city and the president of the pro football writers' association. Between four and seven new members are elected each year, and to get voted into the hall a nominee must gain the votes of approximately 80 per cent of the board.

Anybody may nominate a player or contributor for election, simply by writing to the Hall of Fame. Nominated players however must have been retired for at least five years to be eligible, but a coach can be elected immediately on retirement, and others, such as administrators and owners, may be elected whilst still in office.

At the first election in 1963, 17 members were elected into what has become known as the 'charter' class. Amongst the elected members in that inaugural year were Jim Thorpe, the NFL's first president in 1920; Joe Carr, who was president from 1921–1939; commissioner Bert Bell; Chicago Bears' owner and coach George Halas; veteran players Sammy Baugh, Don Hutson, Bronko Nagurski and the all-star fullback of the 1920s and 1930s Ernie Nevers.

At the time of the 1985 elections, when a further four players were chosen, the membership of professional football's most elite club stands at 128.

O. J. Simpson

It was football's great fortune that young Orenthal James Simpson chose a career on the gridiron; for he could also have become a great athlete. A supreme sprinter with a speed of 9.4 seconds for the 100-yard sprint, O. J. Simpson in the late 1960s was an earlier version of Carl Lewis.

In two years at City College in San Francisco, O. J. Simpson ran for 2552 yards and 54 touchdowns. His efforts were noticed by the scouts from the University of Southern California and in 1967 the fresh faced running back moved to Los Angeles to begin a record breaking career at the Trojans.

Coach John McKay rated Simpson as one of the best prospects he had ever seen and it was not long before his faith was rewarded. 'The Juice', as he became known by his fellow players, ran for 3124 yards, scored 33 touchdowns and either equalled or broke 19 NCAA, Conference or USC records. The University, with Simpson at tailback, won the National Championship in 1967 and in 1968 Simpson himself was awarded the ultimate accolade in College football when he won the prestigious Heisman Trophy.

Because of these feats, Simpson was a first round choice for the Buffalo Bills in the 1969 draft.

On his arrival in the NFL Simpson was heralded by many as a new Jim Brown, but O. J. was not quite the same sort of player.

Where Brown would literally blast his way through defensive lines, Simpson needed a little help from his own linemen to achieve his goals. Many coaches teach young talent to keep their feet moving, and O. J. Simpson was the greatest exponent of this art. He would stand around behind the line of scrimmage, hopping from one foot to another looking for a place to run.

Simpson once described his style as 'cowardly', but the stutter-step, as it became known, was one of his greatest assets.

O. J. Simpson is best remembered for his record breaking season of 1973. In only 14 games, he rushed for an amazing 2003 yards.

The new record was finally established on the final week of the season in New York's Shea Stadium. On a bitterly cold day, during a snow storm, Simpson passed the magic 2000 mark with only 6 minutes left on the clock.

In 1976, O. J. Simpson added another record on national television when he amassed 273 yards in a Thanksgiving Day game against Detroit.

Simpson was transferred to his home team, the San Francisco 49ers in 1977. Sadly, injuries had taken their toll, and with three serious knee operations behind him O. J. Simpson decided to call it a day at the end of the 1979 season.

Simpson was not only a great player on the field, he was a great player off it. It therefore came as no surprise that on his retirement he became a football commentator for the ABC network, and in the spring of 1985 received the ultimate accolade of being elected to the NFL Hall of Fame the first time he was nominated.

Opposite The great O. J. Simpson breaks away for the winning touchdown for U.S.C. against U.C.L.A. in the 1967 game between the two colleges.

O.J. drafted by the Buffalo Bills went on to play brilliantly in the NFL.

1963 Charter Membership of the Hall of Fame

Sammy Baugh Quarterback, Washington Redskins, 1937–1952
Bert Bell Team owner and Commissioner of NFL, 1946–1959
Joe Carr President of the NFL, 1921–1939
Earl (Dutch) Clark Quarterback, Portsmouth Spartans, 1931–1932; Detroit Lions, 1934–1938
Red Grange Halfback, Chicago Bears and New York Yankees, 1925–1934
George Halas Coach, 1920–1967, and team owner of Chicago Bears until death in 1983
Mel Hein Center, New York Giants, 1931–1945
Wilbur (Pete) Henry Tackle, Canton Bulldogs, 1920–23; Canton Bulldogs, 1925–25; New York Giants, 1927; Pottsville Maroons, 1927–1928
Cal Hubbard Tackle, New York Giants, Green Bay Packers and Pittsburgh Pirates, 1927–1936
Don Hutson End, Green Bay Packers, 1935–1945
Earl (Curly) Lambeau Coach, Green Bay Packers, 1919–1949; Chicago Cardinals, 1950–1951; Washington Redskins, 1952–1953
Tim Mara Team Owner, New York Giants, 1925–1959
George Preston Marshall Team Owner, Boston Braves, 1932; Boston Redskins, 1933–1936; Washington Redskins 1936–1969
Johnny (Blood) McNally Halfback, Milwaukee Badgers, Duluth Eskimos, Pottsville Maroons, Green Bay Packers, Pittsburgh Pirates, 1925–1939
Bronko Nagurski Fullback, Chicago Bears, 1930–1937 and 1943
Ernie Nevers Fullback, Duluth Eskimos, 1926–1927; Chicago Cardinals, 1929–1931
Jim Thorpe Halfback, Canton Bulldogs, Cleveland Indians, Oorang Indians, Toledo Maroons, Rock Island Independents, New York Giants, Chicago Cardinals. First President of the American Professional Football Association, forerunner of the NFL, 1920–1928

Did You Know

That NFL commissioner Pete Rozelle's real name is Alvin. The nickname of 'Pete' was given to him by a favourite uncle when he was 5 years old.

That professional footballers were not required to wear protective headgear until 1943. Until then the wearing of helmets was purely optional.

1985 elections to the Hall of Fame

Four players and one administrator (Pete Rozelle) make up the illustrious list of those selected for induction into the Hall of Fame.

Three gridiron giants are at last chosen to enter football's most famous hall: New York Jets' quarterback 'Broadway' Joe Namath; record-breaking running back O. J. Simpson of Buffalo and San Francisco and Dallas Cowboys' star quarter-back of the seventies Roger Staubach. The fifth member in the class of 1985 is former Cleveland and Detroit center Frank Gatski.

Black Players

Black athletes now make up about 60 per cent of professional football rosters. The first black quarterback was the aptly named Willie Thrower who played for the Chicago Bears in 1953. Black players had been part of professional football teams for a long time, one of the first being Fritz Pollard who played for many teams in the early 1920s including Akron, Hammond and the Milwaukee Badgers. As well as playing for these teams Pollard also coached them, thereby becoming the first black professional football coach. Racial prejudice was still rife in America and after retiring from playing the game in 1929, football's coach of a different colour organized the Chicago Blackhawks, the country's first black semi-pro team. He moved from Chicago to New York in 1934 and coached another all black team the 'Brown Bombers'.

In more recent times the name of Emlen Tunnell stands out as a coloured coach of distinction. Tunnell was a defensive back for the New York Giants and the Green Bay Packers from 1948–61, and joined the Giants' coaching staff in 1965.

Although there is a majority of black players in football's ranks today, the position of quarterback still remains predominantly white. The three big exceptions are Houston Oilers' Warren Moon, Arizona Outlaws' playmaker Doug Williams and Memphis Showboats' starting quarterback Walter Lewis.

The Superbowls

The name 'Superbowl' was devised by Kansas City Chiefs' owner Lamar Hunt in 1966. At the meeting in that year of the NFL and the rival AFL (of which Hunt was a member and leading figure), it was decided to hold an inter-league championship game, to be called the 'World Championship of Professional Football', the following year.

The Memorial Coliseum at Los Angeles was chosen as the site of the sporting showdown for which the whole of America had been waiting. On 15 January 1967, Vince Lombardi and his Green Bay Packers, representing the NFL confronted Hunts' Chiefs, who held the AFL title, before a crowd of 61 946 fans.

But the opening round in a long series of inter-league rivalries went to the NFL as the Packers stormed to a memorable 35–10 victory.

The hero of the day was a seventeenth-round draft choice called Bart Starr. Most players selected in such a late round do not survive the rigours of professional football, and Starr recalled after the game that had he followed the usual path, he too would have decided upon a different career in the US Air Force. Instead, Starr served as a 'General' guiding the Packer attack to two consecutive Superbowl victories. In that first game Starr completed 16 of 23 passes for 250 yards and two touchdowns to reserve wide receiver Max McGhee.

Starr was the master tactician, carrying out coach Lombardi's gameplan to near perfection and he was the deserved winner of the very first Superbowl's MVP (most valuable player) award.

Starr continued to dominate in Superbowl II in Miami, Florida. The Packers had just won their third consecutive NFL title and were worthy representatives against the Oakland Raiders. Over 75 000 people provided football with its first $3 million

Greenbay Packers' quarterback Bart Starr was the MVP in both Superbowls 1 and 11. (Greenbay Packers).

dollar gate. The Packers wore down a very strong Raiders team to win the game and the title by 33 points to 14. Starr was again awarded the MVP award for his superb control of a game in which he connected on 13 of 24 passes for 202 yards including a massive 62-yard pass to Boyd Dowler. Kicker Don Chandler was another Green Machine hero, scoring four field goals, which cornerback Herb Adderley capped a victorious day for the Wisconsin outfit with a 60-yard score on an interception late in the fourth quarter.

Walter Payton

In December 1984 Walter Payton broke Jim Brown's long standing NFL rushing record and wrote his name into the history books of pro football.

His list of credits is impressive and is growing all the time, but Walter 'Sweetness' Payton is not himself impressed.

A shy person by nature, Payton is a rarity in football circles, preferring to keep himself to himself off the field. To the public he is a superstar following in the path of former great Chicago Bears players like Red Grange, Bronko Nagurski and Gale Sayers, but that is where the likeness ends.

Despite his dislike of public appearances and his refusal to discuss his private life, Walter Payton is one of the greatest running backs of our time. He is 5ft 10in tall, weighs 205lbs, can bench press 85lbs more than his own weight, and runs the 40-yard dash in an impressive 4.5 seconds. He can walk 40 yards on his hands and has even had the occasion to jump over the top of a 250lb assistant coach.

But to the followers of the gridiron game Walter Payton is a legend. As well as rushing for more yards than any other player, his combined total yardage is greater than any one else and he has rushed 100 yards in more games than anyone else.

Unfortunately, like Simpson at Buffalo, Payton has not shared in any great team successes, and if his immense talents were on parade for a more stylish team then perhaps his superstar status would be more evident.

Born in Columbia, Mississippi on 25 July 1954, the young Payton attended Jackson State University where he quickly gained a reputation as a good running back. The Chicago Bears were looking for some new talent in 1975, in order to rebuild their team.

The legendary Gale Sayers had retired through injury in 1972, and the Bears were keen to find the right replacement. It was on Payton that they pinned their hopes when they chose him in the first round of that year's draft.

Almost immediately Payton began to earn his salary. In 1976 and 1977 he was voted as

Chicago Bears' running back Walter Payton takes a rest between plays.

Payton on one of his record-breaking runs during the 1984 season.

the NFC player of the year and became the NFL player of the year as well. At the age of 24 years he was the youngest man ever to win the award.

On 20 November 1977 in a game against Minnesota Vikings, Payton rushed for 275 yards, breaking the league's single game rushing record. After just five years he had become the Chicago Bears best rusher ever, an immense feat considering the players that had preceded him.

A quiet, unassuming family man, Walter Payton is described as a team man who cares little for personal glory. After his 1000 yards plus season in 1976 he presented all his offensive line with a gold watch, inscribed on the back, 'Thanks for the 1000 yards'.

'Why should I be famous', he once asked. 'I can't heal the World, all I do is carry a football.'

Carrying it the way he does, football's peers need ask for no more.

It wasn't until Superbowl III that the AFL gained credibility in the eyes of most football supporters. The New York Jets came to Miami as the underdogs for their championship game against the all-conquering Baltimore Colts. On the Thursday before the game the Jets' quarterback Joe Namath 'guaranteed' to the world's press that the New York team would win. Namath put his words into action on the day of the game as he led the Jets to a thrilling 16–7 victory. The Colts' star quarterback Johnny Unitas, who had been injured for most of the season, came off the bench late in the fourth quarter to lead the Baltimore team to their only touchdown as the AFL celebrated their coming of age.

The AFL dominance continued the following year in Superbowl IV. A crowd in excess of 80 000 turned out in the New Orleans Tulane Stadium to watch Hank Stram grab a famous 23–7 win. It is customary for presidents of the United States to telephone the winning team after the game, but President Richard Nixon broke the rule by calling the Chiefs before the event. His main purpose was to assure the Kansas quarterback Len Dawson that he had been cleared of any involvement in a federal gambling investigation. Relieved of this pressure, Dawson threw for 122 yards and a touchdown to lead the Chiefs to victory, against a tame Minnesota Vikings team.

Superbowl V created yet another piece of history. Dallas Cowboys' linebacker Chuck Howley became the only player on the losing side to win the prestigious MVP award.

Superbowl V marked the first championship game to be played on artificial turf, in Miami's Orange Bowl. The game was finely balanced until the final seconds as Dallas and Baltimore had scored 13 apiece. Although Howley won the MVP for outstanding work on the Cowboys' defense, the real hero of the day was the Colts' kicker Jim O'Brien. O'Brien, who had dreamt the night before that he would kick the winning field goal, kicked a 32-yard attempt between the posts with only five seconds remaining.

The Cowboys returned to the Superbowl the next year in New Orleans to regain their pride and record a victory over the Miami Dolphins 24–3. The Cowboys' defense under the charge of Howley kept the

Dolphins' offense at bay and they became the first team to stop the opposition from scoring a touchdown in a Superbowl. The player voted MVP, Roger Stanbach, had not competed in the previous year's game, but in Superbowl VI he controlled a potent offense that rushed for a record 252 yards and personally threw for 119 yards and two touchdowns to take the title back to the Lone Star State.

After the Dolphins had finished as bridesmaids in Superbowls III and VI, Don Shula became the second coach to win consecutive titles in games VII and VIII. In Superbowl VII the Dolphins created football history by completing the 'perfect season', that is, going through the whole season unbeaten. Miami's 'no-name' defense suddenly found it had a star worth naming in Jake Scott, who was the right safety and played the whole game, intercepting two passes, including a critical sneak midway through the fourth quarter when a Washington offense had really begun to roll. Miami had marched into a 14–0 lead, but with Scott's help the Dolphins kept the Redskins down to only one touchdown to seal a famous win.

The Dolphins marched proudly into their third consecutive Superbowl appearance in Rice Stadium, Houston on 13 January 1974 for a showdown with the Minnesota Vikings. The game saw the emergence of a new all-American hero, Larry Csonka. Csonka slammed into the Vikings time and time again for a record-breaking total of 145 yards, as the Dolphins, led by quarterback Bob Griese, swamped Minnesota 24–7. Csonka, who carried the football 33 times and scored two touchdowns, was so effective that Griese only had to throw the ball seven times.

The Vikings returned to the fray in Superbowl IX, once again staged in New Orlean's Tulane Stadium. But as had happened in their two previous outings, they had to play second fiddle. The victory this time went to a team playing in its first

Pittsburgh Steelers' Chuck Nolls is the only coach to win the Superbowl four times. (Pittsburgh Steelers).

Superbowl X in January of 1976 saw them once again in the final, this time pitted against another team of distinction, the Dallas Cowboys.

The Steelers won the game late in the fourth quarter when quarterback Terry Bradshaw connected on a pass to wide receiver Lynn Swann, who rounded his marker, Mark Washington, and raced some 64 yards to seal the victory. Swann's agility in pass receiving (he set a Superbowl record of 161 yards), earned him the MVP award, a quite remarkable achievement because in the AFC championship game he had been knocked out by Oakland's Jack Tatum, and hospitalized for three days before joining the team at their pre-game headquarters.

Superbowl XI created many records off the field. A record 103 438 fans packed the Pasadena Rosebowl to witness the event and 81 million TV viewers tuned in as well, the largest audience ever to watch a sporting event. They were not disappointed as the Oakland Raiders and the Minnesota Vikings played some great football. For the Vikings, however, it turned out to be yet another loser's year, but for Oakland it was their first World Championship. The Raiders' stalwart receiver, Fred Biletnikoff, made four key receptions and the Raiders won the game 32–14. Biletnikoff, who reckoned he had smoked two packets of cigarettes in the dressing room before the game, earned the MVP award, while cornerback Willie Brown sealed the game with a record breaking 75-yard interception return late in the match.

An audience of 102 million people throughout the world witnessed Superbowl XII in the Louisiana Superdome in 1978. A capacity crowd of 75 000 sat rivetted to their seats in the air conditioned covered arena as

ever NFL Championship game. It had taken the Pittsburgh Steelers 42 years to reach the final game, and after such a lean period they were determined not to go away empty handed. With a raw young running back called Franco Harris, passing the 1000 yards rushing mark in only his third season, the Steelers gave their owner Art Rooney a present not to be forgotten. Harris rushed for 158 yards against the Vikings, breaking the record set the previous year by Csonka. Harris adopted a policy similar to Csonka's of the season before—powerhouse rushing. In full flight there was hardly a thing that could stop him, and it was no surprise to see him named as the game's MVP as the Steelers marched to a 16–6 victory.

Football like most sports tends to run in dynasties, and the dynasty of the 1970s was undoubtedly that of the Pittsburgh Steelers.

Did You Know
That the Pittsburgh Steelers hold the distinction of being the only Superbowl team to field a team comprised totally of players who have never played for another club. The Superbowl XIV champions included 39 players who had been Pittsburgh draftees and six original free agent signings.

Did You Know

That there are moves afoot in the NFL to stop the retirement of players' numbers. This practice involves the retiring of the number of a team's famous or favourite player upon his own retirement. But as one team official put it, 'If we keep on retiring jersey numbers we will sooner or later run out of numbers and will have to resort to using letters'. The suggestion that has been put forward as an alternative is that the player's jersey only be retired, to the NFL Hall of Fame in Canton, Ohio.

Dallas, always in the lead, kept their cool to run out victors by 27–10. The key to their success was, without doubt, their twin blitz threat of defensive end Harvey Martin and defensive tackle Randy White who gave Denver's quarterback Craig Morton so much trouble that his passing became very, very erratic. So erratic in fact that the Cowboys' defense picked off four interceptions and recovered four fumbles. Martin and White became the first co-owners of the game's MVP trophy.

Superbowl XIII in Miami in 1979 was a victory for the 'Steel Curtain' and the 'Steel Arm'. The Steel Curtain belonged to Pittsburgh's marauding defensive unit consisting of 'Mean' Joe Green, Jack Ham and Jack Lambert. The Steel Arm belonged to quarterback Terry Bradshaw who threw for four touchdowns and a total of 318 yards to win the MVP award. The game was one of the most exciting seen in Superbowl history, as the Steelers rushed into a 35–17 lead with only 7 minutes left on the clock, during which they scored two touchdowns in 19 seconds. Dallas, superbly led by the unflappable Roger Staubach came back to score two themselves before time ran out.

The Steelers' supremacy continued in 1980 as they defeated the Los Angeles Rams by 31 points to 19. In Pasadena's Rosebowl another record breaking crowd of 103 985 witnessed Terry Bradshaw retain the team title as well as the MVP trophy. Bradshaw completed 14 of 21 passes for 309 yards and two touchdowns, and set Superbowl records for most yards gained in Superbowls (932), most yards gained in a single final (318), highest average gain in a career (11.10 yards per pass), highest average gain per game (14.17), most touchdown passes (9), and most touchdown passes in a single final game (4). Jim Plunkett almost came back from the dead to rise to fame in the Superbowl XV game. Plunkett had been discarded by near neighbours San Francisco, after a couple of injury riddled years. The 1970 Heisman trophy winner had been the toast of all football when he was drafted by the New England Patriots in 1971, but five troubled years there, and two with the 49ers, had given him a sound education in the hardships of football life. The Raiders became the first team in NFL history to reach a Superbowl as the wild card entrants. The game, in the New Orleans Superdome against the Philadelphia Eagles, eventually proved to be a one-sided affair as Plunkett threw three touchdown passes, including an amazing 80-yard bomb to Kenny King.

The World Championship stayed in California in 1982 when across the bay the San Francisco 49ers under the leadership of

Superbowl Firsts

Green Bay Packers' quarterback Bart Starr was the first Superbowl MVP, leading the Packers to 35–10 victory over the Kansas City Chiefs in Superbowl I.

Dallas Cowboys' linebacker Chuck Howley became the first and only player on a losing side to win the Superbowl MVP award in game V.

Superbowl V was the first championship game to be played on artificial turf in Miami's Orange bowl.

Dallas Cowboys in Superbowl VI became the first team to prevent the opposition from scoring a touchdown in a Superbowl.

Superbowl XII produced the first dual MVP award when Dallas's Randy White and Harvey Martin were awarded the trophy.

another great quarterback, Joe Montana, eclipsed the Cincinnati Bengals 26–21 in Detroit's Pontiac Silverdome. Freezing weather outside the domed stadium did not stop the Californian sunshine boys from victory as Montana scored himself on a one yard sneak and later connected on an 11-yard pass to Earl Cooper. In spite of all their efforts, the Bengals, who rushed 356 yards compared to the 49ers' 275 yards, could not prevent the title going back west as the well organized and effectively simple game plan of San Francisco paid handsome dividends.

Washington Redskins' remarkable victory in Superbowl XVII was their first NFL championship since 1942. Opponents Miami had amassed a 17–0 lead at the end of the first quarter, and nobody expected the Redskins to return from the brink of disaster. Statistics, amongst other things, proved the difficulty of this, but Washington, with second year head coach Joe Gibbs on the sidelines, quarterback Joe Theismann controlling the offense and a certain John Riggins rushing behind the powerful blocking of the offensive line's aptly named Hogs, rallied in the second half to score 14 unanswered points in the fourth quarter to win the game. Riggins ran in on a 43-yard rush and Charlie Brown caught a 6-yard pass from Theismann with one minute fifty five seconds left to complete the scoring. Miami's Fulton Walker made Superbowl history just before the break with a 98-yard kick-off return, and the MVP award went to John Riggins who rushed for a second 116 yards on 38 carries, an achievement which did much to spark the Washington team to victory.

After winning the previous year's final in such style Washington returned in 1984 to play the Los Angeles Raiders, in what many termed as the toughest final yet. The game turned out to be the most lop-sided victory for the Raiders as their defense snuffed out the potent Washington pass and rush. The

Did You Know

In Superbowl XVI, Cincinnati Bengal head coach Forrest Gregg became the first man to have appeared in the game as both a player for Green Bay in Superbowls I and II and as a head coach.

Superbowl Winners

I	Green Bay Packers 35 Kansas City Chiefs 10
II	Green Bay Packers 33 Oakland Raiders 14
III	New York Jets 16 Baltimore Colts 7
IV	Kansas City Chiefs 23 Minnesota Vikings 7
V	Baltimore Colts 16 Dallas Cowboys 13
VI	Dallas Cowboys 24 Miami Dolphins 3
VII	Miami Dolphins 14 Washington Redskins 7
VIII	Miami Dolphins 24 Minnesota Vikings 7
IX	Pittsburgh Steelers 16 Minnesota Vikings 6
X	Pittsburgh Steelers 21 Dallas Cowboys 17
XI	Oakland Raiders 32 Minnesota Vikings 14
XII	Dallas Cowboys 27 Denver Broncos 10
XIII	Pittsburgh Steelers 35 Dallas Cowboys 31
XIV	Pittsburgh Steelers 31 Los Angeles Rams 19
XV	Oakland Raiders 27 Philadelphia Eagles 10
XVI	San Francisco 49ers 26 Cincinnati Bengals 21
XVII	Washington Redskins 27 Miami Dolphins 17
XVIII	Los Angeles Raiders 38 Washington Redskins 9
XIX	San Francisco 49ers 38 Miami Dolphins 16

Forthcoming Superbowls

XX	26 January 1986, Louisiana Superdome, New Orleans
XXI	25 January 1987, Pasadena Rosebowl, California

Raiders, always in control, took a 21–3 half-time lead and continued to dominate totally on both offense and defense. Marcus Allen typified their domination with a superb 74-yard touchdown run in the third quarter, first going one way, finding the path blocked and magnificently changing direction to find a massive hole in the Redkins' defense. Allen rushed for a record 191 yards and two touchdowns to win the coveted MVP award.

The pre-game talk of a showdown between the two offensive giants of the 1984 season, San Francisco 49ers and Miami Dolphins, proved sadly to be a total miscalculation of events. Both teams had arrived at Superbowl XIX in Stanford's Stadium with high hopes. Both had outstanding quarterbacks in Joe Montana and the record breaking Dan Marino. For Marino the game turned into a real nightmare as the 49ers defense upset his plan of play. Montana on the other hand was Mr Cool, as he cajoled his team to a 38–16 victory almost with ease. Montana completed 24 of 35 passes for a Superbowl record of 331 yards and three touchdowns. Running back Roger Craig was a close second for the MVP award when he became the first player to score three touchdowns in a final. In another one-sided game San Francisco operating a superb double and sometimes triple coverage plan gave Marino nothing to pass to and for the second year running the World Championship stayed on the west coast.

John Riggins

To put it quite simply John Riggins is different. Many of the stars of the gridiron use the media to their own ends. In contrast John Riggins tends to shy away from all the publicity that he has deservedly won.

Riggins was brought up in Centralia, Kansas, the son of Gene, a farmer and one-time fullback for Wichita State. He went to Kansas where he broke all of Gale Sayers rushing records. In four college seasons he never missed a game or a practice. He did

not dare to do so because the alternative to football was to go back to the farm.

Despite his introvertedness, Riggins can be a shocker, and just to prove the point he turned up at the New York Jets' training camp with a Mohican haircut and a gold pearl in his earlobe. The Jets' coach Weeb Ewbank thought he had seen everything the day Joe Namath turned up in a mink coat, but Riggins's approach was different. 'I guess it won't look too bad when he puts

his helmet on', he joked. In 1976 Riggins played out his option in New York and signed a $1.5 million contract with the Washington Redskins. By concidence, their opening match the following season was against the Jets; the Redskins won but Riggins did not have one of his better days. In 1979 John Riggins was suspended for missing practice at the Redskins' training camp. He told Washington general manager Bobby Beathard that he needed time to think and he even mentioned retirement, but he returned two days later and went on to have one of his finest seasons, rushing for 1153 yards and nine touchdowns.

In Superbowl XVII Riggins set a new rushing record with 166 yards on 38 carries to spark the Redskins to a famous last minute victory over Miami, 27–17.

The 1983 season was a personal triumph for the lonesome Riggins. He chalked up 1347 yards rushing and 24 touchdowns and helped the Washington outfit to another Superbowl. But this time it was the turn of another famous running back, Marcus Allen, to make all the headlines as the Redskins lost to the Raiders 38–9.

In 1984 Riggins was plagued with knee injuries, and when the Redskins only succeeded in getting as far as the first round

Two contrasting images. *Opposite left* John Riggins in his days as a rebel running back for the New York Jets. (*Touchdown Magazine*).
Right John Riggins before the Superbowl XVIII against Miami in which he was the MVP. (All-Sport).

of the play-offs, Riggins admitted to some of his team mates that perhaps at the age of 35 it was time to hang up the boots and helmet.

His style of play, which many thought similar to that of the great Jim Brown, was always going to pay a heavy penalty in terms of injuries, and the Hogs of Washington may have to look for another battering ram rusher to replace Riggins who has completed 14 seasons in the NFL.

If 1984 is to be his last competitive season, the Redskins' number 44 will never look quiet the same to British TV viewers, for John Riggins was without doubt their first gridiron hero.

Despite his reclusive nature, John Riggins will be sorely missed by everyone in football, but he will probably be welcomed back with open arms by Dad and the farm in the wheatfields of Kansas.

Did You Know

That three kickers tie for the record number of goals filed in one game, with no misses. Gino Cappelletti, Boston Patriots' kicker, scored six times in a game against Denver on 4 October 1964.

On 18 October 1981, Joe Danelo the New York Giants' kicker did the same in a game against Seattle Seahawks and two years later on 16 October 1983 San Francisco 49ers' Ray Wersching kicked six against the Cincinnati Bengals.

The much publicised battle had become a massacre as the Superbowl left one decade and entered another.

Superbowl Bonus

As well as their normal salaries the players, coaches and administration staff of the competing teams collect massive bonuses for their appearance in a Superbowl.

In Superbowl XVII, between the Washington Redskins and the Miami Dolphins, the winning players collected $36 000 each, whilst the losers received $18 000. As well as the players' pay, the coaching staff and all the backroom staff at both clubs receive a hefty paycheck. A figure in excess of $2.6 million was paid to the two competing clubs in Superbowl XVII.

Attendance History

A total of 1 454 001 people have attended the first 19 Superbowls. The largest crowd was 103 985 at Superbowl XIV, which was played in the Rose Bowl in Pasadena, California.

Rings of War

Unlike most other major sporting finals, the winners of each Superbowl collect not a medal but a ring for their efforts. This is no ordinary ring though; for instance the one made for the victorious Superbowl XVI team, the San Francisco 49ers, contained more than two carats of diamonds and were valued at over $5 000. Each winning club chooses a manufacturer and from various designs submitted the final choice, usually very complex, will be made. Rings are also given to those elected to the Hall of Fame. The rings will be designed and made during the close season, and those returning to the team for pre-season training in July will collect them then. But such is the mystique of these precious objects that many players have been known to fly in from various parts of the USA to collect them as soon as they are ready. Approximately 75 rings are produced for each winning club.

The biggest ring ever produced was for the Green Bay Packers' victory in Superbowl II. The ring cost $1900 to produce in 1968 and weighs 30 pennyweight—a real knuckleduster.

The National Football League Superbowls Most Valuable Player Awards

I	Bart Starr, Quarterback, Green Bay Packers
II	Bart Starr, Quarterback, Green Bay Packers
III	Joe Namath, Quarterback, New York Jets
IV	Len Dawson, Quarterback, Kansas City Chiefs
V	Chuck Howley, Linebacker, Dallas Cowboys
VI	Roger Staubach, Quarterback, Dallas Cowboys
VII	Jake Scott, Safety, Miami Dolphins
VIII	Larry Csonka, Running Back, Miami Dolphins
IX	Franco Harris, Running Back, Pittsburgh Steelers
X	Lynn Swann, Wide Receiver, Pittsburgh Steelers
XI	Fred Biletnikoff, Wide Receiver, Oakland Raiders
XII	Harvey Martin, Defensive End and Randy White, Defensive Tackle, Dallas Cowboys
XIII	Terry Bradshaw, Quarterback, Pittsburgh Steelers
XIV	Terry Bradshaw, Quarterback, Pittsburgh Steelers
XV	Jim Plunkett, Quarterback, Oakland Raiders
XVI	Joe Montana, Quarterback, San Francisco 49ers
XVII	John Riggins, Running Back, Washington Redskins
XVIII	Marcus Allen, Running Back, Los Angeles Raiders
XIX	Joe Montana, Quarterback, San Francisco 49ers

Choice of colours
The AFC and NFC Champions alternate as the home team. The home team always has the choice of wearing coloured or white jerseys.

The largest sized ring produced for an individual was a size 20 ring made for San Francisco 49ers defensive end Lawrence Pillar in 1982. Previously the record was held by Bronco Nagurski for his size 19 Pro-Football Hall of Fame ring.

The winning club is presented immediately after the game with the Vince Lombardi Trophy. Symbolizing the Championship of Professional Football the trophy is made of sterling silver, stands 20 inches high and weighs approximately 7 pounds. It depicts a regulation size football on an elongated base with three concave sides. On the front surface is engraved, *Vince Lombardi Trophy*. Below that appears the NFL shield, and the words, *Superbowl* and *AFC v NFC*. Each year a new trophy is cast, as the winning team gain permanent possession of this supreme professional football award.

The Pro Bowls

The first Pro Bowl of sorts took place at Los Angeles's Wrigley Field on 15 January 1939.

That day the NFL champions, the New York Giants met an all-star team and won 13–10.

The idea for such a game came from Washington Redskins' owner George Preston Marshall who teamed up with a Los Angeles newspaper to launch it. In 1942, largely because of the war, the game was sidelined, and it wasn't until 1951 that it returned in a new format.

The 1951 Bowl matched the all-stars of the National Conference against the American. The AFC won on that day 28–27 in the Los Angeles Coliseum. The Pro Bowl was played for in various ways until 1971, when, after the merger of the two rival leagues (the American Football League and the National Football League), the AFC-NFC end of season game acquired a new significance.

The first game, held in Los Angeles on 24 January 1971 was a victory for the traditional NFC who beat the new AFC 27–6. In 1973 the event moved to the Texas Stadium, the home of the Dallas Cowboys, where the AFC erased a first half deficit of 14 points to win 32–28, thanks largely to the powerful running of one O. J. Simpson. The Pro Bowl then went on a sort of walkabout across the USA as it moved from Texas to Kansas, Miami, New Orleans, Seattle, Tampa and

back to Los Angeles in 1979 before it took up residence in Honolulu the following year.

In the history of the modern day Pro Bowl the NFC has won the game nine times compared to the AFC's six. The most recent game was in 1985 when the AFC, with the New York Jets' defensive end Mark Gastineau dominant with four sacks, won by a 22–14 scoreline.

The players for the Pro Bowl are selected because of their record during the previous season and each conference will also select a coach for each team. In the 1985 game Chicago's Mike Ditka coached the NFC whilst Pittsburgh coach Chuck Knoll had the honour of coaching the AFC.

Results

Year	Date	Winner	Loser	Place	Attendance
1985	27 Jan	AFC 22	NFC 14	Honolulu	46 200
1984	29 Jan	NFC 45	AFC 3	Honolulu	50 445
1983	6 Feb	NFC 20	AFC 19	Honolulu	47 201
1982	31 Jan	AFC 16	NFC 13	Honolulu	49 521
1981	1 Feb	NFC 21	AFC 7	Honolulu	47 879
1980	27 Jan	NFC 37	AFC 27	Honolulu	48 060
1979	29 Jan	NFC 13	AFC 7	Los Angeles	46 281
1978	23 Jan	NFC 14	AFC 13	Tampa	51 337
1977	17 Jan	AFC 24	NFC 14	Seattle	64 151
1976	26 Jan	NFC 23	AFC 20	New Orleans	30 546
1975	20 Jan	NFC 17	AFC 10	Miami	26 484
1974	20 Jan	AFC 15	NFC 13	Kansas City	66 918
1973	21 Jan	AFC 33	NFC 28	Dallas	37 091
1972	23 Jan	AFC 26	NFC 13	Los Angeles	53 647
1971	24 Jan	NFC 27	AFC 6	Los Angeles	48 222

Did You Know

That the biggest win from behind in college football history belongs to the University of Maryland. The Terrapins set the record on 10 November 1984 when they came out for the second half trailing by 31–0. By the end of the game the Maryland outfit had beaten the University of Miami 42–40. The previous record was set three weeks earlier in October when Washington State came back from a 28 point deficit to beat Stanford by 49 points to 42.

Marcus Allen

In the cauldron of Tampa Stadium on 22 January 1984 a young man with an impeccable pedigree came of age. With a swivel of the hips, a quick 180 degree turn and a record-breaking 74-yard touchdown run a quiet unassuming 23-year-old became the latest in a long time of Superbowl heroes.

For Marcus Allen, Superbowl XVIII marked the climax of a brilliant season which saw him named as the game's most valuable player. Suddenly the whole world was talking about Marcus Allen. Superlatives flowed off the tongue with ease whenever his name was mentioned. 'The greatest', said some. 'The best running back since O.J.', said others. Yet Marcus Allen's talents as a running back could have been lost to football had others had their way.

For whilst a student at San Diego's Lincoln High Allen also played as a safety on defense and doubled on offense as one of the school's quarterbacks. It was his quarterbacking activities that were noticed by the University of Oklahoma who tried to recruit him in that position. However, Allen's choice was U.S.C. and he eventually joined the Southern Californian University as a defensive player. When he enrolled at U.S.C. coach John Robinson noticed that the young Allen had more talents as a back on the offense, and during the Autumn training session he tried him out as a fullback. That first practice at the Trojans' camp was one Allen never forgot, because a hefty tackle resulted in a broken nose.

As a sophomore Allen's blocking helped no. 1 Trojan tailback Charles White to the

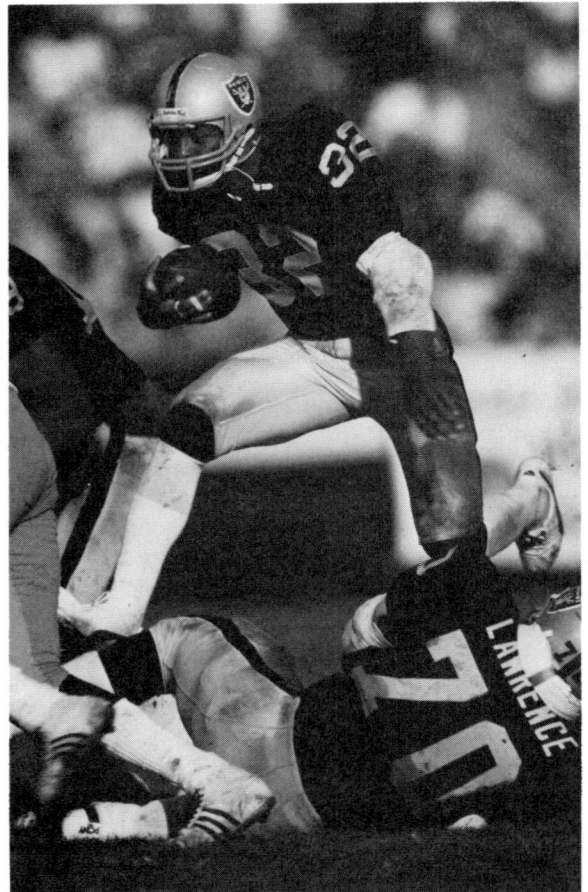

Above right Marcus Allen, the MVP in Superbowl XVIII, always a scoring threat for the raiders. (All-Sport).

Marcus Allen's pro football statistics in regular season play

Rushing

Year	No.	Distance in yards	Average	Touchdowns	Longest run
1982	160	697	4.4	11	53
1983	266	1014	3.8	9	19
1984	275	1168	4.2	13	52

Receiving

1982	38	401	10.6	3	51
1983	68	590	8.7	2	36
1984	64	758	11.8	5	92

Marcus Allen dives for a touchdown. (All-Sport).

Heisman Trophy and in so doing Marcus also ran 606 yards, caught 20 passes and scored 8 touchdowns himself.

As a junior Marcus Allen quickly set about re-writing both college and NCAA records, rushing for 1563 yards and 14 touchdowns. He even found time to throw a touchdown pass in a game against Washington.

In 1981, Marcus Allen became collegiate football's best player winning the Heisman Trophy and setting an all-time single season rushing record with 2342 yards.

After such a successful senior college year many rated the young Allen as a potential no. 1 draft choice but, after being looked over by eight teams (two of which picked running backs ahead of him), it fell to the Los Angeles Raiders to pick him as their first choice.

In view of Allen's popularity at U.S.C. the choice which the Raiders' owner Al Davis made was wise. Davis had just defied the NFL and moved his team from Oakland to the City of Angels and Allen was to be the main draw in the ensuing battle of the turn-stiles with near neighbours Los Angeles Rams. The latter are now coincidentally being coached by Marcus's old U.S.C. mentor, John Robinson.

Davis's first game with the Raiders was played in Atlanta. With slightly less than eight minutes left on the clock in the first quarter, quarterback Jim Plunkett threw the youngster a short pass. At the one-yard line two Falcons waited to greet the rookie. With the agility of a gazelle Allen dived into the air and before the two startled players could re-adjust he had landed in the end-zone.

Before half-time Allen was there again, three times in fact: running for a touchdown, catching a pass that was called back because of a penalty, and throwing a 47-yard pass himself for a score.

It took the new Raider only two games, in which he rushed for 172 yards, caught eight passes for 103 yards and scored three touchdowns, to become the first nomination for the rookie of the year award.

Within two years Marcus Allen's name was on everyone's lips and the third made him an international sports megastar.

If he can stay clear of injuries then the world is in the palm of this young man's hand.

59

Don Shula

A European tourist driving along the Don Shula Expressway in Miami can be forgiven for asking 'Don Who?'. But to the millions of inhabitants of this sun drenched city, and for that matter, to the tens of millions of football fans throughout the USA, the name 'Don Shula' is as much a household word as 'hamburger' or 'coke'. For Don Shula in Miami *is* football.

Under his leadership the Miami Dolphins have become since 1970 one of the greatest teams in NFL history. No self-respecting football fan could ever forget the 'perfect season' of 1972 when he led his team through the regular season with a 14–0 unbeaten record and then proceeded to demolish all the opposition as the Dolphins swept into Superbowl VII. With the elegant Bob Griese at quarterback and a modern day 'Butch Cassidy and the Sundance Kid' in Larry Csonka and Jim Kiick operating out of the backfield Miami crowned their unforgettable season with a 14–7 eclipse of Washington.

Many have described him as the new Lombardi, a strict disciplinarian, with very much his own ideas of how football should be played. Nevertheless his disciplinarian ideas have proved over the past 22 years to be a sure-fire recipe for success.

Not many top coaches today can claim any national fame as players, but Don Shula is different. Born in Painesville, Ohio on 4 January 1930, Shula made his first mark on the world of football as an outstanding offensive player for John Caroll University in Cleveland before moving to the professional ranks in 1951. Cleveland remained 'home' for the young Shula as he signed to play for the Cleveland Browns, but not as an offensive player, instead he specialized as a defensive back. After two strong seasons with the Browns, Shula moved on to Baltimore as part of a massive transfer in which ten Browns moved to the Colts and five Colts went the other way.

In 1957, at the age of 27, Shula moved on to play a season with Washington before retiring in 1958 to the sidelines and a career as a football coach. His baptism as a coach took place in 1958 when he became an assistant at the University of Virginia and then in 1959 at the University Kentucky before entering the pro ranks in 1960 as defensive coach at Detroit Lions.

On 8 January 1963 Don Shula took up his new post as head coach back at Baltimore, where under his guidance the Colts, playing football legends such as Gino Marchetti and Johnny Unitas, became one of the strongest teams in the western conference. In 1964 they reached the NFL championship game only to be beaten by Cleveland 27–0. But revenge was their on 29 December 1968 when a 34–0 victory won them the NFL title, their first in nine years, and gave Baltimore the chance to play the New York Jets in Superbowl III. Unfortunately, despite being odds-on favourites, the day belonged to Joe Namath and the Jets who won the game 16–7.

In April 1970, Shula, who had become disillusioned with the Baltimore job, decided it was time for a move and accepted the head coaching position with Miami Dolphins.

Within two seasons, Miami had been turned from an average team into an exceptional one. The perfect season in 1972 and consecutive world titles in 1972 and 1973 elevated the team to the top of the NFL ladder. In their 14 seasons under Shula the Dolphins have reached the play-offs 11 times, and reached the ultimate game four times, winning two and, more recently, losing in Superbowls XVIII and XIX.

Shula is a brilliant tactician. There are no heroic battle cries in his half-time talks, instead serious tactical work is planned on a blackboard. Among active NFL coaches he has the highest percentage of wins (709). With players like the record-breaking Dan Marino around him, Miami seem destined to take many more honours yet. As well as being the guiding light for the Dolphins as their head coach he is also a vice president of the club, and to continue the family connection, his eldest son David, who played as a professional receiver for Baltimore in 1981, is now the team's receivers coach. At 26 years of age he is one of the youngest coaches in the NFL today.

In 1983 the city of Miami honoured him by naming a street after him, hence the Don Shula Expressway.

Don Shula.

Vince Lombardi

Vincent Thomas Lombardi was born in the Sheepstead Bay area of Brooklyn, New York on 11 June 1913 to Matilda and Henry Lombardi, a meat wholesaler who had emigrated from Italy.

As a boy Lombardi planned to make his mark on the world by entering the priesthood, but his athletic abilities, which became obvious while he was attending the St Francis Preparatory School in Brooklyn, soon changed that. Lombardi played fullback on the school's football team and also starred in the basketball, baseball and track teams.

After graduating from St Francis in 1933 Vince Lombardi enrolled at Fordham University and from 1934 to 1936 played guard on what was the most feared offensive line in college football. The University's famed front row became known as the 'seven blocks of granite' as they played one whole season without conceding a point.

After graduating from Fordham in 1937 with a Batchelor of Science degree, Lombardi worked during the day as as insurance investigator, using the money he earned to continue his education, paying to study law at Fordham's nightschool. At weekends he played football for a minor semi-professional team called the Brooklyn Eagles.

In 1939 Vince Lombardi took his first coaching job, becoming assistant football coach at St Cecilia High School in Englewood, New Jersey. For an annual salary of $1700 he also taught physics, chemistry, algebra and Latin.

Under Lombardi's tutelage St Cecilia won six New Jersey state championships and were unbeaten for 36 games, becoming the most feared high school team in the New York area.

After eight successful years at St Cecilia Lombardi returned to Fordham in 1947 to become the freshman coach.

With two very successful years behind him at Fordham, Lombardi moved on again in 1949, this time to the Army where he was assistant to Colonel 'Red' Blaik, who at the time was one of the top football coaches in the nation. Later in life Vince was to say that the most important thing that ever happened to him was the opportunity to coach under Blaik.

In 1954, after five years of reshaping the Army's T-attack formation, Lombardi made the big jump into the world of professional football, when he signed as offense coach for the New York Giants.

Although only the offensive coach Vince was concerned with the poor state of the club's defense and he persuaded the owners to make several tactical changes that bolstered this department.

In 1956 the Giants won their first NFL championship since 1938; under Vince Lombardi the face of football was changing.

On 2 February 1959, Lombardi signed a five-year contract with one of the greatest clubs in NFL history, the Green Bay Packers. During the post-war years the Packers had been having a lean time, but as soon as he took up his new job Lombardi began to reshape the whole club.

The team had been run by 45 directors from all over the State of Wisconsin, but Lombardi demanded, and got, total control of all on-field policies.

By some shrewd dealing Lombardi picked up four of his first stringers from the Cleveland Browns, and with these and the dormant talent he had inherited at Green Bay he began the mammoth task of rebuilding a once great club.

Lombardi's first task was to polish up the

defense. He launched the team on a vigorous training schedule and established some stringent rules which included players being on time for meals, meetings and workouts, or facing heavy fines, and the imposition of an 11 pm curfew at training camp.

'This is a violent sport', he told his players, 'To play in this league you have got to be tough both physically and mentally'. Minds as well as bodies were shaped for victory. Words like 'Spartanism' and 'total dedication' were hurled at the team by their fiery coach. Defeatism was banned. 'Winning isn't everything', Lombardi insisted, 'It's the only thing'. Such words are still echoed by almost every football coach today.

The effectiveness of his programme was shown in the 1959 league opener against the Chicago Bears. Green Bay won 9–6 and in a spontaneous gesture the players carried their new coach from the field on their shoulders. After winning only one out of 12 games in 1958, Green Bay rolled up a 7–5 winning record in the first year under Lombardi. In his rookie season he was named the National Football League Coach of the year.

In 1960 the Packers won the Western Conference with an 8–4 record, but lost the NFL Championship Game to Philadelphia by a score of 17 to 13. Green Bay again won the Western Conference in 1961, winning 11 out of 14 games. On 31 December 1961 they won their first NFL Championship since 1944 trouncing the New York Giants 37–0.

During the 1962 season the Packers ran up a record 13 wins with only one loss as they once again met the Giants in the final game, winning this time 17–7. Following the victory the Associated Press named the Packers 'The Team of the Year'.

The years 1963 and 1964 proved mediocre as Lombardi began another rebuilding programme in readiness for the winning seasons that were almost certain to come.

In 1965 the Packers again won the NFL Championship, beating Cleveland 23–12 in the final.

1966 saw the first Superbowl World Championship and after winning the NFL title the Packers rolled on to Los Angeles where a convincing 35–10 victory over the AFL

champions, Kansas City Chiefs, saw them acclaimed as the team of the decade.

1967 and Superbowl II once again belonged to Lombardi and his all-conquering Packers. A 9–4–1 regular season record was followed with wins over Los Angeles and Dallas before the yellow and green mean

Vince Lombardi.

machine went into action in Miami's Orange Bowl against the Oakland Raiders in Superbowl II.

After a 33–14 victory had secured an immortal place in the history books for both Lombardi and his Packers, Vince Lombardi announced that this was to be his last game.

But after only one year away from the sport that was his life, Vince Lombardi announced in the spring of 1969 that he was to become part-owner, vice president and head coach of the Washington Redskins.

Lombardi only had one year with the Redskins, because on 3 September 1970 he died suddenly of cancer. He was only 57.

There is little doubt that Vince Lombardi still ranks as one of the greatest football coaches ever. His name still lives in the Lombardi trophy, the official name of the Superbowl award, and in addition the Lombardi award is presented to college football's lineman of the year.

1984 Season Results: National Football League

RUSHING

Yards
NFC: 2105 Eric Dickerson, Rams
AFC: 1179 Earnest Jackson, San Diego

Yards, game
NFC: 215 Eric Dickerson, Rams vs. Houston, December 9 (27 attempts)
AFC: 206 Greg Bell, Buffalo vs. Dallas, November 18 (27 attempts)

Team Leaders, yards
AFC:

BUFFALO	1100	Greg Bell
CINCINNATI	623	Larry Kinnebrew
CLEVELAND	673	Boyce Green
DENVER	1153	Sammy Winder
HOUSTON	785	Larry Moriarty
INDIANAPOLIS	705	Randy McMillan
KANSAS CITY	684	Herman Heard
L. A. RAIDERS	1168	Marcus Allen
MIAMI	606	Woody Bennett
NEW ENGLAND	790	Craig James

Longest (yards)
AFC: 85 Greg Bell, Buffalo vs. Dallas, November 18 – TD
NFC: 81 Billy Sims, Detroit at San Diego, September 30

Attempts
NFC: 407 James Wilder, Tampa Bay
AFC: 296 Earnest Jackson, San Diego
Sammy Winder, Denver

N. Y. JETS	1070	Freeman McNeil
PITTSBURGH	851	Frank Pollard
SAN DIEGO	1179	Earnest Jackson
SEATTLE	327	David Hughes

NFC:

ATLANTA	1486	Gerald Riggs
CHICAGO	1684	Walter Payton
DALLAS	1189	Tony Dorsett
DETROIT	687	Billy Sims
GREEN BAY	581	Gerry Ellis
L. A. RAMS	2105	Eric Dickerson

Attempts, game
NFC: 43 James Wilder, Tampa Bay vs. Green Bay, September 30 (172 yards)
AFC: 34 Sammy Winder, Denver at Raiders, October 28 (126 yards)

Yards per attempt
NFC: 6.0 Hokie Gajan, New Orleans
AFC: 5.0 Joe Carter, Miami

Touchdowns
NFC: 14 Eric Dickerson, Rams
John Riggins, Washington
AFC: 13 Marcus Allen, Raiders

MINNESOTA	773	Alfred Anderson
NEW ORLEANS	914	George Rogers
N. Y. GIANTS	795	Rob Carpenter
PHILADELPHIA	789	Wilbert Montgomery
ST. LOUIS	1174	Ottis Anderson
SAN FRANCISCO	1262	Wendell Tyler
TAMPA BAY	1544	James Wilder
WASHINGTON	1239	John Riggins

Team Champion:
NFC: 2974 Chicago
AFC: 2189 N. Y. Jets

Top Five Rushers

AFC – Individual Rushers

	Att	Yards	Avg	Long	TD
Jackson, Earnest, S. D.	296	1179	4.0	t32	8
Allen, Marcus, Raiders	275	1168	4.2	t52	13
Winder, Sammy, Den.	296	1153	3.9	24	4
Bell, Greg, Buff.	262	1100	4.2	t85	7

NFC – Individual Rushers

	Att	Yards	Avg	Long	TD
Dickerson, Eric, Rams	379	2105	5.6	66	14
Payton, Walter, Chi.	381	1684	4.4	t72	11
Wilder, James, T. B.	407	1544	3.8	37	13
Riggs, Gerald, Atl.	353	1486	4.2	57	13
Tyler, Wendell, S. F.	246	1262	5.1	40	7

American Football Conference – Rushing

	Att	Yards	Avg	Long	TD
Jets	504	2189	4.3	64	17
Cincinnati	540	2179	4.0	33	18
Pittsburgh	574	2179	3.8	52	13
Denver	508	2076	4.1	52	12
New England	482	2032	4.2	73	15
Indianapolis	510	2025	4.0	t31	13
Miami	484	1918	4.0	35	18
Raiders	516	1886	3.7	t52	19
Cleveland	489	1696	3.5	54	10
Houston	433	1656	3.8	t51	13
San Diego	456	1654	3.6	t32	18
Seattle	495	1645	3.3	t40	10
Buffalo	398	1643	4.1	t85	9
Kansas City	408	1527	3.7	t69	12
Conference Total	6797	26305	—	t85	197
Conference Average	485.5	1878.9	3.9	—	14.1

National Football Conference – Rushing

	Att	Yards	Avg	Long	TD
Chicago	674	2974	4.4	t72	22
Rams	541	2864	5.3	66	16
San Francisco	534	2465	4.6	47	21
Washington	588	2274	3.9	31	20
New Orleans	523	2171	4.2	t62	9
St. Louis	488	2088	4.3	39	21
Green Bay	461	2019	4.4	50	18
Detroit	446	2017	4.5	81	13
Atlanta	489	1994	4.1	57	16
Minnesota	444	1844	4.2	39	10
Tampa Bay	483	1776	3.7	37	17
Dallas	469	1714	3.7	t31	12
Giants	493	1660	3.4	28	12
Philadelphia	381	1338	3.5	27	6
Conference Total	7014	29198	—	81	213
Conference Average	501.0	2085.6	4.2	—	15.2

PASSING

Highest Rating
AFC: 108.9 Dan Marino, Miami
NFC: 102.9 Joe Montana, San Francisco

Completion Percentage
NFC: 67.3 Steve Bartkowski, Atlanta (269 attempts, 181 completions)
AFC: 64.2 Dan Marino, Miami (564 attempts, 362 completions)

Attempts
AFC: 564 Dan Marino, Miami
NFC: 560 Neil Lomax, St. Louis

Completions
AFC: 362 Dan Marino, Miami
NFC: 345 Neil Lomax, St. Louis

Yards
AFC: 5084 Dan Marino, Miami
NFC: 4614 Neil Lomax, St. Louis

Yards, game
AFC: 470 Dan Marino, Miami vs. Raiders, December 2 (57 attempts, 35 completions)

NFC: 468 Neil Lomax, St. Louis at Washington, December 16 (46 attempts, 37 completions)

Longest (Yards)
AFC: 92 Marc Wilson (to Marcus Allen), Raiders vs. Seattle, October 7
NFC: 90 Ron Jaworski (to Mike Quick), Philadelphia vs. St. Louis, October 28 – TD

Yards per attempt
AFC: 9.01 Dan Marino, Miami (564 attempts, 5084 yards)
NFC: 8.40 Joe Montana, San Francisco (432 attempts, 3630 yards)

Touchdown passes
AFC: 48 Dan Marino, Miami
NFC: 28 Neil Lomax, St. Louis
Joe Montana, San Francisco

Touchdown passes, game
AFC: 5 John Elway, Denver vs. Minnesota, November 18; Dave Krieg, Seattle vs. Detroit, December 2; Dan

Marino, Miami at Washington, September 2; Marc Wilson, Raiders at San Diego, October 21
NFC: 4 Gary Danielson, Detroit vs. Minnesota, September 23; Lynn Dickey, Green Bay vs. Detroit, October 28; Lynn Dickey, Green Bay vs. Minnesota, November 11; Phil Simms, Giants vs. Philadelphia, September 2; Joe Theismann, Washington at Indiana, October 7; Danny White, Dallas vs. Washington, December 9

Lowest interception percentage
AFC: 1.9 Tony Eason, New England (431 attempts, 8 intercepted)
NFC: 2.3 Joe Montana, San Francisco (432 attempts, 10 intercepted)

Team Champion (Net Yards)
AFC: 5018 Miami
NFC: 4257 St. Louis

	Att	Comp	Pct Comp	Yds	Avg Gain	TD	Pct TD	Long	Int	Pct Int	Rating Points
Marino, Dan, Mia	564	362	64.2	5084	9.01	48	8.5	t80	17	3.0	108.9
Eason, Tony, N. E.	431	259	60.1	3228	7.49	23	5.3	t76	8	1.9	93.4
Fouts, Dan, S. D.	507	317	62.5	3740	7.38	19	3.7	t61	17	3.4	83.4
Krieg, Dave, Sea.	480	276	57.5	3671	7.65	32	6.7	t80	24	5.0	83.3

NFC – Individual Qualifiers

	Att	Comp	Pct Comp	Yds	Avg Gain	TD	Pct TD	Long	Int	Pct Int	Rating Points
Montana, Joe, S. F.	432	279	64.6	3630	8.40	28	6.5	t80	10	2.3	102.9
Lomax, Neil, St. L.	560	345	61.6	4614	8.24	28	5.0	t83	16	2.9	92.5
Bartkowski, Steve, Atl.	269	181	67.3	2158	8.02	11	4.1	61	10	3.7	89.7
Theismann, Joe, Wash.	477	283	59.3	3391	7.11	24	5.0	t80	13	2.7	86.6
Dickey, Lynn, G. B.	401	237	59.1	3195	7.97	25	6.2	t79	19	4.7	85.6

American Football Conference – Passing

	Att	Comp	Pct Comp	Gross Yards	Tkd	Yds Lost	Net Yards	Avg Yds Att	Avg Yds Comp	TD	Pct TD	Long	Int	Pct Int
Miami	572	367	64.2	5146	14	128	5018	9.00	14.02	49	8.6	t80	18	3.1
San Diego	662	401	60.6	4928	36	285	4643	7.44	12.29	25	3.8	t88	21	3.2
Kansas City	593	305	51.4	3869	33	301	3568	6.52	12.69	21	3.5	t65	22	3.7
Seattle	497	283	56.9	3751	42	328	3423	7.55	13.25	32	6.4	t80	26	5.2
Raiders	491	266	54.2	3718	54	360	3358	7.57	13.98	21	4.3	92	28	5.7
Cincinnati	496	306	61.7	3659	45	358	3301	7.38	11.96	17	3.4	t80	22	4.4
Pittsburgh	443	240	54.2	3519	35	278	3241	7.94	14.66	25	5.6	t80	25	5.6
New England	500	292	58.4	3685	66	454	3231	7.37	12.62	26	5.2	t76	14	2.8
Houston	487	282	57.9	3610	49	382	3228	7.41	12.80	14	2.9	76	15	3.1
Cleveland	495	273	55.2	3490	55	358	3132	7.05	12.78	14	2.8	64	23	4.6
Jets	488	272	55.7	3341	52	382	2959	6.85	12.28	20	4.1	49	21	4.3
Denver	475	263	55.4	3116	35	257	2859	6.56	11.85	22	4.6	73	17	3.6
Buffalo	588	298	50.7	3252	60	554	2698	5.53	10.91	18	3.1	t70	30	5.1
Indianapolis	411	206	50.1	2543	58	436	2107	6.19	12.34	13	3.2	t74	22	5.4
Conference Total	7198	4054	—	51627	634	4861	46766	—	—	317	—	t88	304	—
Conference Average	514.1	289.6	56.3	3687.6	45.3	347.2	3340.4	7.17	12.73	22.6	4.4	—	21.7	4.2

National Football Conference – Passing

	Att	Comp	Pct Comp	Gross Yards	Tkd	Yds Lost	Net Yards	Avg Yds Att	Avg Yds Comp	TD	Pct TD	Long	Int	Pct Int
St. Louis	566	347	61.3	4634	49	377	4257	8.19	13.35	28	4.9	t83	16	2.8
San Francisco	496	312	62.9	4079	27	178	3901	8.22	13.07	32	6.5	t80	10	2.0
Giants	535	288	53.8	4066	55	434	3632	7.60	14.12	22	4.1	t65	18	3.4
Dallas	604	322	53.3	3995	48	389	3606	6.61	12.41	19	3.1	t68	26	4.3
Tampa Bay	563	334	59.3	3907	45	362	3545	6.94	11.70	22	3.9	t74	23	4.1
Green Bay	506	281	55.5	3740	42	310	3430	7.39	13.31	30	5.9	t79	30	5.9
Philadelphia	606	331	54.6	3823	60	463	3360	6.31	11.55	19	3.1	t90	17	2.8
Detroit	531	298	56.1	3787	61	486	3301	7.13	12.71	19	3.6	t77	22	4.1
Washington	485	286	59.0	3417	48	341	3076	7.05	11.95	24	4.9	t80	13	2.7
Atlanta	478	294	61.5	3546	67	496	3050	7.42	12.06	14	2.9	61	20	4.2
Minnesota	533	281	52.7	3337	64	465	2872	6.26	11.88	18	3.4	t70	25	4.7
New Orleans	476	246	51.7	3198	45	361	2837	6.72	13.00	21	4.4	74	28	5.9
Chicago	390	226	57.9	2695	36	232	2463	6.91	11.92	14	3.6	t61	15	3.8
Rams	358	176	49.2	2382	32	240	2142	6.65	13.53	16	4.5	68	17	4.7
Conference Total	7127	4022	—	50606	679	5134	45472	—	—	298	—	t90	280	—
Conference Average	509.1	287.3	56.4	3614.7	48.5	366.7	3248.0	7.10	12.58	21.3	4.2	—	20.0	3.9

PASS RECEIVING

Receptions
NFC: 106 Art Monk, Washinton
AFC: 89 Ozzie Newsome, Cleveland

Receptions, game
AFC: 15 Kellen Winslow, San Diego at Green Bay, October 7 (157 yards)
NFC: 12 Ottis Anderson, St. Louis at Washington, December 16 (124 yards)

Yards
NFC: 1555 Roy Green, St. Louis

AFC: 1395 John Stallworth, Pittsburgh

Yards, game
NFC: 206 James Lofton, Green Bay at Denver, October 15 (11 receptions)
AFC: 191 Steve Largent, Seattle at Denver, November 25 (12 receptions); Ozzie Newsome, Cleveland at Jets, October 14 (14 receptions)

Longest (Yards)
AFC: 92 Marcus Allen (from Marc Wilson), Raiders vs. Seattle, October 7

NFC: 90 Mike Quick (from Ron Jaworski), Philadelphia vs. St. Louis, October 28 – TD

Yards per reception
NFC: 22.0 James Lofton, Green Bay (62 receptions, 1361 yards)
AFC: 20.4 Daryl Turner, Seattle (35 receptions, 715 yards)

Touchdowns
AFC: 18 Mark Clayton, Miami
NFC: 12 Roy Green, St. Louis

AFC: Team Leaders, Receptions

BUFFALO	69	Byron Franklin
CINCINNATI	65	Cris Collinsworth
CLEVELAND	89	Ozzie Newsome
DENVER	69	Steve Watson
HOUSTON	69	Tim Smith
INDIANAPOLIS	43	Raymond Butler
KANSAS CITY	62	Henry Marshall
L. A. RAIDERS	80	Todd Christensen
MIAMI	73	Mark Clayton
NEW ENGLAND	66	Derrick Ramsey
N. Y. JETS	68	Mickey Shuler
PITTSBURGH	80	John Stallworth
SAN DIEGO	61	Charlie Joiner
SEATTLE	74	Steve Largent

NFC:				L. A. RAMS	34	Henry Ellard	PHILADELPHIA	65	John Spagnola
ATLANTA	67	Stacey Bailey	MINNESOTA	47	Leo Lewis	ST. LOUIS	78	Roy Green
CHICAGO	45	Walter Payton	NEW ORLEANS	35	Hokie Gajan	SAN FRANCISCO	71	Roger Craig
DALLAS	60	Doug Cosbie	N. Y. GIANTS	48	Bob Johnson &	TAMPA BAY	85	James Wilder
DETROIT	77	James Jones			Zeke Mowatt	WASHINGTON	106	Art Monk
GREEN BAY	62	James Lofton						

AFC – Individual Receivers

	No	Yards	Avg	Long	TD
Newsome, Ozzie, Clev.	89	1001	11.2	52	5
Stallworth, John, Pitt.	80	1395	17.4	51	11
Christensen, Todd, Raiders	80	1007	12.6	38	7
Largent, Steve, Sea.	74	1164	15.7	65	12
Clayton, Mark, Mia.	73	1389	19.0	t65	18

AFC – Top Five Receivers by Yards

	No	Yards	Avg	Long	TD
Stallworth, John, Pitt.	1395	80	17.4	51	11
Clayton, Mark, Mia.	1389	73	19.0	t65	18
Duper, Mark, Mia.	1306	71	18.4	t80	8
Watson, Steve, Den.	1170	69	17.0	73	7
Largent, Steve, Sea.	1164	74	15.7	65	12

NFC – Individual Receivers

	No	Yards	Avg	Long	TD
Monk, Art, Wash	106	1372	12.9	72	7
Wilder, James, T. B.	85	685	8.1	50	0
Green, Roy, St. L.	78	1555	19.9	t83	12
Jones, James. Det.	77	662	8.6	39	5
House, Kevin, T. B.	76	1005	13.2	55	5

NFC – Top Five Receivers by Yards

	No	Yards	Avg	Long	TD
Green, Roy, St. L.	1555	78	19.9	t83	12
Monk, Art, Wash.	1372	106	12.9	72	7
Lofton, James, G. B.	1361	62	22.0	t79	7
Bailey, Stacey, Atl.	1138	67	17.0	61	6
Quick, Mike, Phil.	1052	61	17.2	t90	9

INTERCEPTIONS

Interceptions
AFC: 10 Ken Easley, Seattle
NFC: 9 Tom Flynn, Green Bay

Longest (Yards)
AFC: 99 Gill Byrd, San Diego at Kansas City, October 14 – TD
NFC: 99 Tim Lewis, Green Bay vs. Rams, November 18 – TD

Top Five Interceptors

	No	Yards	Avg	Long	TD
Easley, Ken, Sea.	10	126	12.6	t58	2
Flynn, Tom, G. B.	9	106	11.8	31	0
Brown, Dave, Sea.	8	179	22.4	t90	2
Lewis, Tim, G. B.	7	151	21.6	t99	1
Downs, Mike, Dall.	7	126	18.0	t27	1

PUNT RETURNS

Yards Per Return
AFC: 15.7 Mike Martin, Cincinnati
NFC: 13.4 Henry Ellard, Rams

Longest (Yards)
NFC: 83 Henry Ellard, Rams vs. Giants, September 30
AFC: 76 Louis Lipps, Pittsburgh at New Orleans, November 19

Top Five Punt Returners

	No	FC	Yards	Avg	Long	TD
Martin, Mike, Cin.	24	5	376	15.7	55	0
Ellard, Henry, Rams	30	3	403	13.4	t83	2
Lipps, Louis, Pitt.	53	2	656	12.4	t76	1
McLemore, Dana, S. F.	45	11	521	11.6	t79	1
Willhite, Gerald, Den.	20	9	200	10.0	35	0

KICK OFF RETURNS

Yards Per Return
AFC: 30.7 Bobby Humphery, Jets
NFC: 23.0 Barry Redden, Rams

Longest (Yards)
NFC: 97 Del Rodgers, Green Bay at Chicago, December 9 – TD
AFC: 97 Bobby Humphery, Jets vs. Pittsburgh, September 6 – TD

Top Five Kick off Returners

	No	Yards	Avg	Long	TD
Humphery, Bobby, Jets	22	675	30.7	t97	1
Williams, Dokie, Raiders	24	621	25.9	62	0
Anderson, Larry, Ind.	22	525	23.9	69	0
Redden, Barry, Rams	23	530	23.0	40	0
Mitchell, Stump, St. L.	35	804	23.0	56	0

PUNTING

Average Yards per Punt
AFC: 44.9 Jim Arnold, Kansas City (98 punts, 4397 yards)
NFC: 43.8 Brian Hansen, New Orleans (63 punts, 3020 yards)

Longest (Yards)
AFC: 89 Luke Prestridge, New England vs. Miami, October 21
NFC: 87 David Finzer, Chicago vs. New Orleans, October 7

Top Five Individual Punters

	No	Yards	Long	Avg	Total Punts	TB	Blk	Opp Ret	Ret Yds	In 20	Net Avg
Arnold, Jim, K. C.	98	4397	63	44.9	98	13	0	60	461	22	37.5
Roby, Reggie, Mia.	51	2281	69	44.7	51	10	0	17	138	15	38.1
Stark, Rohn, Ind.	98	4383	72	44.7	98	7	0	62	600	21	37.2
Hansen, Brian, N. O.	69	3020	66	43.8	70	7	1	47	550	9	33.3
Cox, Steve, Clev.	74	3213	69	43.4	76	8	2	43	489	16	33.7

SCORING

Points
Non-Kickers
AFC: 108 Marcus Allen, Raiders

Mark Clayton, Miami
NFC: 84 Eric Dickerson, Rams
John Riggins, Washington

Kickers
NFC: 131 Ray Wersching, San Francisco
AFC: 117 Gary Anderson, Pittsburgh

Touchdowns
AFC: 18 Marcus Allen, Raiders (13-rush, 5-pass)
Mark Clayton, Miami (18-pass)
NFC: 14 Eric Dickerson, Rams (14-rush)
John Riggins, Washington (14-rush)

Extra Points
AFC: 66 Uwe von Schamann, Miami (70 attempts)
NFC: 56 Ray Wersching, San Francisco (56 attempts)

Field Goals
NFC: 30 Paul McFadden, Philadelphia (37 attempts)
AFC: 24 Gary Anderson, Pittsburgh (32 attempts)
    Matt Bahr, Cleveland (32 attempts)

Most Points, Game
AFC: 24 Marcus Allen, Raiders vs. San Diego, September 24 (4 TD, 3-rush, 1-pass); Larry Kinnebrew, Cincinnati at Houston, October 28 (4 TD, 3-rush, 1-pass)
NFC: 18 Lynn Cain, Atlanta at Rams, October 7 (3 TD, rush); Eric Dickerson, Rams at Tampa Bay, November 25 (3 TD, rush);

Longest Field Goal (Yards)
AFC: 60 Steve Cox, Cleveland at Cincinnati, October 21
NFC: 54 Jan Stenerud, Minnesota vs. Atlanta, September 16

Eddie Lee Ivery, Green Bay vs. Rams, November 18 (3 TD, rush); Art Monk, Washington at Indianapolis, October 7 (3 TD, pass); Joe Morris, Giants vs. Washington, October 28 (3 TD, rush); Leonard Thompson, Detroit vs. Minnesota, September 23 (3 TD, pass); Otis Wonsley, Washington vs. Detroit, November 11 (3 TD,   rush)

Team Leaders

AFC:

BUFFALO	48	Greg Bell
CINCINNATI	103	Jim Breech
CLEVELAND	97	Matt Bahr
DENVER	101	Rich Karlis
HOUSTON	46	Joe Cooper
INDIANAPOLIS	47	Raul Allegre
KANSAS CITY	104	Nick Lowery
L. A. RAIDERS	108	Marcus Allen
MIAMI	108	Mark Clayton
NEW ENGLAND	108	Tony Franklin
N. Y. JETS	89	Pat Leahy
PITTSBURGH	117	Gary Anderson
SAN DIEGO	92	Rolf Benirschke
SEATTLE	110	Norm Johnson

NFC:

ATLANTA	91	Mick Luckhurst
CHICAGO	101	Bob Thomas
DALLAS	102	Rafael Septien
DETROIT	91	Ed Murray
GREEN BAY	61	Al Del Greco
L. A. RAMS	112	Mike Lansford
MINNESOTA	90	Jan Stenerud
NEW ORLEANS	94	Morten Andersen
N. Y. GIANTS	83	Ali Haji-Sheikh
PHILADELPHIA	116	Paul McFadden
ST. LOUIS	117	Neil O'Donoghue
SAN FRANCISCO	131	Ray Wersching
TAMPA BAY	95	Obed Ariri
WASHINGTON	120	Mark Moseley

Team Champion
AFC. 513 Miami
NFC: 475 San Francisco

AFC – Individual Scorers
Kickers

	XP	XPA	FG	FGA	PTS
Anderson, Gary, Pitt.	45	45	24	32	117
Johnson, Norm, Sea.	50	51	20	24	110
Franklin, Tony, N. E.	42	42	22	28	108
Lowery, Nick, K. C.	35	35	23	33	104
Breech, Jim, Cin.	37	37	22	31	103

Non-Kickers

	TD	TDR	TDP	TDM	PTS
Allen, Marcus, Raiders	18	13	5	0	108
Clayton, Mark, Mia.	18	0	18	0	108
Johnson, Pete, S.D.-Mia.	12	12	0	0	72
Largent, Steve, Sea.	12	0	12	0	72
Lipps, Louis, Pitt.	11	1	9	1	66

NFC – Individual Scorers
Kickers

	XP	XPA	FG	FGA	PTS
Wersching, Ray, S. F.	56	56	25	35	131
Moseley, Mark, Wash.	48	51	24	31	120
O'Donoghue, Neil, St. L.	48	51	23	35	117
McFadden, Paul, Phil.	26	27	30	37	116
Lansford, Mike, Rams	37	38	25	33	112

Non-Kickers

	TD	TDR	TDP	TDM	PTS
Dickerson, Eric, Rams.	14	14	0	0	84
Riggins, John, Wash.	14	14	0	0	84
Riggs, Gerald, Atl.	13	13	0	0	78
Wilder, James, T. B.	13	13	0	0	78
Green, Roy, St. L.	12	0	12	0	72

American Football Conference – Scoring

	TD	TDR	TDP	TDM	XP	XPA	FG	FGA	SAF	POINTS
Miami	70	18	49	3	66	70	9	19	0	513
Seattle	51	10	32	9	50	51	20	24	1	418
San Diego	48	18	25	5	46	47	20	29	0	394
Pittsburgh	45	13	25	7	45	45	24	32	0	387
Raiders	44	19	21	4	40	44	20	27	2	368
New England	42	15	26	1	42	42	22	28	1	362
Denver	42	12	22	8	38	42	21	28	0	353
Cincinnati	39	18	17	4	37	39	22	31	1	339
Jets	40	17	20	3	39	40	17	24	1	332
Kansas City	35	12	21	2	35	35	23	33	0	314
Buffalo	31	9	18	4	31	31	11	21	0	250
Cleveland	25	10	14	1	25	25	25	35	0	250
Houston	28	13	14	1	27	28	15	19	0	240
Indianapolis	28	13	13	2	27	28	14	23	1	239
Conference Total	568	197	317	54	548	567	263	373	7	4759
Conference Average	40.6	14.1	22.6	3.9	39.1	40.5	18.8	26.6	0.5	339.9

National Football Conference – Scoring

	TD	TDR	TDP	TDM	XP	XPA	FG	FGA	SAF	POINTS
San Francisco	57	21	32	4	56	57	25	35	1	475
Washington	51	20	24	7	48	51	24	31	0	426
St. Louis	51	21	28	2	48	51	23	35	0	423
Green Bay	51	18	30	3	48	51	12	21	0	390
Rams	38	16	16	6	37	38	25	33	3	346
Tampa Bay	40	17	22	1	38	40	19	26	0	335
Chicago	37	22	14	1	35	37	22	28	1	325
Dallas	34	12	19	3	33	34	23	29	1	308
Giants	36	12	22	2	32	36	17	33	0	299
New Orleans	34	9	21	4	34	34	20	27	0	298
Detroit	32	13	19	0	31	31	20	27	0	283
Atlanta	31	16	14	1	31	31	20	27	2	281
Philadelphia	27	6	19	2	26	27	30	37	0	278
Minnesota	31	10	18	3	30	31	20	23	0	276
Conference Total	550	213	298	39	527	549	300	412	8	4743
Conference Average	39.3	15.2	21.3	2.8	37.6	39.2	21.4	29.4	0.6	338.8

All-Time National Football League Records
(Through 1984 Season)

SERVICE

Most Seasons, Active Player
26 George Blanda, Chi Bears, 1949–58; Balt, 1950; AFL: Hou, 1960–66; Oak, 1967–75

Most Games Played, Lifetime
340 George Blanda, Chi Bears, 1949–58; Balt, 1950; AFL: Hou, 1960–66; Oak, 1967–75

Most Consecutive Games Played, Lifetime
282 Jim Marshall, Cleve, 1960; Minn, 1961–79

Most Seasons, Head Coach
40 George Halas, Chi Bears, 1920–29, 33–42, 46–55, 58–67

SCORING

Most Seasons Leading League
5 Don Hutson, GB, 1940–44
Gino Cappelletti, Bos, 1961, 63–66 (AFL)

Most Points, Lifetime
2,002 George Blanda, Chi Bears, 1949–58; Balt, 1950; AFL: Hou, 1960–66; Oak, 1967–75 (9-td, 943-pat, 335-fg)

Most Points, Season
176 Paul Hornung, GB, 1960 (15-td, 41-pat, 15-fg)

Most Points, Rookie Season
132 Gale Sayers, Chi, 1965 (22-td)

Most Points, Game
40 Ernie Nevers, Chi Cards vs Chi Bears, Nov 28, 1929 (6-td, 4-pat)

Most Points, One Quarter
29 Don Hutson, GB vs Det, Oct 7, 1945 (4-td, 5-pat) 2nd Quarter

Touchdowns

Most Seasons Leading League
8 Don Hutson, GB, 1935–38, 41–44

Most Touchdowns, Lifetime
126 Jim Brown, Cleve, 1957–65 (106-r, 20-p)

Most Touchdowns, Season
24 John Riggins, Wash (24-r), 1983

Most Touchdowns, Rookie Season
22 Gale Sayers, Chi, 1965 (14-r, 6-p, 1-prb, 1-krb)

Most Touchdowns, Game
6 Ernie Nevers, Chi Cards vs Chi Bears, Nov 28, 1929 (6-r)
William (Dub) Jones, Cleve vs Chi Bears, Nov 25, 1951 (4-r, 2-p)
Gale Sayers, Chi vs SF, Dec 12, 1965 (4-r, 1-p, 1-prb)

Most Consecutive Games Scoring Touchdowns
18 Lenny Moore, Balt, 1963–65

Field Goals

Most Seasons Leading League
5 Lou Groza, Cleve, 1950, 52–54, 57

Most Field Goals, Lifetime
338 Jan Stenerud, KC 1967–69; Gr Bay 1980–83

Most Field Goals, Season
35 Ali Haji-Sheikh, NY Giants, 1983

Most Field Goals, Game
7 Jim Bakken, St L vs Pitt, Sept 24, 1967

Most Consecutive Games, Field Goals
31 Fred Cox, Minn, 1968–70

Highest Field Goal Percentage, Season
95.24 Mark Mosely, Wash, 1982 (20–21)

Most Consecutive Field Goals
23 Mark Mosely, Wash, 1981–82

Longest Field Goal
63 yd Tom Dempsey, NO vs Det, Nov 8, 1970

RUSHING

Most Seasons Leading League
8 Jim Brown, Cleve, 1957–61, 63–65

Most Yards Gained, Lifetime
13,309 Walter Payton, Chi, 1975–84

Most Yards Gained, Season
2,105 Eric Dickerson, LA Rams, 1984

Most Yards Gained, Game
275 Walter Payton, Chi vs Minn, Nov 20, 1977

Longest Run from Scrimmage
99 yd Tony Dorsett, Dall vs Minn, Jan 3, 1983 (td)

Highest Average Gain, Lifetime (799 att)
5.2 Jim Brown, Cleve, 1957–65 (2,359–12,312)

Highest Average Gain, Game (10 att)
17.1 Marion Motley, Cleve vs Pitt, Oct 29, 1950 (11–188)

Most Touchdowns Rushing, Lifetime
17.1 Marion Motley, Cleve vs Pitt, Oct 29, 1950 (11–188)

Most Touchdowns Rushing, Lifetime
106 Jim Brown, Cleve, 1957–65

Most Touchdowns Rushing, Season
24 John Riggins, Wash, 1983

Most Touchdowns Rushing, Game
6 Ernie Nevers, Chi Cards vs Chi Bears, Nov 28, 1929

PASSING

Most Seasons Leading League
6 Sammy Baugh, Wash, 1937, 40, 43, 45, 47, 49

Most Passes Completed Lifetime
3,686 Fran Tarkenton, Minn, 1961–66, 72–78; NY Giants, 1967–71 (6,467 attempts)

Most Passes Completed Season
362 Dan Marino, Miami, 1984 (564 attempts)

Most Passes Completed, Game
42 Richard Todd, NY Jets vs SF, Sept 21, 1980 (59 attempts)

Most Consecutive Passes Completed
20 Ken Anderson, Cin vs Hou, Jan 2, 1983

Longest Pass Completion (all tds)
99 Frank Filchock (to Farkas), Wash vs Pitt, Oct 15, 1939
George Izo (to Mitchell), Wash vs Cleve, Sept 15, 1963
Karl Sweetan (to Studstill), Det vs Balt, Oct 16, 1966
C. A. Jurgensen (to Allen), Wash vs Chi, Sept 16, 1968
Jim Plunkettt (to Branch) LA Raiders vs Wash Oct 2, 1983

Most Yards Gained Passing, Lifetime
47,003 Fran Tarkenton, Minn, 1961–66, 72–78; NY Giants, 1967–71

Most Yards Gained Passing, Game
554 Norm Van Brocklin, LA vs NY Yanks, Sept 28, 1951 (41–27)

Most Yards Gained Passing, Season
5,084 Dan Marino, Miami, 1984

Most Touchdown Passes, Lifetime
342 Fran Tarkenton, Minn, 1961–66, 72–78; NY Giants, 1967–71

Most Touchdown Passes, Season
48 Dan Marino, Miami, 1984

Most Touchdown Passes, Game
7 Sid Luckman, Chi Bears vs NY, Nov 14, 1943
Adrian Burk, Phil vs Wash, Oct 17, 1954
George Blanda, Hou vs NY, Nov 19, 1961 (AFL)
Y. A. Tittle, NY vs Wash, Oct 28, 1962
Joe Kapp, Minn vs Balt, Sept 28, 1969

Most Consecutive Games, Touchdown Passes
47 John Unitas, Balt, 1956–60

Passing Efficiency, Lifetime (1,500 att)
63.7 Joe Montana, SF 1979–84; (1,324–2,077)

Passing Efficiency, Season (100 att)
70.55 Ken Anderson, Cin, 1982 (309–218)

Passing Efficiency, Game (20 att)
90.9 Ken Anderson, Cin vs Pitt, Nov 10, 1974 (22–20)

Passes Had Intercepted

Most Passes Intercepted, Game
8 Jim Hardy, Chi Cards vs Phil, Sept 24, 1950 (39 attempts)

Most Consecutive Passes Attempted, None Intercepted
294 Bryan (Bart) Starr, GB, 1964–65

Fewest Passes Intercepted, Season (Qualifiers)
1 Joe Ferguson, Buff, 1976 (151 attempts)

PASS RECEPTIONS

Most Seasons Leading League
8 Don Hutson, GB, 1936–37, 39, 41–45

Most Pass Receptions, Lifetime
657 Charley Joiner, SD, 1969–84

Most Pass Receptions, Season
106 Art Monk, Wash, 1984

Most Pass Receptions, Game
18   Tom Fears, LA vs GB, Dec 3, 1950 (189 yd)

Longest Pass Reception (all tds)
99   Andy Farkas (Filchock), Wash vs Pitt, Oct 15, 1939
     Bobby Mitchell (Izo), Wash vs Cleve, Sept 15, 1963
     Pat Studstill (Sweetan), Det vs Balt, Oct 16, 1966
     Gerry Allen (Jurgensen), Wash vs Chi, Sept 15, 1968
     Cliff Branch (Plunkett), LA Raiders vs Wash, Oct 2, 1983

Most Consecutive Games, Pass Receptions
127   Harold Carmichael, Phil, 1972–1980

Most Pass Receptions by a Running Back, Game
17   Clark Gaines, NY Jets vs SF, Sept 21, 1980

Most Yards Gained Pass Receptions, Game
303   Jim Benton, Cleve vs Det, Nov 22, 1945

Touchdowns Receiving

Most Touchdown Passes, Lifetime
99   Don Hutson, GB, 1935–45

Most Touchdown Passes, Season
18   Mark Clayton, Miami, 1984

Most Touchdown Passes, Game
5   Bob Shaw, Chi Cards vs Balt, Oct 2, 1950
    Kellen Winslow, SD vs Oak, Nov 22, 1981

Most Consecutive Games, Touchdown Passes
11   Elroy (Crazy Legs) Hirsch, LA, 1950–51
     Gilbert (Buddy) Dial, Pitt, 1959–60

PASS INTERCEPTIONS

Most Interceptions by, Lifetime
81   Paul Krause, Wash (28), 1964–67; Minn (53), 1968–79

Most Interceptions by, Season
14   Richard (Night Train) Lane, LA, 1952

PUNTING

Most Seasons Leading League
4   Sammy Baugh, Wash, 1940–43
    Jerrel Wilson, AFL: KC, 1965, 68; NFL: KC, 1972–73

Most Punts, Season
114   Bob Parsons, Chi, 1981

Most Punts, Game
14   Dick Nesbitt, Chi Cards vs Chi Bears, Nov 30, 1933
     Keith Molesworth, Chi Bears vs GB, Dec 10, 1933
     Sammy Baugh, Wash vs Phil, Nov 5, 1939
     John Kinscherf, NY vs Det, Nov 7, 1943
     George Taliaferro, NY Yanks vs LA, Sept 28, 1951

Longest Punt
98 yd   Steve O'Neal, NY Jets vs Den, Sept 21, 1969 (AFL)

Average Yardage Punting

Highest Punting, Average, Lifetime (300 punts)
45.1 yd   Sammy Baugh, Wash, 1937–52 (338)

Highest Punting Average, Season (20 punts)
51.4 yd   Sammy Baugh, Wash, 1940 (35)

Highest Punting Average, Game (4 punts)
61.8 yd   Bob Cifers, Det vs Chi Bears, Nov 24, 1946

PUNT RETURNS

Yardage Returning Punts

Most Yards Gained, Lifetime
3,008   Rick Upchurch, Den, 1975–83

Most Yards Gained, Season
655   Neal Colzie, Oak, 1975

Most Yards Gained, Game
205   George Atkinson, Oak vs Buff, Sept 15, 1968

Longest Punt Return (all tds)
98   Gil LeFebvre, Cin vs Brk, Dec 3, 1933
     Charlie West, Minn vs Wash, Nov 3, 1968
     Dennis Morgan, Dall vs St L, Oct 13, 1974

Touchdowns Returning Punts

Most Touchdowns, Lifetime
8   Jack Christiansen, Det, 1951–58
    Rick Upchurch, Den, 1975–83

Most Touchdowns, Season
4   Jack Christiansen, Det, 1951
    Rick Upchurch, Den, 1976

Most Touchfowns, Game
2   Jack Christiansen, Det vs LA, Oct 14, 1951; vs GB, Nov 22, 1951
    Dick Christy, NY Titans vs Den, Sept 24, 1961
    Rick Upchurch, Den vs Cleve, Sept 26, 1976
    Leroy Irvin, LA vs Atl, Oct 11, 1981

KICK OFF RETURNS

Yardage Returning Kickoffs

Most Yards Gained, Lifetime
6,922   Ron Smith, Chi, 1965, 70–72; Atl, 1966–67, LA, 1968–60; SD, 1973; Oak, 1974

Most Yards Gained, Season
1,317   Bobby Jancik, Hou, 1963 (AFL)

Most Yards Gained, Game
294   Wally Triplett, Det vs LA, Oct 29, 1950 (4)

Longest Kickoff Return for Touchdown
106   Al Carmichael, GB vs Chi Bears, Oct 7, 1956
      Noland Smith, KC vs Den, Dec 17, 1967 (AFL)
      Roy Green, St L vs Dall, Oct 21, 1979

Highest Average, Lifetime (75 returns)
30.6   Gale Sayers, Chi, 1965–71

Average Yardage Returning Kickoffs

Highest Average, Season (15 returns)
41.1   Travis Williams, GB, 1967 (18)

Highest Average, Game (3 returns)
73.5   Wally Triplett, Det vs LA, Oct 29, 1950 (4–294)

Touchdowns Returning Kickoffs

Most Touchdowns, Lifetime
6   Ollie Matson, Chi Cards, 1952 (2), 54, 56, 58 (2)
    Gale Sayers, Chi, 1965, 66 (2), 67 (3)
    Travis Williams, GB, 1967 (4), 69, 71

Most Touchdowns, Season
4   Travis Williams, GB, 1967
    Cecil Turner, Chi, 1970

Most Touchdowns, Game
2   Thomas (Tim) Brown, Phil vs Dall, Nov 6, 1966
    Travis Williams, GB vs Cleve, Nov 12, 1967

Super Bowl Records
Super Bowl Composite Standings

	W	L	Pct	Pts	OP
Pittsburgh Steelers	4	0	1.000	103	73
Green Bay Packers	2	0	1.000	68	24
San Francisco 49ers	2	0	1.000	64	37
New York Jets	1	0	1.000	16	7
Oakland/L. A. Raiders	3	1	.750	111	66
Baltimore Colts	1	1	.500	23	29
Kansas City Chiefs	1	1	.500	33	42
Dallas Cowboys	2	3	.400	112	85
Miami Dolphins	2	3	.400	74	103
Washington Redskins	1	2	.333	43	69
Cincinnati Bengals	0	1	.000	21	26
Denver Broncos	0	1	.000	10	27
Los Angeles Rams	0	1	.000	19	31
Philadelphia Eagles	0	1	.000	10	27
Minnesota Vikings	0	4	.000	34	95

Individual Records

SERVICE

Most Games
5   Marv Fleming, Green Bay, 1967–68, Miami, 1972–74; Larry Cole, Dallas, 1971–72, 1976, 1978–79; Cliff Harris, Dallas, 1971–72, 1976, 1978–79; D. D. Lewis, Dallas, 1971–72, 1976, 1978–79; Preston Pearson, Baltimore, 1969, Pittsburgh, 1975, Dallas, 1976, 1978–79; Charlie Waters, Dallas, 1971–72 1976, 1978–79, Rayfield Wright, Dallas, 1971–72, 1976, 1978–79

Most Games, Coach
6   Don Shula, Baltimore, 1969; Miami, 1972–74, 1983, 1985
5   Tom Landry, Dallas, 1971–72, 1976, 1978–79

4 Bud Grant, Minnesota, 1979,
1974–75, 1977
Chuck Noll, Pittsburgh, 1975–76,
1979–80

Most Games, Winning Team, Coach
4 Chuck Noll, Pittsburgh, 1975–76,
1979–80
2 Vince Lombardi, Green Bay,
1967–68
Tom Landry, Dallas, 1972, 1978
Don Shula, Miami, 1973–74
Tom Flores, Oakland, 1981; L.
A. Raiders, 1984

SCORING

Points

Most Points, Career
24 Franco Harris, Pittsburgh, 4
games (4-td)
20 Don Chandler, Green Bay, 2
games (8-pat, 4-fg)

Most Points, Game
18 Roger Craig, San Francisco vs.
Miami, 1985 (3-td)
15 Don Chandler, Green Bay vs.
Oakland, 1968 (3-pat, 4-fg)

Touchdowns

Most Touchdowns, Career
4 Franco Harris, Pittsburgh, 4
games (4-r)
3 John Stallworth, Pittsburgh, 4
games (3-p)
Lynn Swann, Pittsburgh, 4
games (3-p)
Cliff Branch, Oakland/L. A.
Raiders, 3 games (3-p)

Most Touchdowns, Game
3 Roger Craig, San Francisco vs.
Miami, 1985 (2-p, 1-r)

Field Goals

Most Field Goals, Career
5 Ray Wersching, San Francisco,
2 games (5 att)
4 Don Chandler, Green Bay, 2
games (4 att)
Jim Turner, N. Y. Jets/Denver, 2
games (6 att)

Most Field Goals, Game
4 Don Chandler, Green Bay vs.
Oakland, 1968
Ray Wersching, San Francisco
vs. Cincinnati, 1982

Longest Field Goal
48 Jan Stenerud, Kansas City vs.
Minnesota, 1970

RUSHING

Attempts

Most Attempts, Career
101 Franco Harris, Pittsburgh, 4
games
64 John Riggins, Washington, 2
games
57 Larry Csonka, Miami, 3 games

Most Attempts, Game
38 John Riggins, Washington vs.
Miami, 1983

Yards gained

Most Yards Gained Career
354 Franco Harris, Pittsburgh, 4
games
297 Larry Csonka, Miami, 3 games

Most Yards Gained, Game
191 Marcus Allen, L. A. Raiders vs.
Washington, 1984

Longest Run from Scrimmage
74 Marcus Allen, L. A. Raiders vs.
Washington, 1984

PASSING

Completions

Most Passes Completed, Career
61 Roger Staubach, Dallas, 4 games
49 Terry Bradshaw, Pittsburgh, 4
games

Most Passes Completed, Game
29 Dan Marino, Miami vs. San
Francisco, 1985

Most Consecutive Completions, Game
8 Len Dawson, Kansas City vs.
Green Bay, 1967
Joe Theismann, Washington vs.
Miami, 1983

Yards gained

Most Yards Gained, Career
932 Terry Bradshaw, Pittsburgh, 4
games
734 Roger Staubach, Dallas, 4 games

Most Yards Gained, Game
331 Joe Montana, San Francisco vs.
Miami, 1985

Longest Pass Completion
80 Jim Plunkett (to King), Oakland
vs. Philadelphia, 1981 (TD)

Touchdowns

Most Touchdown Passes, Career
9 Terry Bradshaw, Pittsburgh, 4
games
8 Roger Staubach, Dallas, 4 games

Most Touchdown Passes, Game
4 Terry Bradshaw, Pittsburgh vs.
Dallas, 1979

PASS RECEIVING

Receptions

Most Receptions Career
16 Lynn Swann, Pittsburgh, 4 games
15 Chuck Foreman, Minnesota, 3
games

Most Receptions, Game
11 Dan Ross, Cincinnati vs. San
Francisco, 1982

Yards Gained

Most Yards Gained Career
364 Lynn Swann, Pittsburgh, 4
games
268 John Stallworth, Pittsburgh, 4
games

Most Yards Gained, Game
161 Lynn Swann, Pittsburgh vs.
Dallas, 1976

Longest Reception
80 Kenny King (from Plunkett),
Oakland vs. Philadelphia,
1981 (TD)

INTERCEPTIONS BY

Most Interceptions By, Career
3 Chuck Howley, Dallas, 2 games
Rod Martin, Oakland/L. A.
Raiders, 2 games

Most Interceptions By, Game
3 Rod Martin, Oakland vs.
Philadelphia, 1981

Yards gained

Longest Return
75 Willie Brown, Oakland vs.
Minnesota, 1977 (TD)

PUNTING

Most Punts, Career
17 Mike Elscheid, Oakland/
Minnesota, 3 games

Most Punts, Game
9 Ron Widby, Dallas vs.
Baltimore, 1971

Longest Punt
61 Jerrel Wilson, Kansas City vs.
Green Bay, 1967

PUNT RETURNS

Most Punt Returns, Career
6 Willie Wood, Green Bay, 2
games
Jake Scott, Miami, 3 games
Theo Bell, Pittsburgh, 2 games
Mike Nelms, Washington, 1
game

Most Punt Returns, Game
6 Mike Nelms, Washington vs.
Miami, 1983

Longest Return
34 Darrell Green, Washington vs.
L. A. Raiders, 1984

KICKOFF RETURNS

Most Kickoff Returns, Game
5 Larry Anderson, Pittsburgh vs.
Los Angeles, 1980
Billy Campfield, Philadelphia vs.
Oakland, 1981
David Verser, Cincinnati vs. San
Francisco, 1982

Yards gained

Most Yards Gained, Career
283 Fulton Walker, Miami, 2 games
207 Larry Anderson, Pittsburgh, 2
games

Most Yards Gained, Game
190 Fulton Walker, Miami vs.
Washington, 1983

Longest Return
98 Fulton Walker, Miami vs.
Washington, 1983 (TD)

COMBINED NET YARDS GAINED

Yards gained

Most Yards Gained, Career
468 Franco Harris, Pittsburgh, 4
games
391 Lynn Swann, Pittsburgh, 4
games

Most Yards Gained, Game
209 Marcus Allen, L. A. Raiders vs.
Washington, 1984

Team Records

SCORING

Most Points, Game
38 L. A. Raiders vs. Washington,
1984
San Francisco vs. Miami, 1985

Fewest Points, Game
3 Miami vs. Dallas, 1972

CHAPTER THREE

College Football

Introduction

Football in the USA is big business, and nowhere is it bigger than in the colleges throughout this vast country. Under the aegis of the National Collegiate Athletic Association, over 650 Universities compete at four levels of excellence in probably one of the toughest schedules in the world.

Just as professional as its senior counterparts, in management terms at least, the college football circuit is the breeding ground for the stars of tomorrow.

Under NCAA rules players do not receive salaries, although rumours abound every year of inducements being made that break the rules. Colleges found guilty by the tough disciplinarian NCAA of violating their rules are usually banned from the lucrative Bowl games at the end of the season.

Whilst the players are not paid, their mentors, the coaches, are among the highest paid sports coaches in the USA. Alabama's Paul Bryant was reported to have earned in excess of $450 000 in 1981. Not only do the coaches earn substantial basic salaries, but they can command huge fees for seminars and summer training camps and from the media.

Almost all of today's NFL and USFL coaches started life in college ranks. Los Angeles Rams' head coach John Robinson was for many years the top man at the University of Southern California, and Darryl Rogers, one of the newest coaches in the NFL at Detroit Lions, served his time until last spring at Arizona State.

Everything about College football is on a big scale. The Division One Universities use stadiums that are big enough to attract massive crowds, and massive crowds do turn up. In 1981 the University of Michigan averaged a crowd of 104 292 for their regular season games. The top twenty teams will have an average crowd attendance for a season of over 60 000 people who cram into huge dome-like stadiums to cheer on their favourites.

In 1979, Michigan again set a new record for crowd attendance at a single game when over 106 000 fans packed into the Ann Arbor Stadium to watch the Wolverines play their arch rivals in the Big Ten, Ohio State.

Nearly 37 million fans attended college football games in 1984, compared to only 11 million who watched NFL action.

Football has certainly come a long way from its early pioneering days back in the latter part of the last century. In 1892 Stanford and the University of Calfornia met in the first recorded west coast game, and three years later the first conference or league was formed. Originally called the Western Athletic Conference, it is known today as the 'Big Ten'.

Over the past century many more conferences have been formed, not only to play football but to enable groups of universities to participate in all sports.

Many of these conferences are based on geographical areas, with teams vying every year for their conference championship and a chance to represent their league in a money-spinning Bowl game.

The teams in each conference will play a certain number of games against local conference rivals. Other games will be played against colleges from other conferences and some will arrange schedules that include fixtures with Universities who are labelled as 'Independents'. Notre Dame, Pittsburgh, Miami and Penn State number in these ranks, and choose to run their own athletic policies and play games against some of the top colleges in the USA. Some of these games have longstanding traditions predating the formation of conferences. The U.S.C. versus Notre Dame fixture is an annual affair that can be traced back to the 1920s.

Like any sport, college-style football has a habit of developing dynasties, and these have constantly varied over the years.

The team from the University of Michigan in the early 1900s, with Willie 'The Wisp' Heston at the helm, was undefeated for 56 games between 1901 and 1905. Because of their ability to score almost at will, they became known as the 'Point-a-Minute' team, and their record in the year 1901 (11–0), with a total score of 550 points for and none

---

Did You Know

That President Gerald Ford was center and captain of Michigan University in the mid 1930s. In 1934 he was voted their most valuable player. He played in the annual college all-star game but chose not to enter into the professional ranks, opting for a brilliant political career instead.

Other famous presidents of the gridiron include John F. Kennedy, who played for Harvard as an end; Franklin D. Roosevelt, who captained Harvard's freshman team in 1900; Dwight D. Eisenhower, who played for Army until he broke a leg against the Carlisle Indians on 12 November 1912; and although President Ronald Reagan played only prep-school football, he achieved fame when he played Notre Dame's legendary George Gipp in a 1940 Warner Brothers film. Reagan sped some 50 yards downfield for a touchdown, where he bounced the ball on the ground, and became the very first player to spike a football in the end-zone.

---

against, showed how powerful they were.

A few hundred miles to the west, and some twenty years later, Illinois, under Red Grange, set about rewriting the record books with four touchdowns in 12 minutes during one game.

The 1920s saw Notre Dame rise to prominence, with the legendary Knute Rockne as coach. Rockne is still regarded by many as the greatest coach ever.

The 'Thundering Herd' of U.S.C. became almost invincible during the 1930s on the west coast, whilst on the eastern seaboard New York's Fordham went a whole season in 1936 without conceding a single touchdown.

The war years naturally saw the emergence of the military academies, and the Army with Glenn Davis and Doc Blanchard achieved an NCAA record high of 56 points per game.

The post-war years once again saw the emergence of Notre Dame, before Oklahoma and Texas decided it was time that the southwest achieved some fame.

The late 1950s saw the arrival of new coaches with new ideas. One of the leading lights of this era was John McKay of U.S.C. McKay favoured a new I-version for his offensive formations, and after going through only 8 wins and 11 losses, a powerful I-formation gave the Trojans three national titles and perfect seasons of 11–0–0 and 12–0–0.

The formations used by colleges are much more varied than those used in the professional leagues. College football tends to try the unusual and some say is far more exciting than its big league brothers.

Naturally, the large colleges across the nation play their football within one of the major division IA conferences, or as a division IA Independent. There are a few exceptions such as Baylor, a small baptist University from Waco, Texas, which plays in the Southwest Conference.

The major conferences are the Big Ten, comprising colleges from the northern midwest; the Big Eight, whose teams come predominantly from the farming belt of the midwest (Nebraska and Kansas to name but two); the Pacific Ten Conference, the major Universities from the far west; the Southeastern Conference, whose members are located, as the name suggests, in the deep

The Major Conferences

Division 1A:

Atlantic Coast
Clemson
Duke
Georgia Tech.
Maryland
North Carolina
North Carolina State
Wake Forest
Virginia

Big Eight
Colorado
Iowa State
Kansas
Kansas State
Missouri
Nebraska
Oklahoma
Oklahoma State

Big Ten
Illinois
Northwestern
Indiana
Iowa
Michigan
Michigan State
Minnesota
Ohio State
Purdue
Wisconsin

Pacific 10
Arizona
Arizona State
California
Oregon
Oregon State
Southern California
Stanford
University of California
  at Los Angeles
Washington
Washington State

Southeastern
Florida
Louisiana State
Alabama
Auburn
Georgia
Kentucky
Mississippi
Mississippi State

Tennessee
Vanderbilt

Southwest
Arkansas
Baylor
Houston
Rice
Southern Methodist
Texas
Texas A&M
Texas Christian
Texas Tech.

Western Athletic
Air Force
Brigham Young
Colorado State
Hawaii
New Mexico
San Diego State
Texas-El Paso
Utah
Wyoming

Mid-American
Toledo
Western Michigan
Miami, Ohio
Ball State
Bowling Green
Central Michigan
Eastern Michigan
Kent State
Northern Illinois
Ohio University

Division 1A Independents
Boston College
West Virginia
Florida State
South Carolina
Syracuse
Virginia Tech.
Temple
Penn State
Miami, Florida
Southwest Louisiana
Memphis State
Notre Dame
Southern Mississippi
Pittsburgh
Rutgers
Tulane

Louisville
East Carolina

Missouri Valley
Illinois State
Tulsa
Southern Illinois
Drake
Indiana State
West Texas State
Wichita State

Ohio Valley
Eastern Kentucky
Youngstown State
Akron
Austin Peay
Middle Tennessee
Morehead State
Murray State
Tennessee Tech.

Pacific Coast
Nevada-Las Vegas
San Jose State
New Mexico State
Fresno State
Long Beach State
Pacific
Utah State

Southern
Western Carolina
Davidson
Appalachian State
Citadel
East Tennessee State
Furman
Marshall
Tennessee-Chattanooga

Division 1AA:

Big Sky
Boise State
Idaho
Idaho State
Montana
Montana State
Nevada-Reno
Northern Arizona
Weber State

Gulf Star
Southwest Texas State
Stephen F. Austin
Sam Houston State

Northwest Louisiana
Southeast Louisiana
Nicholls State

Ivy League
Brown
Columbia
Cornell
Dartmouth
Harvard
Penn
Princeton
Yale

Southland
Arkansas State
Lamar
Louisiana Tech.
McNeese State
North Texas State
Northeast Louisiana
Texas-Arlington

Southwestern
Alcorn State
Jackson State
Southern University
Texas Southern
Grambling
Alabama State
Mississippi Valley State
Prairie View A&M

Yankee
New Hampshire
Maine
Boston University
Connecticut
Massachusetts
Rhode Island

Division 1AA Independents
Tennessee State
Delaware
Cincinnati
William and Mary
LeHigh
Bucknell
Colgate
Richmond
Western Kentucky
Lafayette
Florida A&M

---

south of the country; the Southwest Conference, with some of the best known teams in the land: Texas, Houston, Arkansas, S.M.U; the Atlantic Coast Conference, geographically not far from the Southeastern, but with most of the colleges from the Carolinas, Virginia and Georgia; and the Western Athletic Conference, whose biggest college is without doubt the Mormon Brigham Young University, the 1984 National Champions. Other major conferences are the Pacific Coast Athletic Conference, the Missouri Valley Conference and of course the grandfather of them all the Ivy League, with such distinguished members as Harvard, Princeton, Yale, Brown, Dartmouth and Cornell. The Ivy League has, though, in recent years decided to downgrade its athletic ability and is now rated in football as a division IAA league.

Knute Rockne

Knute Rockne received a rather nasty introduction to football. As a young Norwegian immigrant to the Logan Square district of Chicago, Rockne first played the game with his immigrant friends in the streets. It was at one of these impromptu games that the young Rockne received a bad mauling by an opposing team. When he finally arrived home, his clothes tattered and in shreds, his parents announced that that was the end of his football career.

But a few bumps and bruises did not put Rockne off and soon he was back on the gridiron playing and starring first for his high school and later for the Irving Park Athletic Club.

Rockne worked at the Chicago Post Office for four years until he had saved enough money to continue his education at Notre Dame University.

After a difficult first year at South Bend, Knute Rockne turned his attention to the track where he excelled in the pole vault, of all things, and later set a school indoor record of 12ft 4ins.

Those achievements gave him the incentive to give football another try and eventually he won a place in the 'Fighting Irish' team as an end, being named captain of the team in 1913.

Rockne, who was also a semi-professional boxer, continued his studies at Notre Dame and graduated in 1913 with a first class chemistry degree.

Rockne was something of an all-rounder at South Bend, writing for the student newspaper, playing the flute in the school orchestra, taking a major role in every school play and even reaching the finals of the school marbles tournament.

Upon graduation Knute Rockne was offered a post in the University's chemistry department as an assistant and he accepted the post on the condition that he could help coach the football team, known as the Fighting Irish.

When head coach Jesse Harper retired in 1917, Rockne was named as his successor.

Under Rockne's guiding hand Notre Dame skyrocketed to national prominence and became American's favourite team. With their penchant for upsetting the stronger, more established football powers throughout the land the Irish captured the hearts of millions of Americans who viewed Notre Dame's victories as hope for their achievements against the struggle of every day.

During Rockne's 13-year career Notre Dame won six national championships, beat Stanford in the 1925 Rosebowl and achieved five unbeaten seasons.

His overall winning percentage of 0.881 (won 105, lost 12, drew 5), still tops the list for both college and professional football.

Knute Rockne was a football revolutionary. His many ideas changed the face of football overnight. He was the first football coach to take his team all over the country and to initiate intersectional rivalries. He made use of his medical and anatomical knowledge to design his own equipment and uniforms. He reduced the weight and bulk of the equipment and introduced satin and silk pants that cut down wind resistance. Rockne believed that passing made up half of football strategy, whilst most of his peers kept the ball almost totally on the ground.

Football, however, was never enough for Knute Rockne. He served as Notre Dame's athletic director, business manager, ticket distributor, track coach and equipment manager. He wrote a weekly column for a local newspaper, was the author of three books, including a series of children's books, and was one of the main designers of the Notre Dame stadium.

Knute Rockne was also a dedicated family man with four children, and a keen gardener, growing much of the family's food in their small garden.

Knute Rockne, the father of Notre Dame Football. (University of Notre Dame).

Rockne also made several public speeches and had begun to make coaching films for football followers throughout America. It was whilst he was on a filming trip to Hollywood on 31 March 1931, that the plane he was travelling in crashed in a storm in Bazaar, Kansas, and Knute Rockne was killed.

The death of Knute Rockne shook football, and it was many years before Notre Dame would rise to prominence again.

> *'A pro game is motion. A college game is emotion'.* Bob Zuppke.

> *'Football is all very well as a game for rough girls, but it's hardly suitable for delicate boys'.* Oscar Wilde.

Other division IAA conferences worth a mention are the Big Sky, Ohio Valley, Southern, Mid-Continent, Mid-Eastern and the Yankee.

Below this grade of football are the smaller divisions II and III conferences, normally situated within one or two states. Some of the titles of these conferences are quite delightful. Lone Star, Rocky Mountain and Little Three are amongst their number with quaintly named colleges like Slippery Rock, Wooster, Bowie State and Kutztown.

At this end of the scale really small-town football is to be found; most of these colleges only have two or three thousand students, whereas some of the giants of the division 1A circuit will have an enrolment in excess of 40 000.

But whatever the size, every August over 50 000 young men the length and breadth of the USA are going through the pain barrier in an attempt to lift their 'alma mater' to glory and fame.

The College Game of the Century: Notre Dame v. Ohio State on 2 November 1935.

Fifty years have passed since Notre Dame's unbelievable 18–13 upset of Ohio State, but the 1935 confrontation is still labelled as the 'game of the century'.

Although both teams were undefeated before the clash, the top-ranked Buckeyes were strong favourites. The Irish were good but not that good and one sports writer even went as far as to favour the Ohio team by 40 points.

Coach Elmer Layden, a former member of the famed Four Horsemen, said later, 'The 1935 team was one that believed in itself to an extraordinary extent. It was fired emotionally because death walked with it in every game'.

The captain-elect Joe Sullivan, a starting tackle, had died of pneumonia several months before the season began, and instead of electing another captain his team mates dedicated each contest to his memory.

The atmosphere in Columbus, Ohio had been electric for weeks before the big game. There were parades and rallies and university officials and city politicians went into hiding to avoid 'friends' seeking tickets. Black market touts were scoffing at anything less than $50 for a ticket. On the Friday before the game Layden took his team to a secluded school outside the city hoping to avoid the carnival-like atmosphere that had built up. But when the Irish arrived they were greeted by thousands of Buckeye fans chanting, 'Catholics go home'.

When Saturday came over 81 000 fans jammed into the Ohio Stadium. The Buck-

Former Pittsburgh linebacker Chris Doleman prepares to sack the opposition quarterback. (University of Pittsburgh).

eyes got off to a quick start and held a commanding 13–0 lead at halftime. All the pre-game predictions were coming true. The Ohio offense operated almost at will and Notre Dame could not do anything right.

In the dressing room at half-time Layden announced that the second team would start the second half. 'They won the first half', he said, 'Now it's your turn. Go out and win this half for yourselves'.

At the end of the third quarter the Buckeyes were still 13–0 ahead but the Irish were on the move.

On the Ohio 12-yard line quarterback Andy Pilney passed to Francis Gaul and the Irish were on the two-yard line. On the next play Steve Miller went over for the touchdown. The conversion kick hit the crossbar and bounced back on to the field, but Notre Dame had at last got on to the scoreboard. Notre Dame's defense forced Ohio to punt on their fourth down and the Irish were on the march again.

Pilney's zig-zag run brought Notre Dame back into Buckeye territory and a 33-yard pass to Mike Layden brought the Irish right back into the game. A kick would make the game a draw, but again they missed and Ohio State clung on to a precarious 13–12 lead.

Layden called for an onside kick, but Ohio were not to be fooled, and after recovering the ball they began a series of time-wasting moves that would run the clock down and win them the game. But a fumble by Dick Beltz fell to second string center Henry Pojman thus giving the Irish one last crack at the nut on the Ohio 49-yard line with only a minute remaining.

The crowd were going wild. Coach Layden was crouching on the sideline chain-smoking. He sent in a play. The ball came back to Pilney, who dropped back to throw. But all his receivers were covered. So he took off, trying to get out of the reach of the

Buckeyes' rushing defenders. They finally forced him out of bounds on the Ohio 19-yard line. But Pilney didn't get up. He had torn a cartilage and had to be carried from the field on a stretcher.

Back-up quarterback Bill Shakespeare entered the fray with less than 30 seconds remaining. He threw the ball straight at Buckeye defender Beltz who got his hands to the ball, but couldn't hang on to it.

So Layden then sent in scrub quarterback Jim McKenna with another play. McKenna had sneaked on board the team train to Columbus, and his team-mates had helped hide him in one of the berths. When he couldn't get a ticket for the game, he talked his way into the Notre Dame locker room. When Layden saw him, he ordered the young man to get dressed. He did, but in his obvious excitement he forgot his pads. Now he was bringing in the winning play.

Shakespeare threw another pass. Wayne Millar caught the ball in the end-zone and the miracle was complete.

College Nicknames

Over the years several colleges have adopted nicknames for their teams or units within them. The practise has become so common today that nearly every team in the land has a nickname for their favourite players.

The Four Horsemen

Just over 60 years ago a dramatic nickname was coined by an enterprising sportswriter as he reported Notre Dame's 13–7 victory over Army.

The Notre Dame backfield of Stuhldreher, Crowley, Miller and Layden was transformed overnight into one of the most fabled quartets in football history.

Quarterback Harry Stuhldreher, left half back Jim Crowley, right half back Don Miller and fullback Elmer Layden had just run rampant through the Army team at New York's Polo Grounds on 18 October 1924.

Grantland Rice, a sports reporter for the *New York Herald Tribune*, witnessed the event and penned possibly one of the most famous reports in sports history.

The Four Horsemen of Notre Dame. Left to right: Don Miller, Elmer Layden, Jim Crowley, Harry Stuhldreher.

Outlined against a blue-grey sky the Four Horsemen rode again. In dramatic lore they are known as Famine, Pestilence, Destruction and Death. These are only aliases, their real names are: Stuhldreher, Crowley, Miller and Layden. They formed the crest of the South Bend cyclone before which the fighting Army team was swept over the precipice at the Polo Grounds this afternoon as 55 000 spectators peered down in bewilderment upon the panorama spread out on the green plain below.

The name stuck, the radio networks throughout America picked up the story and soon every football fan in the land knew of the exploits of four diminutive figures known from that day to this as 'The Four Horsemen'.

One for the Gipper

George Gipp, perhaps the greatest all-round player in college football history would have become a legend even if he had overcome the throat infection that claimed his life in 1920 at the age of 25. However it was his.

deathbed speech to Notre Dame's coach Knute Rockne which assured Gipp's place in football's history books.

As he lay dying, Gipp, who had contracted the throat infection while helping the Irish defeat Northwestern late in the 1920 season, made a passionate plea to Rockne:

> I've got to go now Rock, it's all right, I'm not afraid. Sometime Rock, when the team is up against it, when things are wrong and the breaks are beating the boys, tell them to go in there and win just one for the Gipper. I don't know where I will be then Rock, but I'll know about it and I'll be happy.

Rockne waited eight years to relay Gipp's parting request. On 10 November 1928, after losing two of its four games, an injury-riddled Notre Dame team travelled to New York's Yankee Stadium to play the unbeaten Army.

At halftime, Rockne told the players of Gipp's request and informed them, 'This is the day and you are the team'.

All-American halfback George Gipp who inspired the Notre Dame slogan, 'One for the Gipper'.

Notre Dame won the game 12–6. Jack Chevigny scored the first and upon reaching the end-zone said, 'That's one for the Gipper'. Football experts who witnessed the game said it was the greatest demonstration of inspired football they had ever seen.

Even now, nearly 60 years later, every aspiring young footballer or anyone facing insurmountable odds hears the tale of the Gipper.

The Iron Men of Suwanee

In 1899 a team of 14 men set out from their tiny Tennessee mountain school and played five games in six days against top-ranking colleges spread over 3000 miles and won them all!

The Praying Colonels

This team was the pride of the south. They came from Kentucky to upset the mighty Harvard 6–0 in 1921. Their nickname came about because of a prayer issued before every game.

The Thundering Herd

This was the name given to Southern California's dazzling teams of the 1930s which were coached by Howard Headman Jones. The Herd won the Rosebowl five times and produced more All-Americans than any other college: seven backs and eleven linemen.

Seven Blocks of Granite

Fordham University's rugged line of 1936 acquired this name. In that season they didn't allow one single touchdown. The legendary Vince Lombardi played guard for the team which was coached by one of the 'Four Horsemen', Jim Crowley.

Lonely End

In 1957 Army had a rather unique wingman called Bill Carpenter. He would split far out, never joined in the huddle, and mysteri-

---

'Tackling is more natural than blocking. If a man is running down the street with everything you own, you won't let him get away. That's tackling'. Vince Lombardi.

The University of Southern California's Arab stallion mascot, Traveller III.

ously received his signals from elsewhere. Nobody knew exactly where they came from but his achievements were nevertheless remarkable. Because of his exploits poems were written about him entitled: *To the lonely End*.

College Mascots

Traveller III: A 16-hand Arabian horse who races around the Los Angeles Coliseum track with a Trojan soldier on its back every time the University of Southern California scores a touchdown.

Albert the Alligator: A 12ft-long swamp alligator who has been adopted by the University of Florida whose nickname happens to be the 'Gators'.

Mike: A snarling Bengal tiger owned by Louisiana State University.

Ragnar: The 'Razorbacks' of Arkansas have at their games 300lbs of untamed boar called Ragnar who has been known to chase some frightened students up trees on the college campus.

Ab and Daisy: The University of Baylor in Texas has adopted twin bear cubs who live in splendid surroundings in the college grounds. Some say their den is more palatial than the students' quarters.

Bevo: The Longhorns of Texas University have as their mascot a genuine Texas Longhorn known to all the college as Bevo.

War Eagle: A huge eagle trained by Auburn to emit a deafening scream when the team scores a touchdown.

Freddie Fang: The University of Montana's pet bobcat who has also made several appearances on TV and in films.

Ralphie: A massive 1500lb American bison, adopted by the University of Colorado. Ralphie is thought to be the largest mascot of any sport or association in captivity.

Bill XXVII: The most recent in a long line of mascots used by the Naval Academy at Annapolis. Bill is the latest in a series of so-called good luck billy goats used by the midshipmen, a practice which dates back to 1890.

Superfan

Giles Pellerin, a 77-year-old retired telephone engineer from San Marino, California, is probably football's most loyal fan.

Until the 1984 season Pellerin had viewed 618 consecutive University of Southern California games, both home and away. In all he has travelled by plane, train and car more than 600 000 miles and spent more than $60 000 in doing so.

Pellerin's unbroken run began at the start of the 1926 season when he watched the Trojans defeat Whittier 74–0. He has come very close to missing a game or two, including one in 1949 when he was hospitalized five days before a home game for an emergency appendicitis operation. On the day of the game, Pellerin told a nurse that he was going for a walk in the hospital grounds and instead he went to the Los Angeles Coliseum. He returned to his bed several hours later after witnessing U.S.C. defeat Washington 40–28.

The superfan tag could also be given to his two brothers: Oliver aged 75, has not missed a Trojan game since 1947 and younger brother Max had seen more than 300 consecutive matches until work forced him to move overseas several seasons ago.

The Bowl Games

Every year the major college teams vie for places in the 18 Bowl games that currently take place around the country. In late November and early December the scouts from the various bowl organizations travel the land signing up the best teams in the country to play in the games, which usually start the week before Christmas.

A trip to a Bowl game can mean money for a college, and the chance to appear on National TV. In the 1985 Rose Bowl, the teams were paid a staggering $5.6 million in a very different game from that of 1 January 1902 when the University of Michigan played Stanford in the first 'East-West' Bowl game.

The tournament of Roses had begun in 1890 as a winter floral celebration and parade in Pasadena, California. The first parade took place along the dirt streets of Pasadena and was organized by the local Valley Hunt Club. Flowers grown by local residents adorned the parading horses and carriages. The festival quickly caught the attention of people throughout the nation, and many travelled to the west coast to see the unique parade. Within five years the parade had become so famous and complex that the Valley Hunt Club relinquished its sponsorship to a committee of community leaders who formed the Pasadena Tournament of Roses Association.

At the end of the 1901 season, Michigan was prevailed upon to play Stanford in an 'East-West' game at Tournament Park. The contest took place on 1 January 1902, and Michigan won by a score of 49–0. The game was played on a 110-yard field and 8000 spectators turned out to watch this very first Bowl game.

College Football can be rough as a University of Southern California running back takes a tackle from a Washington State linebacker.

In the summer of 1983 the Baltimore Stars and the Tampa Bay Bandits brought the United States Football League to England for an exhibition game.

Eric Dickerson, the Los Angeles Rams running back set records in High School and in the NFL.

Doug Flutie, the 1984 Heisman Trophy Winner now passes for the New Jersey Generals in the United States Football League.

A fisheye view of the hole in the roof of the Dallas Stadium.

Luckily, the helmets are strong in American Football.

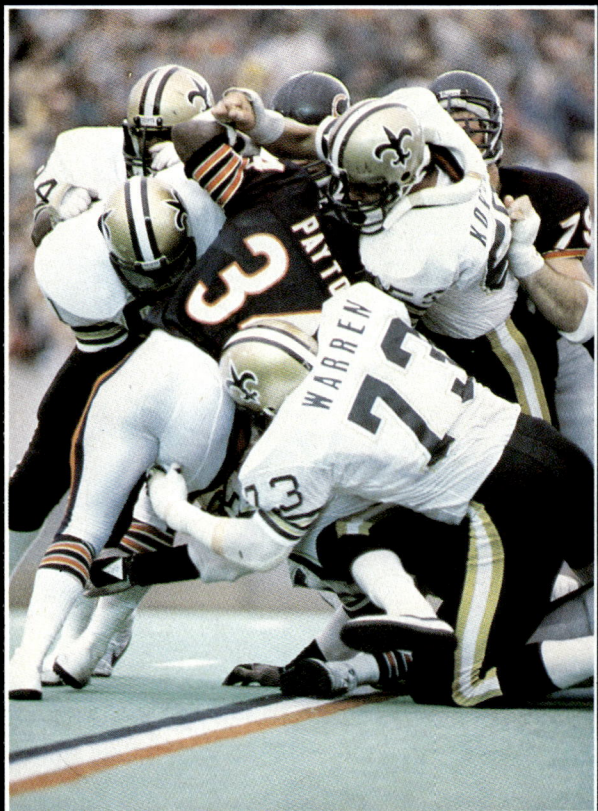

Walter Payton, Chicago Bears running back, tries to break the plane of the goal line against the New Orleans defense.

Quarterback Joe Theismann rolls out as John Riggins protects.

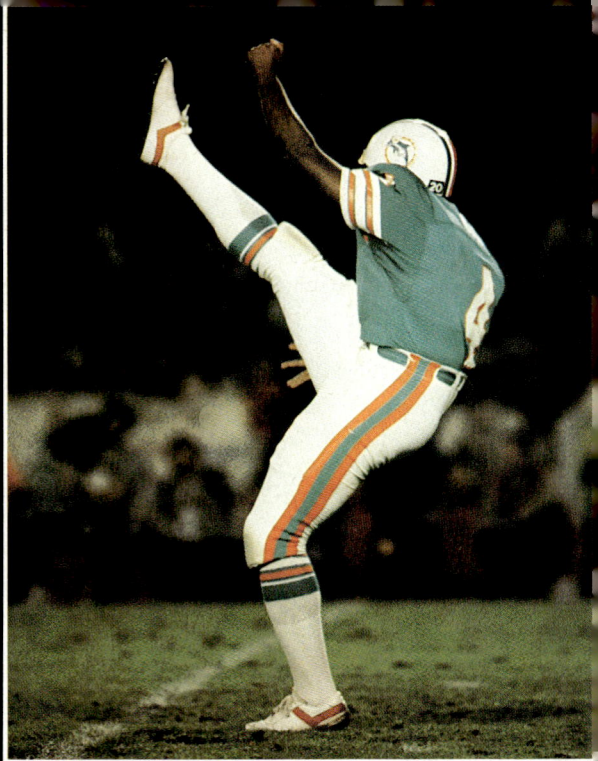

Miami Dolphin Reggie Roby shows the correct form of a "punt".

Dallas Cowboys defenders celebrate their "Quarterback Sack" or mauling of Joe Theismann.

In 1903 polo replaced football as the sports attraction, but lured a crowd of only 2000 people. So in 1904 the tournament decided to introduce chariot races. These were very popular and the 1915 event attracted 25 000 spectators. Eventually interest dwindled and in view of this fact, and the high cost of staging the races, the tournament committee decided to return to football as its main attraction for 1916.

Southern California has long been famous for its temperate climate, but the 1916 Bowl game was hit by a rain storm and the game between Washington State and Brown University was played in atrocious conditions as the Cougars became the first western winners, defeating Brown 14–0.

In 1918 the country was at war and college football was virtually non-existent. However a game was arranged between two military teams: the Mare Island Marines and Camp Lewis Army. President Woodrow Wilson approved the game and all the profits were handed over to the Red Cross. For the record the Marines won the game 19–7, largely thanks to Hollis Hunington, who had played for Oregon in 1917. Hollis ran for 111 yards and was named player of the game.

The 1919 game was a similar affair to that of the previous year. Great Lakes Navy travelled out west and handed a 17–0 defeat to the Mare Island Marines. One of the stars that day was a certain George Halas, who ran a 45-yard pass for the final touchdown. Halas was later to become one of the founding fathers of the NFL.

The 1920 bowl game between Harvard and Oregon attracted a capacity crowd of 30 000 fans paying a mere 65 cents for their seats, and because of the success of the event, the City of San Diego decided to inaugurate their own bowl. Called the Christmas Classic, the first game took place on Boxing Day 1921 when Center, a small college from Danville, Kentucky, walloped a lack-lustre Arizona team 38–0.

The Christmas Classic only lasted that one year though. Crippling financial problems forced the premature death of the only other bowl game to challenge the Pasadena 'East-West' event.

In 1923 the new Rosebowl stadium was officially opened and the 'East-West' bowl was given its new name.

In the first game played in the new

'Football is not a contact sport. It's a collision sport. A good example of a contact sport is ballroom dancing'. **Duffy Daugherty,** *former head coach of Michigan State and College Hall of Fame.*

stadium, the University of Southern California, a late replacement for California, who had declined the invitation, beat Penn State 14–3.

The Nittany Lions arrived 45 minutes late for the game due to a traffic jam and the game was concluded in moonlight as sportwriters struck matches to complete their stories.

The 1925 Rosebowl classic was the confrontation the country wanted to see: Notre Dame v. Stanford; the Four Horsemen v. Ernie Nevers; Knute Rockne v. Pop Warner. Although Pop Warner's Cardinals won the battle of the statistics—beating Notre Dame in virtually every offensive category—the Irish, led superbly by Rockne,

The 1954 Rosebowl game between U.C.L.A. and Michigan: U.C.L.A. quarterback Paul Cameron in action.

capitalized on Stanford's mistakes and came out on top on the scoreboard.

Stanford's Ernie Nevers, recovering from two broken ankles, rushed for 114 yards but Elmer Layden's three touchdowns for Notre Dame proved the decisive factor. Another of the fabled horsemen quartet, Harry Stuhldreher, actually broke his ankle early in the game, but despite the painful injury continued to play in what proved to be the Indiana college's finest hour.

The 1929 game produced one of the most famous bone-headed moves in history. California center Roy Riegels picked up a Georgia Tech. fumble on the Tech.'s 20-yard line. In those days a fumble could be advanced, so Riegels then proceeded to race down the pitch, but in the wrong direction, towards his own goal! As his team mates block fiercely, Cal's Benny Lom saw the mistake and chased Riegels down on his own one-yard line. In the next play, Lom's punt was blocked by Georgia and a two point safety resulted that won the game 8–7. The play, one of the most bizarre in all football history, brought the capacity 53 000 crowd to their feet. Riegels was later to explain that he had thought that the noise he had heard was the fans yelling encouragement!

Riegel's mistake gained him overnight fame. He received a proposal of marriage in which the couple would walk up the aisle and not down, and daft sponsorship ideas were put forward like an upside-down cake and a new necktie with the stripes the wrong way round.

Despite the depression, the 1930s saw the emergence of new games to rival the Rose. El Paso, Pittsburgh and New York tried to stage games in 1931, but as in San Diego,

Did You Know

That during the 1929 Rosebowl in which California's Roy Riegels became famous for his wrong-way run, the ball burst. On a quick California kick the air went completely out of the ball during its flight and it fell to the ground like a pancake, denying the Bears much needed ground in the battle with Georgia Tech.

their games did not go as planned, and financial problems once again forced their abandonment.

It was not until 1935 that the Rosebowl received worthy competition. The newly completed Orange Bowl Stadium in Miami decided to stage its own east coast game, and in that year on New Year's Day the Orange Bowl game was born. The neighbouring state of Louisiana was also preparing for a new Bowl game. New Orleans, a city already known for its mardigras festivities and other festivals, inaugurated the Sugar Bowl on 1 January 1935. Playing in Tulane Stadium, the local Tulane University beat Temple 20–14.

Bowl fever had once again hit the nation, and two years later football-mad Texas at last got the formula right with their own festival of football. The Cotton Bowl was designed to add attraction to the annual state fair in Dallas and almost overnight became a hit.

Football went to Cuba in 1937 when the first and only Bacardi Bowl was staged in Havana. Organized by the Cuban National Festival it was the first major game to have been played outside the USA.

During the Second World War the major Bowl games continued to thrive, and it was in 1942 that the Orange Bowl came of age. The first seven games in Miami had failed to attract the big college teams, and until 1942 the Bowl was a confrontation between small schools.

1942 also saw a change of venue for the Rosebowl. Because of a threatened Japanese air attack on the US mainland, the game was switched to Durham, North Carolina. The game between Oregon State and the local Duke University was a sell-out three days after the tickets went on sale. 56 000 crammed into the Durham Stadium to watch the west coast team beat Duke 20–16 on a 68-yard pass from quarterback Bob Dethman to Gene Gray.

After the war a new era began at the Pasadena-based Rose. Until then a western team was always invited to participate by the tournament committee, then the western University would itself select its opponents. In 1946 the two conferences, the old Pacific coast (now the Pacific Ten), and the Big Ten selected their own competing teams. 1947 and 1948 saw Bowl hysteria hit football. Over night games came and went as every city in the country wanted to stage their own version. San Antonio in Texas staged the Alamo Bowl in 1947, and in California Fresno held the Raisin Bowl. There were Grape bowls, Dixie Bowls, Delta Bowls, even the Salad Bowl in Phoenix, Arizona.

Of the 15 or so Bowl games inaugurated during this period, only 2 remain today. The Gator Bowl in Jacksonville, Florida and the

year, with over 100 000 fans packed into the Pasadena Stadium, and the same is true of the other three 'big' Bowl games: the Orange, Sugar, and Cotton, which all receive enormous patronage.

The TV coverage of these games is not only financially beneficial, it also gives the players a national audience for their skills.

Because of the time zones, it is possible,

The first and only British running back in top class football, Iowa's Owen Gill finds a gap in the Iowa State defense. (University of Iowa).

Tangerine Bowl across state in Orlando. Beginning, as the Orange had done, with small town colleges and even with high schools, these two Bowl games now attract some of the best college teams in the division IA ranks. The Bluebonnet Bowl in Houston, Texas started life in 1959 as did the Liberty Bowl. The Liberty is one of the most travelled of all bowls. It started in Philadelphia in 1959 then moved to Atlantic City in 1964, before settling down for good in Memphis, Tennessee the following year. With the inevitable TV coverage, the 1960s saw the establishment of many more Bowl games, until today there are 18 major Bowls for division IA teams.

There are Bowl games as well for division IAA and division II and III colleges. Until recently the division III championship game was known as the 'Amos Alonzo Stagg' Bowl, after one of the founding fathers of football.

Bowl games attract huge attendances. The annual Rosebowl classic is a sell-out every

by switching channels, to watch all four of the major Bowl games on New Year's Day.

The Orange Bowl has a tendency to try and match up the country's top two teams, and in recent years with the appearance of Nebraska, Miami, Oklahoma and Penn State it has achieved National Championship status. The Sugar Bowl is region-proud and puts together the champions of the southeast with one of the other major local teams. The Cotton Bowl like the Sugar matches the champions of the southwest conference with another of the top colleges across the USA. The University of Texas,

Did You Know
That U.C.L.A. is the only college to win New Year's Day Bowl games in the last three years: the 1983 and 1984 Rose Bowl and the 1985 Fiesta Bowl in which they triumphed over Miami.

83

which is one of the teams most often selected, has taken part in the Cotton 18 times, winning on 10 occasions. For some unknown reason the Cotton Bowl produces some of the closest battles in college history. Because of the number of Bowl games now being played (there are 18 in all), many observers feel that the status of the Bowl has been reduced, but in today's money-go-round of football fantasia, the colleges find the Bowl circuit very attractive.

College Bowl Records

Alabama, The Nation's Number 1 Bowl Team

Alabama has appeared in more Bowl games (37), than any other team in collegiate football.

Its 1983 Sun Bowl victory equalled U.S.C.'s record of 20 victories in Bowl games.

The Crimson Tide's 29 appearances in the four major Bowls (the Rose, Sugar, Cotton and Orange) also places them top of the college teams. Alabama is the only team to have won all four major Bowl games twice. The following is a listing of the nation's top twenty Bowl teams according to the number of games played:

Team	No. of Games	All Bowls			Big Four		
		W	L	T	W	L	T
1 Alabama	37	20	14	3	17	11	1
2 Texas	31	15	14	2	12	9	1
3 U.S.C.	28	21	7	0	18	6	0
4 Tennessee	26	12	14	0	4	9	0
5 Oklahoma	25	16	8	1	13	5	0
6 Georgia	24	10	13	1	7	9	1
7 Louisiana State	24	11	11	2	7	6	0
8 Georgia Tech.	22	14	8	0	9	3	0
9 Nebraska	23	13	10	0	8	9	0
10 Penn State	22	14	6	2	6	4	1
11 Mississippi	21	11	10	0	6	6	0
12 Arkansas	21	8	10	3	4	7	1
13 Missouri	19	8	11	0	2	5	0
14 Ohio State	19	9	10	0	6	8	0
15 Texas Tech.	16	3	12	1	0	1	0
16 Auburn	17	9	7	1	2	2	0
17 Pittsburgh	16	7	9	0	3	5	0
18 Florida	15	7	8	0	1	2	0
19 Michigan	16	6	10	0	5	8	0
20 North Carolina	15	6	9	0	0	3	0

'Football is like committee meetings, called huddles, separated by outbursts of violence'. George Will.

The 1984–85 Season Bowl Games

California Bowl
15 December, Fresno California
$150 000 per team
Nevada-Las Vegas 30, Toledo 13

Independence Bowl
15 December, Shreveport Louisiana
$425 000 per team
Air Force 23, Virginia Tech 7

Holiday Bowl
21 December, San Diego California
$475 000 per team
Brigham Young 24, Michigan 17

Florida Citrus Bowl (formerly the Tangerine)
22 December, Orlando Florida
$600 000 per team
Georgia 17, Florida State 17

Sun Bowl
22 December, El Paso Texas
$550 000 per team
Maryland 28, Tennessee 27

Cherry Bowl
22 December, Pontiac Silverdome Michigan
$750 000 per team
Army 10, Michigan State 6

Freedom Bowl
26 December, Anaheim California
$500 000 per team
Iowa 55, Texas 17

Liberty Bowl
27 December, Memphis Tennessee
$700 000 per team
Auburn 21, Arkansas 15

Gator Bowl
28 December, Jacksonville Florida
$900 000 per team
Oklahoma State 21, South Carolina 14

Aloha Bowl
29 December, Honolulu Hawaii
$400 000 per team
Southern Methodist 27, Notre Dame 20

Hall of Fame Bowl
29 December, Birmingham Alabama
$650 000 per team
Kentucky 20, Wisconsin 19

Bluebonnet Bowl
31 December, Houston Texas
$465 000 per team
West Virginia 31, Texas Christian 14

Peach Bowl
31 December, Atlanta Georgia
$580 000 per team
Virginia 27, Purdue 24

Cotton Bowl
1 January 1985, Dallas Texas
$2 million
Boston College 45, Houston 28

Fiesta Bowl
1 January, Tempe Arizona
$1.1 million
U.C.L.A. 39, Miami 36

Orange Bowl
1 January, Miami Florida
$2 million
Washington 28, Oklahoma 17

Rose Bowl
1 January, Pasadena California
$5.6 million
U.S.C. 20, Ohio State 17

Sugar Bowl
1 January, New Orleans Louisiana
$2.1 million per team
Nebraska 28, Louisiana State 10

Bowl Games No Longer With Us

Alamo (San Antonio, Texas); 1947
Aviation (Dayton, Ohio); 1961
Bacardi (Havana, Cuba); 1937
Bluegrass (Louisville, Kentucky); 1958
Camelia (Lafayette, Louisiana); 1948
Charity (New York); 1930–31
Charity (El Paso, Texas); 1933
Charity (Pittsburgh, Pennsylvania); 1931
Christmas (Los Angeles, California); 1924
Christmas (San Diego, California); 1921–22
Delta (Memphis, Tennessee); 1948–49
Dixie (Birmingham, Alabama); 1948–49
Dixie Classic (Dallas, Texas); 1922 and 1925
Fort Worth Classic (Fort Worth, Texas); 1922
Garden State (East Rutherford, New Jersey); 1978–81
Gotham (New York); 1961–62
Grape (Lodi, California); 1947–48
Great Lakes (Cleveland, Ohio); 1947
Harbor (San Diego, California); 1947–49
Mercy (Los Angeles, California); 1961
Oil (Houston, Texas); 1946–47
Pasadena (Pasadena, California); 1967 and 1969–70
Presidential Cup (College Park, Maryland); 1950
Raisin (Fresno, California); 1946–49
Salad (Phoenix, Arizona); 1948–52
Shrine (Little Rock, Arkansas); 1948

Most Bowl Appearances
Alabama 37
Texas 31
U.S.C. 28
Tennessee 26
Oklahoma 25
Louisiana State 24
Georgia 24

Best Bowl Record:
U.S.C. with 21 wins, 7 losses in 28 appearances

Worst Bowl Record:
Iowa State and Utah State with 4 defeats in 4 appearances.

'And now football fans, it's time for the kiss-off'. TV presenter 'Dandy' Don Meredith.

National Champions

Every season all the newspapers and journalists throughout the land hold their own weekly polls to see which college is given top rating. At the end of the season, usually sometime in late December, the sportswriters get together in a national poll organized by the Associated Press and vote for their top team of the year.

Occasionally this poll will be put off until after the New Year's Day Bowl games and sometimes the results of these games will determine who carries the mantle of America's no. 1 college.

The first poll took place way back in 1936, when Minnesota won the crown. During the war years (1941–1945), the United Press took a poll of football coaches to determine the winners and from 1946–49 the National Football Foundation undertook the role. These bodies have in recent years revived their ballots but the Associated Press poll still stands as the best guide to the National Championships.

Did you know

The University of Notre Dame has won the title more times than anyone else, with eight victories between 1943 and 1977. Alabama is next with six and Oklahoma and Ohio State have five each, then comes Minnesota, U.S.C. and Texas with four, finally Ohio State with three national titles.

Only eight colleges have won titles in consecutive seasons: Army, Nebraska, Alabama, Notre Dame, Minnesota, Oklahoma, Texas and Ohio State. The only Universities to have won consecutive titles twice are Oklahoma in 1955–56 and 1974–75, and Alabama in 1964–65 and 1978–79.

National Champions from 1936

1936	Minnesota	1961	Alabama
1937	Pittsburgh	1962	U.S.C.
1938	Texas Christian	1963	Texas
1939	Texas A&M	1964	Alabama
1940	Minnesota	1965	Alabama
1941	Minnesota (UP)	1966	Notre Dame
1942	Ohio State (UP)	1967	U.S.C.
1943	Notre Dame (UP)	1968	Ohio State
1944	Army (UP)	1969	Texas
1945	Army (UP)	1970	Nebraska
1946	Notre Dame (NFF)	1971	Nebraska
1947	Notre Dame (NFF)	1972	U.S.C.
1948	Michigan (NFF)	1973	Notre Dame
1949	Notre Dame (NFF)	1974	Oklahoma
1950	Oklahoma	1975	Oklahoma
1951	Tennessee	1976	Pittsburgh
1952	Michigan State	1977	Notre Dame
1953	Maryland	1978	Alabama
1954	Ohio State	1979	Alabama
1955	Oklahoma	1980	Georgia
1956	Oklahoma	1981	Clemson
1957	Auburn	1982	Penn State
1958	Louisiana State	1983	Miami, Florida
1959	Syracuse	1984	Brigham Young
1960	Minnesota		

Charles White, U.S.C. back and Heisman Trophy winner, 1979.

The Heisman Trophy

The John W. Heisman Memorial Trophy Award is presented each year to the oustanding college football player by the Downtown Athletic Club of New York.

Originally known as the D.A.C. Trophy, the award was renamed in 1936 after John W. Heisman, the first athletic director of the Downtown Athletic Club, a football player for Penn State and Brown University, and a coach for 36 years at Auburn, Oberlin, Clemson, Akron, Penn State, Rice, Washington and Jefferson and Georgia Tech.

(Cont. p. 88)

Winners of the Heisman Trophy

1935	Jay Berwanger	Halfback	Chicago	1960	Joe Bellino	Halfback	Navy
1936	Larry Kelley	End	Yale	1961	Ernie Davis	Halfback	Syracuse
1937	Clint Frank	Halfback	Yale	1962	Terry Baker	Quarterback	Oregon State
1938	Davey O'Brien	Quarterback	Texas Christian	1963	Roger Staubach	Quarterback	Navy
1939	Nile Kinnick	Halfback	Iowa	1964	John Huarte	Quarterback	Notre Dame
1940	Tom Harmon	Halfback	Michigan	1965	Mike Garrett	Tailback	U.S.C.
1941	Bruce Smith	Halfback	Minnesota	1966	Steve Spurrier	Quarterback	Florida
1942	Frank Sinkwich	Halfback	Georgia	1967	Gary Beban	Quarterback	U.C.L.A.
1943	Angelo Bertelli	Quarterback	Notre Dame	1968	O. J. Simpson	Tailback	U.S.C.
1944	Les Horvath	Halfback	Ohio State	1969	Steve Owens	Halfback	Oklahoma
1945	Doc Blanchard	Fullback	Army	1970	Jim Plunkett	Quarterback	Stanford
1946	Glenn Davis	Halfback	Army	1971	Pat Sullivan	Quarterback	Auburn
1947	John Lujack	Quarterback	Notre Dame	1972	Johnny Rodgers	Flanker	Nebraska
1948	Doak Walker	Halfback	Southern Methodist	1973	John Cappelletti	Halfback	Penn State
				1974	Archie Griffin	Halfback	Ohio State
1949	Leon Hart	End	Notre Dame	1975	Archie Griffin	Halfback	Ohio State
1950	Vic Janowicz	Halfback	Ohio State	1976	Tony Dorsett	Tailback	Pittsburgh
1951	Dick Kazmaier	Halfback	Princeton	1977	Earl Campbell	Tailback	Texas
1952	Billy Vessels	Halfback	Oklahoma	1978	Billy Sims	Halfback	Oklahoma
1953	John Lattner	Halfback	Notre Dame	1979	Charles White	Tailback	U.S.C.
1954	Alan Ameche	Fullback	Wisconsin	1980	George Rogers	Halfback	South Carolina
1955	Howard Cassady	Halfback	Ohio State	1981	Marcus Allen	Tailback	U.S.C.
1956	Paul Hornung	Quarterback	Notre Dame	1982	Herschel Walker	Tailback	Georgia
1957	John Crow	Halfback	Texas A. & M.	1983	Mike Rozier	Tailback	Nebraska
1958	Pete Dawkins	Halfback	Army	1984	Doug Flutie	Quarterback	Boston College
1959	Billy Cannon	Halfback	Louisiana State				

The Korean Kicker

Min Jong Lee grew up in Seoul, South Korea, playing soccer and baseball.

He even played for the national Korean little league team against Japan, Taiwan and Hong Kong. But Lee was not destined for the life of a baseball star, instead a career in the ranks of professional football seems certain for this U.C.L.A. star kicker.

A move from Korea to Downey, California changed not only his fortunes but also his name. From then on he was just plain John Lee, and, so the story goes, a chance meeting with a stray football one day during baseball practice changed his sporting habits as well.

The football came flying on to the baseball diamond, and Lee calling upon his soccer skills picked it up and returned it with a mighty kick to the coach. The coach was impressed and asked the youngster to try out as kicker for the football team. Every kick that Lee took in practice went straight through the uprights and thus a kicker was born.

In 1984 John Lee became the top scorer in U.C.L.A. history with 272 points, passing the previous best set by Gary Beban, the Bruins' only Heisman winner.

1984 saw records fall both locally and nationally as Ming Jong Lee became the hottest kicking prospect since Arizona State's Luis Zendejas.

Over the course of the season Lee set the National Collegiate Athletic Association record for the most field goals in one season when he kicked no. 29 in the final victory over U.S.C. on 17 November 1984.

In the 1985 Fiesta Bowl against Miami, Lee scored a massive 30 points including a last minute field goal to win the game for the Bruins by 39 to 37.

In the three years he has attended U.C.L.A. John has converted 63 of 75 attempts in his regular season average of 0.853, which is the highest in NCAA history for players who have made 60 or more attempts in their career.

Because of his success, John Lee was voted All-America kicker at the end of the 1984 season, and, as he has another year as a college player, 1985 is certain to see every other college scoring record fall to this remarkable young man from Seoul, Korea.

U.C.L.A.'s All-American kicker John Lee scores the winning points in the 1985 Fiesta Bowl. (U.C.L.A.)

The bronze trophy was sculpted by Frank Eliscu, with the advice of one of Notre Dame's famous 'Four Horsemen', Jim Crowley, by then coaching at Fordham University in New York.

The first winner of the prized award was Chicago University's halfback Jay Berwanger in 1935. A year later it was Berwanger who again wrote his name into the record books by being selected as the first choice in the NFL's inaugural draft.

The award is made to college football's player of the year, but it is interesting to note that only twice has the prize gone to a lineman, and then not an interior one. In 1936 Yale's end Larry Kelley won and in 1949 Notre Dame's star end Leon Hart was chosen.

Boston College's talented quarterback Doug Flutie became the fiftieth recipient in 1984, but only 13 quarterbacks have ever won the award, the majority of triumphs belonging to running backs.

Since its inception Notre Dame players have won the award more times than any other college with 6 winners: quarterback Angelo Bertelli in 1943, quarterback John Lujack in 1947, end Leon Hart in 1949, halfback John Lattner in 1953, quarterback Paul Hornung in 1956 (Hornung later went onto become a star running back with the Green Bay Packers), and John Huarte, the Fighting Irish quarterback of 1964, who was their last winner.

The college with the next highest number of winners is the University of Southern California who are represented by some of the best known names in football today: Mike Garrett, O. J. Simpson, Charles White and Marcus Allen in 1965, 1968, 1979, and 1981 respectively.

The Heisman Trophy is without doubt the biggest single award a college player can receive, and as multi-million dollar contracts are offered to the winners, the announce-ment of the results every December is awaited with bated breath.

The Outland Trophy

The Outland Trophy is presented each year to the outstanding interior lineman in collegiate football by the Football Writers' Association of America.

The award was first presented in 1946 to Notre Dame's talented tackle George Connor, and has been greatly prized by the 39 footballers who have won it since.

The 1962 Gotham Bowl, played in New York's Yankee Stadium, provided one of the smallest Bowl crowds ever. Only 6166 fans turned out in sub-zero temperatures to witness Nebraska beat the Miami Hurricanes by 36 to 34.

U.C.L.A.'s Heisman-winning quarterback of 1967, Gary Beban. (U.C.L.A.).

Because of its similarity to the Lombardi Award many winners have won both in the same year, but nevertheless the Outland Trophy is one of the highest honours in college football a lineman can receive.

Winners have included Merlin Olsen, who later starred for the Los Angeles Rams and after retiring from football became a movie star and sports TV presenter; Randy White, Dallas Cowboys' defensive tackle who won the Superbowl XII MVP award as part of the now famous 'Doomsday II' defense; and Tommy Nobis, the Texas All-American who won it for his play both ways—as a guard and a middle linebacker.

1946	George Connor	Tackle	Notre Dame
1947	Joe Steffy	Guard	Army
1948	Bill Fischer	Guard	Notre Dame
1949	Ed Badgon	Guard	Michigan State
1950	Bob Gain	Tackle	Kentucky
1951	Jim Weatherall	Tackle	Oklahoma
1952	Dick Modzelewski	Tackle	Maryland
1953	J. D. Roberts	Guard	Arkansas
1954	Bill Brooks	Guard	Arkansas
1955	Calvin Jones	Guard	Iowa
1956	Jim Parker	Guard	Ohio State
1957	Alex Karras	Tackle	Iowa
1958	Zeke Smith	Guard	Auburn
1959	Mike McGhee	Tackle	Duke
1960	Tom Brown	Guard	Minnesota
1961	Merlin Olsen	Tackle	Utah State
1962	Bobby Bell	Tackle	Minnesota
1963	Scott Appleton	Tackle	Texas
1964	Steve DeLong	Tackle	Tennessee
1965	Tommy Nobis	Linebacker	Texas
1966	Lloyd Phillips	Defensive Tackle	Arkansas
1967	Ron Yary	Offensive Tackle	U.S.C.
1968	Bill Stanfill	Defensive Tackle	Georgia
1969	Mike Reid	Defensive Tackle	Penn State
1970	Jim Stillwagon	Middle Guard	Ohio State
1971	Larry Jacobsen	Defensive Tackle	Nebraska
1972	Rich Glover	Middle Guard	Nebraska
1973	John Hicks	Offensive Tackle	Ohio State
1974	Randy White	Defensive Tackle	Maryland
1975	Leroy Selmon	Defensive Tackle	Oklahoma
1976	Ross Browner	Defensive End	Notre Dame
1977	Brad Shearer	Defensive Tackle	Texas
1978	Greg Roberts	Guard	Oklahoma
1979	Jim Richter	Center	N. Carolina St.
1980	Hugh Green	Defensive End	Pittsburgh
1981	Dave Rimington	Center	Nebraska
1982	Dave Rimington	Center	Nebraska
1983	Dean Steinkuhler	Offensive Guard	Nebraska
1984	Bruce Smith	Defensive End	Virginia Tech.

'Pro Football is like nuclear warfare, there are no winners, only survivors'. Frank Gifford.

The Lombardi Award

The Lombardi Award was instituted in 1970 by the Rotary Club of Houston. It was set up as a memorial to the legendary Vince Lombardi who played as guard for Fordham University from 1934 to 1936.

The Lombardi Award is presented annually to the country's best lineman, and like the Heisman, it is of vital importance, as the winners can almost guarantee themselves a money spinning career in professional football.

1970	Jim Stillwagon	Middle Guard	Ohio State
1971	Walt Patulski	Defensive End	Notre Dame
1972	Rich Glover	Middle Guard	Nebraska
1973	John Hicks	Offensive Tackle	Ohio State
1974	Randy White	Defensive Tackle	Maryland
1975	Leroy Selmon	Defensive Tackle	Oklahoma
1976	Wilson Whitley	Defensive Tackle	Houston
1977	Ross Browner	Defensive End	Notre Dame
1978	Bruce Clark	Defensive Tackle	Penn State
1979	Brad Budde	Offensive Guard	U.S.C.
1980	Hugh Green	Defensive End	Pittsburgh
1981	Kenneth Sims	Defensive Tackle	Texas
1982	Dave Rimington	Center	Nebraska
1983	Dean Steinkuhler	Offensive Guard	Nebraska
1984	Bill Fralic	Offensive Tackle	Pittsburgh

'Winning is the ONLY thing'. Vince Lombardi.

Most successful Division 1A Coaches

Coach, School	Yrs	W	L	T	%	Rank
Barry Switzer, Oklahoma	12	115	23	4	0.824	1
Tom Osborne, Nebraska	12	118	27	2	0.810	2
Joe Paterno, Penn State	19	176	43	2	0.801	3
Bo Schembechler, Michigan	22	186	54	6	0.768	4
Danny Ford, Clemson	7	52	15	2	0.768	4
Herb Deromedi, Central Michigan	7	57	17	3	0.760	6
La Vell Edwards, Brigham Young	13	118	37	1	0.760	6
Howard Schnellenberger, Louisville	5	41	16	0	0.719	8
Vince Dooley, Georgia	21	168	64	8	0.717	9
Dick Crum, N. Carolina	11	89	35	3	0.713	10
Fred Akers, Texas	10	83	34	2	0.706	11
Pat Dye, Auburn	11	88	37	1	0.702	12
Terry Donahue, U.C.L.A.	9	71	29	5	0.700	13
Bobby Bowden, Florida State	19	146	62	2	0.700	13
Bobby Collins, S.M.U.	10	79	34	3	0.694	15

Joe Namath

It was a green Lincoln convertible that clinched the signing of Alabama's young quarterback in Miami on 2 January 1965.

The cocky youngster had just played the game of his life trying to prevent the 'Crimson Tide' from going down 21–17 to Texas in that year's Orange Bowl.

Joe Namath came to the New York Jets via Beaver Falls, Pennsylvania, where he was born and brought up, and the University of Alabama.

Despite the fact that he sat out part of his junior year for rule violations and part of his

A youthful looking Joe Namath at the University of Alabama in 1964.

Joe Namath at the end of his career as Los Angles Rams' quarterback.

third because of a knee injury, in the spring of 1965 he attracted almost every scout in the country.

In the Orange Bowl game, Namath limped on to the field in the second quarter with a heavily strapped knee and completed 18 passes for 255 yards as the 'Tide' came back from a 14–0 deficit to frighten the life out of the Longhorns and nearly cause one of the major upsets of Bowl history.

New York Jets' owner Sonny Werblin completed the signing of Namath the day after the game and, as well as the obvious inducement of the car, a $400 000 long-term contract sealed one of the greatest deals in football.

After a slow start in his first pro season Namath lived up to all expectations three years later as he took the Jets to the AFL championship and on to Superbowl III against the Baltimore Colts.

The Colts, with the legendary Johnny Unitas at the helm, were the pre-game favourites by a mile, but Namath paid no attention to the odds and in the week preceding the game went about telling almost everybody that the Jets would win. His confidence-boosting speeches came to a head on the Thursday before when at a press conference he publicly 'guaranteed' that the title would go to New York.

Superbowl III will always be remembered as 'Namath's Bowl'. Although he didn't personally set the game alight, because of his pre-game attitude and the sheer playboy image he put over 'Broadway Joe' re-wrote the history books that day.

With his dark curly hair and the white game shoes that were his trade mark, he created a new image for football overnight. He would often be seen dancing the night away in one of New York's top discos, and some said that it was there that he did his training.

There were other, and possibly technically better quarterbacks, but none had the magic of Joe. An expectant buzz could be heard at every game he played and nine times out of ten Namath performed brilliantly.

Sadly, Joe's career was beset with injury. He had suffered from knee injuries all his footballing life, and the rough and tough world of the NFL only made matters worse.

After more than a decade of piloting the Jets' offense Namath finished his career in, of all places, the showbiz capital of the world: Los Angeles, with the L.A. Rams. In 1978 time at last caught up with the first quarterback to pass for more than 4000 yards in a season and he retired. But the name of Joe Namath was never just another statistic in the record books.

Records

Most Victories achieved by Active Coaches

Bo Schembechler, Michigan	186
Joe Paterno, Penn State	176
Vince Dooley, Georgia	168
Bill Yeoman, Houston	155
Jerry Claiborne, Kentucky	153
Bobby Bowden, Florida State	146
Hayden Fry, Iowa	131
Tom Osborne, Nebraska	118
La Vell Edwards, B.Y.U.	118
Bill Dooley, Virginia Tech.	117
Barry Switzer, Oklahoma	115
Grant Teaff, Baylor	114
Lou Holtz, Minnesota	110

Most victories won by Division 1A Teams

1	Michigan	655
2	Notre Dame	641
3	Texas	632
4	Alabama	606
5	Penn State	593
6	Nebraska	593
7	Ohio State	589
8	Oklahoma	579
9	USC	565
10	Tennessee	558
11	Army	532
12	Pittsburgh	520
13	Navy	520
14	Georgia	522
15	Louisiana State	516

No. of appearances in Consecutive Bowl Games

1	Alabama	25
2	Nebraska	16
3	Penn State	13
4	Ohio State	12
5	Pittsburgh	9
5	Michigan	9
6	Texas	7

Most successful Coaches in Collegiate Football History

Name	Victories	Years	Average no. of Wins Per Season
1 Paul 'Bear' Bryant	323	38	8.5
2 Amos Alonzo Stagg	314	57	5.5
3 Glen 'Pop' Warner	313	44	7.1
4 Woody Hayes	238	32	7.4
5 Jess Neely	207	40	5.2
6 Warren Woodson	207	37	5.6
7 Dr Eddie Anderson	201	39	5.1
8 Dana X. Bible	198	33	6.0
9 Dan McGugin	197	30	6.7
10 Fielding Yost	196	29	6.8

The most successful coach of all time, Paul Bear Bryant of Alabama University.

America's Top Teams

For Last 25 years (1960–84)

		All Games			Regular Season		
		W	L	T	%	W	L	T	%
1	Alabama	235	46	8	0.827	222	36	6	0.852
2	Texas	221	55	5	0.795	210	46	4	0.815
3	Penn State	220	60	2	0.784	207	55	1	0.789
4	Nebraska	220	63	5	0.772	208	55	5	0.785
5	Ohio State	197	58	6	0.766	192	50	6	0.786
6	U.S.C.	206	62	11	0.758	196	58	11	0.760
7	Arizona State	204	67	2	0.751	197	66	2	0.747
8	Oklahoma	204	70	8	0.737	195	65	5	0.745
9	Arkansas	200	73	7	0.727	193	65	6	0.742
10	Michigan	191	73	5	0.719	188	64	5	0.741

For Last 10 years (1975–84)

		W	L	T	%	W	L	T	%
1	Alabama	100	19	1	0.837	92	17	1	0.841
2	Oklahoma	96	21	2	0.815	90	19	2	0.820
3	Nebraska	99	23	1	0.809	94	18	1	0.836
4	Pittsburgh	94	23	2	0.798	88	20	2	0.809
5	Penn State	95	21	1	0.789	88	22	1	0.797
6	Michigan	92	25	2	0.781	90	18	2	0.827
6	Ohio State	92	25	2	0.781	89	19	2	0.818
8	Brigham Young	93	27	1	0.773	90	22	1	0.801
9	U.S.C.	89	25	4	0.771	83	24	4	0.766
10	Texas	89	28	2	0.756	86	22	2	0.791

For Last 5 Years (1980–84)

		W	L	T	%	W	L	T	%
1	Nebraska	53	9	0	0.855	51	6	0	0.895
2	Brigham Young	53	9	0	0.855	50	7	0	0.877
3	Pittsburgh	50	9	1	0.842	47	7	1	0.864
4	Georgia	49	9	1	0.839	47	7	1	0.864
5	Clemson	46	11	2	0.797	43	10	2	0.800
6	Alabama	47	12	1	0.792	43	11	1	0.791
7	Ohio State	47	13	0	0.783	44	11	0	0.800
8	Texas	46	13	1	0.775	45	9	1	0.827
9	Penn State	45	13	1	0.771	42	13	1	0.759
10	Southern Methodist	44	13	1	0.767	43	11	1	0.791
11	Washington	46	14	0	0.767	43	12	0	0.782

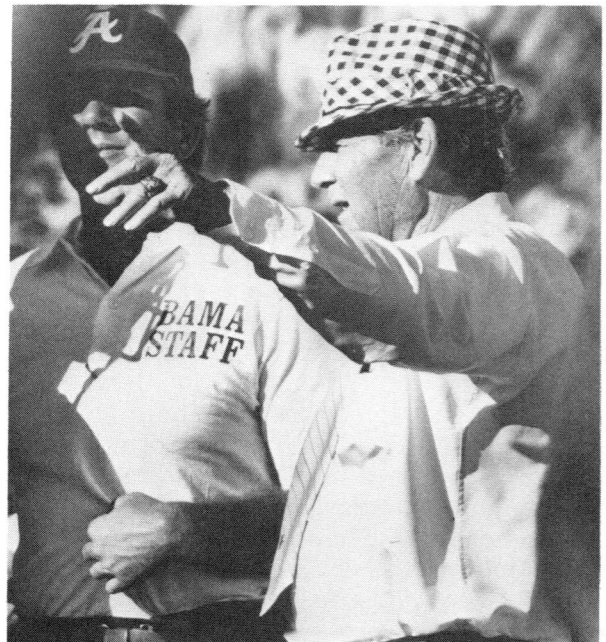

NCAA 1984 Final Statistics

Division 1–A individual leaders

Rushing

	CL	G	CAR	YDS	AVG	TD	YDSPG
Keith Byars, Ohio State	Jr	11	313	1655	5.3	22	150.5
Rueben Mayes, Washington State	Jr	11	258	1637	6.3	11	148.8
Kenneth Davis, Texas Christian	Jr	11	211	1611	7.6	15	146.5
Curtis Adams, Central Michigan	Sr	10	222	1204	5.4	13	120.4
Johnnie Jones, Tennessee	Sr	11	229	1290	5.6	10	117.3

Scoring

	CL	G	TD	XP	FG	PTS	PTPG
Keith Byars, Ohio State	Jr	11	24	0	0	144	13.1
Allen Pinkett, Notre Dame	Jr	11	18	0	0	108	9.8
John Lee, UCLA	Jr	11	0	17	29	104	9.5
Bobby Raymond, Florida	Sr	11	0	34	23	103	9.4
Chris White, Illinois	Jr	11	0	31	24	103	9.4

Passing Efficiency
(Min. 15 att. per game)

	CL	G	ATT	CMP	CMP PCT	INT	INT PCT	YDS	YDS/ATT	TD	TD PCT	RATING POINTS
Doug Flutie, Boston Col	Sr	11	386	233	60.36	11	2.85	3454	8.95	27	6.99	152.9
Robbie Bosco, Brigham Young		12	458	283	61.79	11	2.40	3875	8.46	33	7.21	151.8
Bernie Kosar, Miami (Fla.)		12	416	262	62.98	16	3.85	3642	8.75	25	6.01	148.7
Kerwin Bell, Florida		11	184	98	53.26	7	3.80	1614	8.77	16	8.70	148.0
Randall Cunningham, Nev-LV		12	332	208	62.65	9	2.71	2628	7.92	24	7.23	147.6

Receiving

	CL	G	CT	YDS	TD	ctpg
David Williams, Illinois	Jr	11	101	1278	8	9.2
Charles Lockett, Long Beach State	So	11	75	1112	4	6.8
Larry Willis, Fresno State	Sr	12	79	1251	8	6.6
Gerard Phelan, Boston College	Sr	11	64	971	3	5.8
Tracy Henderson, Iowa State	Jr	11	64	941	6	5.8

Total Offense

	RUSHING CAR	GAIN	LOSS	NET	PASSING ATT	YDS	PLS	TOTAL OFFENSE YDS	YD PL	TDR*	YDPSG
Robbie Bosco, Brigham Young	85	291	234	57	458	3875	543	3932	7.2	35	327.7
Doug Flutie, Boston Col	62	328	179	149	386	3454	448	3603	8.0	30	327.5
Doug Gaynor, Long Beach St.	93	320	307	13	385	3230	478	3243	6.8	20	324.3
Bernie Kosar, Miami (Fla.)	52	40	270	−230	416	3642	468	3412	7.3	29	284.3
Jim Everett, Purdue	50	134	186	−52	389	3003	439	2951	6.7	16	268.3

Field Goals

	CL	G	FGA	FG	PCT	FGPG
John Lee, UCLA	Jr	11	33	29	0.879	2.64
Chris White, Illinois	Jr	11	28	24	0.857	2.18
Mike Prindle, Western Michigan	Sr	11	30	24	0.800	2.18
Bobby Raymond, Florida	Sr	11	26	23	0.885	2.09
Kevin Butler, Georgia	Sr	11	28	23	0.821	2.09

Division 1–A team leaders

Passing offense

	G	ATT	CMP	INT	PCT	YDS	YDS/ATT	TD	YDSPG
Brigham Young	12	496	305	13	61.5	4154	8.4	34	346.2
Miami (Florida)	12	450	279	17	62.0	3826	8.5	25	318.8
Boston College	11	392	236	11	60.2	3473	8.9	27	315.7
Long Beach State	11	431	271	20	62.9	3423	7.9	16	311.2
Illinois	11	423	276	10	65.2	3130	7.4	22	284.5

Passing defense

	G	ATT	CMP	INT	PCT	YDS	YDS/ATT	TD	YDS
Texas Tech	11	196	89	12	45.4	1263	6.4	9	114.8
Wichita State	11	221	109	9	49.3	1278	5.8	9	116.2
Syracuse	11	220	108	10	49.1	1312	6.0	4	119.3
Memphis State	11	227	95	11	41.9	1349	5.9	10	122.6
Nebraska	11	256	115	16	44.9	1369	5.3	7	124.5

Punt Returns
(Min. 1.2 per game)

	CL	NO	YDS	TD	AVG
Ricky Nattiel, Florida	So	22	346	1	15.7
Jeff Smith, Nebraska	Sr	15	225	0	15.0
Shane Swanson, Nebraska	Sr	19	275	1	14.5
Scott Thomas, Air Force	So	24	304	0	12.7
Ron Milus, Washington	Jr	17	211	1	12.4

Kick-off Returns
(Min. 1.2 per game)

	CL	NO	YDS	TD	AVG
Ricky Calhoun, Fullerton	So	13	396	1	30.5
K. Henderson, Tex. Tech	Fr	13	376	1	28.9
Joe Rowley, N. Mex. St	Fr	15	411	1	27.4
Willie Drewrey, W. Vir	Sr	20	546	1	27.3
Curt Duncan, N. western	So	17	464	1	27.3

Punting
(Min. 3.6 per game)

	CL	NO	AVG
Ricky Anderson, Vanderbilt	Sr	58	48.2
Bill Smith, Mississippi	So	44	47.7
Randall Cunningham, Nev-L.V.	Sr	59	47.5
Rick Donnelly, Wyoming	Sr	63	47.5
Tom Tupa, Ohio State	Fr	41	47.0

Division 1–A team leaders

Rushing offense

	G	CAR	YDS	AVG	TD	YDSPG
Army	11	779	3798	4.9	34	345.3
Air Force	11	659	3591	5.4	36	326.5
Nebraska	11	695	3422	4.9	39	311.1
TCU	11	605	3126	5.2	34	284.2

Rushing defense

	G	CAR	YDS	AVG	TD	YDSPG
Oklahoma	11	386	757	2.0	4	68.8
Virginia Tech	11	437	787	1.8	7	71.5
Arizona	11	383	831	2.2	9	75.5
Nebraska	11	438	867	2.0	6	78.8
Cal St. Fullerton	12	426	1183	2.8	8	98.6
Iowa	12	439	1193	2.7	7	99.4

Total offense

	G	PLYS	YDS	AVG	TD	YDSPG
Brigham Young	12	902	5838	6.5	55	486.5
Boston Col	11	825	6317	6.4	50	483.4
TCU	11	835	5103	6.1	47	463.9
Florida St	11	807	4959	6.1	42	450.8

Total defense

	G	PLYS	YDS	AVG	TD	YDSPG
Nebraska	11	694	2236	3.2	12	203.3
Oklahoma	11	726	2477	3.4	13	225.2
Virginia Tech	11	772	2574	3.3	14	234.0
Central Mich	11	746	2899	3.9	14	263.5

Scoring offense

	G	PTS	AVG
Boston Col	11	404	36.7
Brigham Young	12	432	36.0
Florida St	11	389	35.4
Ohio State	11	374	34.0

Division 1–A single game highs

Player

Rushing and Passing	Player, Team (opponent, date)	Total
Rushing and passing plays	Gym Kimball, Utah State (Nevada Las-Vegas, Nov. 17)	64
	Gym Kimball, Utah State (Brigham Youn, Nov. 24)	64
Rushing and passing yards	Jeff Van Raaphorst, Arizona State (Florida State, Nov 3)	532
Rushing plays	Glenn Hunter, Ohio (Miami of Ohio, Nov. 3)	42
Net rushing yards	Rueben Mayes, Washington State (Oregon, Oct 27)	*357
Passes attempted	Paul Berner, Pacific (Long Beach State, Nov. 3)	60
Passes completed	Jeff Van Raaphorst, Arizona State (Florida State, Nov. 3)	38
Passing yards	Jeff Van Raaphorst, Arizona State (Florida State, Nov 3)	532

Receiving and kick returns

Passes caught	Larry Willis, Fresno State (Montana State, Nov. 17)	16
Receiving yards	Larry Willis, Fresno State (Montana State, Nov. 17)	282
Punt return yards	Ricky Nattiel, Florida (Mississippi State, Sept. 29)	120
Kickoff return yards	Tony Cherry, Oregon (Washington State, Oct. 27)	240

Scoring

Field goals made	Mike Prindle, Western Michigan (Marshall, Sept. 29)	*7
Points scored	Keith Byars, Ohio State (Illinois, Oct. 13)	30
	Reuben Mayes, Washington State (Stanford, Oct. 20)	30
Points scored by kicking	Mike Prindle, Western Michigan (Marshall, Sept. 29)	*24

Team

Team	Team (opponent, date)	Total
Rushing plays	Army (Navy, Dec. 1)	84
Net rushing yards	Army (Montana, Nov. 17)	628
Rushing and passing yards	Wyoming (New Mexico, Oct. 20)	695
Passing yards	Arizona State (Florida State, Nov. 3)	532
Fewest rush-pass yards allowed	Iowa (Northwestern, Oct. 6)	49
Fewest rushing yards allowed	Iowa State (Colorado, Oct. 13)	−16
Passes attempted	Pacific (Long Beach State, Nov. 3)	61
Passes completed	Arizona State (Florida State, Nov. 3)	38
Points scored	Air Force (Northern Colorado, Sept 8)	75

*All-time record

Modern Major-College Individual Records
(Through 1984 Season)

Points

Most in a Game	43	____
Most in a Season	174	____
	174	____
Most in a Career	368	____

Touchdowns

Most in a Game	7	____
Most in a Season	29	____
	29	____
Most in a Career	59	____
	59	____

Field Goals

Most in a Game	7	____
Most in a Season	28	____
Most in a Career	60	____
Most Consecutively (Career)	30	____

Other Season Records

Yards Gained Rushing	2,342 yd	____
Highest Average Gain per Rush (min. 150 attempts)	9.35 yd	____
Most Passes Attempted	509	____
Most Passes Completed	296	____
Most Touchdown Passes	47	____
Most Yards Gained Passing	4,571 yd	____
Most Passes Caught	134	____
Most Yards Gained on Catches	1,779 yd	____
Most Touchdown Passes Caught	18	____
Most Passes Intercepted by	14	____
Highest Punting Average (min. 30 punts)	49.8 yd	____

Division 1–AA individual leaders

Rushing

	CL	G	CAR	YDS	AVG	TD	YDSPG
Gene Lake, Delaware State	Jr	10	238	1722	7.2	20	172.2
Vince Hall, Middle Tennessee State	Sr	11	260	1439	5.5	5	130.8
Mike Clark, Akron	So	10	258	1172	4.5	4	117.2
Paul Lewis, Boston U	Sr	10	269	1165	4.3	9	116.5
Robbie Gardner, Furman	Jr	11	169	1232	7.3	14	112.0

Scoring

	CL	G	TD	XP	FG	PTS	PTPG
Jerry Rice, Mississippi Valley	Sr	10	27	0	0	162	16.2
Gene Lake, Delaware State	Jr	10	20	0	0	120	12.0
Gerald Harris, Georgia Southern	So	9	17	0	0	102	11.3
Roy Banks, Eastern Illinois	So	11	17	0	0	102	9.3
Martin Zendejas, Nevada-Reno	Fr	11	0	35	22	101	9.2

Passing Efficiency
(Min 15 att. per game)

	CL	G	ATT	CMP	CMP PCT	INT	INT PCT	YDS	YDS/ATT	TD	TD PCT	RATING POINTS
Willie Totten, Miss. Valley	Jr	10	518	324	62.55	22	4.25	4557	8.80	66	10.81	163.6
Gilbert Renfroe, Tenn. St	Jr	11	165	95	57.58	5	3.03	1458	8.84	17	10.30	159.7
Bobby Lamb, Furman	Jr	11	191	106	55.50	7	3.66	1781	9.32	19	9.95	159.3
Kenneth Biggles, Tenn. St	Sr	11	258	157	60.85	7	3.24	2242	8.69	24	9.30	159.1
Mickey Corwin, Middle Tenn.	Sr	11	196	120	61.22	9	4.59	1566	7.99	21	10.71	154.5

Receiving

	CL	G	CT	YDS	TD	CTPG
Jerry Rice, Mississippi Valley	Sr	10	103	1682	27	10.3
Joe Thomas, Mississippi Valley	Jr	10	80	1119	11	8.0
Jerry Wright, Eastern Illinois	Sr	10	76	1029	7	7.6
Dave Kucera, Bucknell	Sr	10	73	1029	6	7.3
Ronnie Benn, Lehigh	Jr	11	77	1149	10	7.0

Total Defense

	RUSHING			PASSING			TOTAL OFFENSE				
	CAR	GAIN	LOSS	NET	ATT	YDS	PLS	YDS	YDPL	TDR*	YDSPG
Willie Totten, Miss. Valley	46	148	133	15	518	4557	564	4572	8.1	61	457.2
Sean Payton, Eastern Ill	111	167	349	−182	473	3843	584	3661	6.3	31	332.8
Kelly Bradley, Montana St	99	251	304	−53	439	3508	598	3455	5.8	35	314.1
Vein Harris, Idaho State	60	88	303	−215	441	3469	501	3254	6.5	18	295.8
Scott Lineham, Idaho	97	381	187	194	318	2407	415	2601	6.3	21	289.0

Punt returns
(Min. 1.2 per game)

	CL	NO	YDS	TD	AVG
Willie Ware, Miss. Val.	Jr	19	374	3	19.7
John Taylor, Del. St	Jr	17	255	2	15.0
Tim Chambers, Penn	Sr	25	372	0	14.9
Melvin Bell, Ga South	Jr	18	252	1	14.0
Herb Harbison, N C. A&T	So	17	225	1	13.2

Kickoff Returns
(Min. 1.2 per game)

	CL	NO	YDS	TD	AVG
C. Richardson, E. Wash	So	21	729	2	34.7
John Armstrong, Rich	Jr	18	531	0	29.5
Steve Ortman, Penn	Sr	22	620	1	28.2
Oscar Smith, Nicholls	Jr	17	471	0	27.7
Harvey Reed, Howard	Fr	14	374	1	26.7

Punting
(Min. 3.6 per game)

	CL	NO	AVG
Steve Kornegay, Western Caro	Jr	49	43.4
Dirk Nelson, Montana St	Sr	55	43.3
Scott Seyner, SE Louisiana	Jr	63	43.3
Bob Hagedorn, Weber State	Sr	54	43.3
Ron Knowlton, Eastern Wash	Sr	53	42.3

Jim Brown (Syracuse) — 1956
Lydell Mitchell (Penn State) — 1971
Mike Rozier (Nebraska) — 1983
Luis Zendejas (Ariz State) — 1981–84

Arnold Boykin (Mississippi) — 1951
Lydell Mitchell (Penn State) — 1971
Mike Rozier (Nebraska) — 1983
Glenn Davis (Army) — 1943–46
Tony Dorsett (Pittsburgh) — 1973–76

Mike Prindle (W Mich) — 1984
Paul Woodside (West Virginia) — 1982
Obed Ariri (Clemson) — 1977–80
Chuck Nelson (Washington) — 1981–82

Marcus Allen (So Cal) — 1981
Greg Pruitt (Oklahoma) — 1971

Bill Anderson (Tulsa) — 1965
Bill Anderson (Tulsa) — 1965
Jim McMahon (Brigham Young) — 1980
Jim McMahon (Brigham Young) — 1980
Howard Twilley (Tulsa) — 1965
Howard Twilley (Tulsa) — 1965
Tom Reynolds (San Diego St) — 1969
Al Worley (Washington) — 1968
Reggie Roby (Iowa) — 1981

Division 1–AA individual leaders (cont.)

Field Goals

	CL	G	FGA	FG	PCT	FGPG
Martin Zendejas, Nevada-Reno	Fr	11	27	22	0.815	2.00
Kirk Roach, Western Carolina	Fr	10	24	16	0.667	1.60
Mike Molstead, Northern Iowa	Sr	11	30	17	0.567	1.55
George Benyola, Louisiana Tech	Jr	11	24	16	0.667	1.45
Scott Bridges, Indiana State	Jr	11	20	15	0.750	1.36

Divsion 1-AA team leaders

Passing offense

	G	ATT	CMP	INT	PCT	YDS	YDS/ATT	TD	YDSPG
Mississippi Valley	10	558	351	24	62.9	4968	8.9	64	496.8
Easter Illinois	11	508	288	16	56.7	4071	8.0	29	370.1
Tennessee State	11	425	253	12	59.5	3760	8.8	42	341.8
Montana State	11	529	301	24	56.9	3672	6.9	32	333.8

Passing defense

	G	ATT	CMP	INF	PCT	YDS	YDS/ATT	TD	YDS
Louisiana Tech	11	254	112	20	44.1	1161	4.6	2	105.5
Tennessee State	11	235	85	28	36.2	1240	5.3	8	112.7
McNeese State	11	224	94	23	42.0	1257	5.6	5	114.3
Dartmouth	9	174	94	9	54.0	1062	6.1	9	118.0
Northern Louisiana	11	258	105	16	40.7	1886	5.4	5	126.0

Division 1-AA single game highs

Player

Rushing and Passing	Player Team (opponent date)	Total
Rushing and passing plays	Willie Totten, Mississippi Valley (Southern B.R., Sept.29)	73
Rushing and passing yards	Willie Totten, Mississippi Valley (Prairie View, Oct. 27)	621
Rushing play	Steve Harris, Northern Iowa (NW Missouri St., Nov. 17)	42
Net rushing yards	Gene Lake, Delaware State (Liberty Baptist, Nov. 10)	336
Passes attempted	Willie Totten, Mississippi Valley (Southern B.R., Sept.29)	66
	Bernard Hawk, Bethune-Cookman (Georgia Southern, Oct. 6)	66
Passes completed	Willie Totten, Mississippi Valley (Southern B.R., Sept. 29)	*46
Passing yards	Willie Totten, Mississippi Valley (Prairie View, Oct. 27)	*599
Touchdown passes	Willie Totten, Mississippi (Kentucky State, Sept. 1)	9
Receiving and kick returns		
Passes caught	Jerry Rice, Mississippi Valley (Kentucky State, Sept. 1)	17
	Jerry Rice, Mississippi Valley (Southern B.R., Sept. 29)	17
Receiving yards	Jerry Rice, Mississippi Valley (Kentucky State, Sept. 1)	*294
Touchdown passes caught	Jerry Rice, Mississippi Valley (Kentucky State, Sept. 1)	*5
	Jerry Rice, Mississippi Valley (Prairie View, Oct. 2)	*75
Punt return yards	Willie Totten, Mississippi Valley (Washburn, Sept. 15)	*216
Kickoff return yards	Michael Smith, Florida A&M (Alcorn State, Oct. 27)	200
Scoring		
Touchdowns and points	Gene Lake, Delaware State (Howard, Nov. 3)	**6 & ***36
Field goals	Tim McMonigle, Idaho (Northern Arizona, Nov. 3)	**5
	Martin Zendejas, Nevada-Reno (Idaho State, Nov. 17)	**5

Team	Team (opponent, date)	
Rushing plays	Boston U (Morgan State, Sept. 15)	79
Net rushing yards	Arkansas State (Tennessee-Martin, Sept. 15)	*621
Rushing and passing yards	Mississippi Valley (Prairie View, Oct. 27)	762
Passing yards	Mississippi Valley (Kentucky State, Sept. 1)	*699
Fewest rushing yards allowed	Eastern Washington (Angelo State, Sept. 22)	60
Fewest rush-pass yards allowed	Tennessee State (Hampton, Sept. 1)	33
Passes attempted	Mississippi Valley (Southern-B.R., Sept. 29)	70
	Texas Southern (Mississippi Valley, Oct. 20)	70
Passes completed	Mississippi Valley (Southern-B.R., Sept. 29)	*50
	Mississippi Valley (Prairie View, Oct. 27)	*50
Touchdown passes	Mississippi Valley (Kentucky State, Sept. 1)	*11
Points scored	Mississippi Valley (Kentucky State, Sept. 1)	86

*All-time record **Ties all-time record

Division 1–AA team leaders (cont.)

Rushing offense

	G	CAR	YDS	AVG	TD	YDSPG
Delaware St	10	581	3773	6.5	44	377.3
Furman	11	569	3100	5.4	29	281.8
Arkansas St	11	615	3074	5.0	35	279.5
Ga, Southern	11	539	2914	5.4	32	264.9
SW Missouri St	10	485	2474	5.1	20	247.4

Rushing defense

	G	CAR	YDS	AVG	TD	YDSPG
Grambling	11	344	489	1.4	4	44.5
Northern Iowa	11	353	704	2.0	9	64.0
Alcorn State	9	291	578	2.0	6	64.2
Tennessee State	11	397	817	2.1	7	74.3
Arkansas State	11	419	863	2.1	8	78.5

Total offense

	G	PLYS	YDS	AVG	TD	YDSGP
Miss. Valley	10	866	6401	7.4	84	640.1
Delaware St.	10	725	5103	7.0	58	510.3
Tennessee St.	11	790	5085	6.4	58	462.3
Furman	11	779	4982	6.4	50	452.9

Total defense

	G	PLYS	YDS	AVG	TD	YDSPG
Tennessee St.	11	632	2057	3.3	15	187.0
Alcorn State	9	544	2001	3.7	16	222.3
Louisiana Tech	11	797	2568	3.2	12	233.5
NW Louisiana	11	700	2637	3.8	12	239.7
McNeese St.	11	695	2720	3.9	18	247.3

Scoring Offense

	G	PTS	AVG
Miss. Valley	10	609	60.9
Delaware St.	10	425	42.5
Tennessee St.	11	450	40.9
Alcorn State	9	354	39.3
Northern Iowa	11	366	33.3

CHAPTER FOUR

The United States Football League

The collapse of the ill-fated World Football League in 1975 brought to an end another in a long series of challenges to the NFL's monopoly of the professional football scene. With it went most people's dreams and ambitions of a pro football team in their town.

The NFL, which had 26 teams at that time, was enjoying an astonishing amount of support, mainly because of the TV networks' saturation coverage of the game. In a country as vast as the USA many thought that 26 teams were not enough to sate the appetites of a sports-hungry public, but in 1976 the NFL compensated the public a little by adding another two franchises to their operation, in Seattle and Tampa, to bring the league up to today's strength of 28.

Many more cities and many aspiring owners were pressing the NFL to extend still further, but their continued refusal led to an historic press conference in New York on 11 May 1982 at which was announced the formation of the United States Football League. The USFL, as it has become known, decided to start with 12 franchises: in Arizona, Birmingham (Alabama), Boston (Mass.), Chicago, Denver, Detroit (Michigan), Los Angeles, New Jersey, Oakland, Philadelphia, Tampa Bay and Washington.

Within two weeks a TV agreement was reached with the giant ABC network, and within a month, on 14 June 1982, the fledgling USFL had appointed its very first commissioner. Chester R. (Chet) Simmons had formerly been President of the Entertainment and Sports Programming Network (ESPN), a sports-only cable channel making tremendous inroads into the world of televised sports events. The most astounding part of the new league's plans was not to oppose the NFL's monopoly of autumn football, but to switch their season to the spring. It would run from March until July.

Most observers (including those at the NFL), scoffed at the idea, but the USFL went ahead with its plans for the first season to begin on 6 March of the following year.

The initial nine-month period saw the groundwork being laid with great precision. Celluloid heart-throb and former Florida State footballer Burt Reynolds was named as a co-owner of the Tampa franchise, and not surprisingly the team was to be called the 'Bandits'. It was a dream come true for Reynolds, who had starred in a film drama about a team of convicts whipped into shape to play their guardians called *The Longest Yard* (re-titled *The Mean Machine* in Europe).

The USFL were already attracting good coaching and administration staff, but to attract good players the USFL instituted its own first draft on 4 January 1983.

The 12 teams selected a total of 312 players in a territorial draft where clubs were given first choice of graduating college players within their own geographical area. A further 288 were taken in the round-by-round draft. The order of the draft had been settled by lots at a meeting in Tampa the previous autumn, Los Angeles being first out of the hat.

The first player selected, by the Express, was a quarterback who had broken all NCAA records whilst playing at the University of Pittsburgh: Dan Marino. Despite offers of money beyond his wildest dreams

Marino decided against the USFL and was drafted by the NFL's Miami Dolphins three months later. Finance was one of the major reasons for the failure of the WFL but the USFL had, it seemed, no such problems.

Many good players who would almost certainly have been drafted in the NFL's first round were signing long term contracts and the biggest shot in the arm came on 23 February when the Heisman Trophy winner, running back Herschel Walker signed a multi-million dollar contract with the New Jersey Generals.

Walker's signing from the University of Georgia brought harsh criticism for the talented back was still an undergraduate who could have played for his college for another year. NFL and the NCAA joined forces to condemn the move, but their anger was a small price to pay for a player of Walker's obvious stature.

Herschel Walker not only brought his vast array of talents to the USFL, he also brought instant credibility and more importantly, he sold tickets. The inaugural season opened with five matches on 6 March 1983. A crowd of 45 167 turned out at Phoenix to watch the Wranglers lose 24–0 to the Oakland Invaders. The average crowd of 39 171 was heartwarming. The public's curiosity no doubt had much to do with this high level of patronage, as did the signing of several top college players. North Carolina's running back Kelvin Bryant had joined the Philadelphia Stars, Ohio State's talented Tim Spencer moved in with the Chicago Blitz as did Grambling's high-flying wide receiver Trumaine Johnson; whilst Birmingham Stallions grabbed S.M.U.'s gifted quarterback Reggie Collier. The new league, however, learned two major lessons within its first month of operation. Firstly, in spring it tends to rain a lot, and spring 1983 was no exception. In week four it rained at all six matches. To find a football game, said some,

all one had to do was to follow the windscreen wipers! The second mistake was that the league had not played pre-season games; this is like going on stage without having had a dress rehearsal. The original idea not to play any, but to launch the new season with a bang, had seemed a good one at the time, until the first two games of the year ended up looking like Keystone Cops movies!

Before the start of the season the 12 owners had supposedly come to a 'gentleman's agreement' to limit the size of salaries. But some teams were better than others at abiding by it. Chicago's George Allen spared no expense in building up his Blitz outfit and many teams feared that the Blitz would go through the season with an unbeaten 18–0 record. Luckily, money cannot always buy success. Allen's team didn't even win their division and had to sneak into the play-offs by the back door, by way of a wild card.

The winners of the central division were the Michigan Panthers. The Panthers, with quarterback Bobby Hebert and wide receiver Anthony Carter creating havoc with the game-plans of opposing defensive co-ordinators became the USFL's first champions

Quarterback Steve Young broke all records when he signed for the Los Angeles Express in a $40 million deal in 1984.

when they beat Philadelphia 24–22 in Denver's Mile High Stadium on 17 July.

The game drew nearly 51 000 spectators, the second largest crowd of the year. 60 237 had packed into the Pontiac Silverdome the week before to witness the Michigan outfit rip into a powerful Oakland Invaders team and win 37–21.

The Michigan triumph had not looked possible when the season began. The team lost four of their first five games and their offensive line was so weak that poor quarterback Hebert was fast becoming a candidate for the record of most sacked player ever.

At this point the Panthers' coach Jim Stanley decided to bring in the reinforcements. Almost overnight he changed the face of the offensive line-up by grabbing tackle Ray Pinney and guard Tyrone McGriff from Pittsburgh and by signing ex-steeler Thom Dornbrook. This made all the difference to the team. The Panthers won 11 of their next 13 games and nosed out the Blitz for the division championship. Now that Hebert was gaining the pass protection he so sorely needed, Michigan went into the championship game with the Stars determined to give all. After the third quarter the Panthers held a comfortable 17–3 lead, but a 19-point fourth quarter by Philadelphia brought the game to a nail-biting end as Carter caught a 48-yard pass from the game's MVP to seal a great victory.

Despite the early season problems, the

Did You Know

That the USFL has signed the last three Heisman winners, Herschel Walker, Mike Rozier and Doug Flutie.

And that of the four Heisman winners playing in the NFL today, two play for the New Jersey Generals (Herschel Walker and Doug Flutie), and the Jacksonville Bulls have the other two on their books (Mike Rozier and Archie Griffin).

That Archie Griffin of Jacksonville Bulls is the only player to have won the Heisman trophy twice.

USFL was sufficiently delighted with their endeavours to announce a programme of expansion for the 1984 season. Six new franchises—in Pittsburgh, Jacksonville, Memphis, Houston, San Antonio and Oklahoma—were announced. The original franchise for Oklahoma was intended to be sited in San Diego, California, but difficulties with the local stadium authorities prevented this and the team was switched to Tulsa. The following winter months proved to be exciting times. The new teams announced their owners, coaches and nicknames and the second annual draft on 4 January 1984 once again stole the show from the rival NFL. The Pittsburgh Maulers selected and later signed the 1983 Heisman Trophy winner Mike Rozier from Nebraska. Some of the very best college players from the 1983 season were now signing for USFL teams. San Antonio Gunslingers took UCLA's Rose Bowl winning quarterback Rick Neuheisel, whilst near neighbours Houston decided on Miami's Jim Kelly to lead their offense. The 1983 season had seen a distinct lack of quality quarterbacks, with most of the play concentrating on rushing. To balance this nearly all the USFL teams were now looking for the big play maker to lead their attacks in the 1984 season.

Cleveland's Brian Sipe signed a multi-million dollar contract with New Jersey, and Pittsburgh's Cliff Stoudt decided that a career with the Birmingham Stallions seemed a better deal than sitting out most of the year as a reserve on the Steelers squad. Everything was set for the biggest and best show the USFL could put together.

The league now had ten teams in NFL cities, the Boston franchise had moved to New Orleans and the Arizona and Chicago teams had quite literally swopped cities. The Wranglers of 1983 became the Blitz of 1984 and vice versa. Los Angeles Express had set the pace by signing Brigham Young's highly rated quarterback Steve Young in a deal said to be worth $40 million, and everything in the garden was looking rosy. The TV audiences were up and so were attendance figures: Jacksonville provided the league with its first 70 000-plus crowd.

The press were at last beginning to take some notice, and the introduction of so many talented players had raised the standard of play dramatically. Everything was set for the showpiece in Tampa Stadium on 15 July. 1983 runners-up Philadelphia were again representing the Eastern conference, whilst from the West came the Arizona Wranglers. The USFL wanted an exciting 'edge of the seat' game to entice yet more converts, but what they got was a dull, one-sided affair in which Philadelphia's powerful offensive attack swarmed over a lack-lustre Arizona defense to win 23–3.

The following week the USFL went international as the all-conquering Stars paraded their talents against the Tampa Bay Bandits in London's Wembley Stadium. Some 35 000 British football fans turned out for the game which never really lived up to its billing as both teams put on more of an exhibition game than the blood and guts thriller the British were expecting. The Stars eventually ran out 24–21 winners after being 14 points adrift at half-time.

Back home in the USA the cold winds of Autumn were beginning to sour the USFL's 1984 year. Rumours abounded of teams in financial difficulties, and the situation worsened with the announcement that the USFL was to switch to an autumn season in 1986. Philadelphia found that they wouldn't be able to play in their home stadium because they would clash with the NFL's Eagles, so they moved their operation to Baltimore, the city deserted by the Colts some six months previously.

Oklahoma, which had never felt quite at home in Tulsa, was rumoured to be moving to nearly every city in the nation, including Hawaii and Washington; after a disastrous season, they announced their intentions of moving first to Miami and then to Orlando.

The Pittsburgh team meanwhile was

Denver Gold's nose tackle Pat Ogrin tries to break past a Michigan Panther offensive linesman. (Denver Gold).

Did You Know

That the President and General Manager of the Oakland Invaders is Vince Lombardi Jr, son of the famous Green Bay Packers' coach.

That the President of the Chicago White Sox Baseball team, Eddie Einhorn, is to take over the Chicago Blitz franchise when the team returns to play in the 1986 autumn programme.

---

suffering the most, as their signing of Rozier and other star players had cost them dear. With losses estimated at $5 million they eventually filed for bankruptcy and disappeared from the league altogether.

Michigan, the league's first champions, were also having problems and eventually decided upon a merger with Oakland. Oklahoma eventually gave up hope of moving to another city and followed suit, this time merging with Arizona to form a team for the 1985 season called the Arizona Outlaws. Washington's fate had at last been resolved when the franchise was bought by a group of businessmen who moved it to the Disney town of Orlando and renamed the team the Renegades.

The mardi-gras city of New Orleans didn't take too well to spring-time football either and the New Orleans Breakers moved for the second time to Portland, Oregon. Chicago, meanwhile, had decided to opt out of the league altogether for the new season, and will not be returning until the 1986 autumn season begins.

Thus, after an optimistic start, the close season saw the United States Football League shrink to 14 teams and talks of a final collapse could be heard on every street corner. The change to an autumn season brought the USFL in direct conflict with the NFL, and it consequently suffered problems regaining TV rights, the contract for which was worth millions of dollars.

The apparent negative response from the TV networks brought about in early January 1985 the resignation of Commissioner Simmons. He was immediately replaced by Harry Usher, who had assisted Peter Ueberoth in running the highly successful Los Angeles Olympics.

So, in a mood of great pessimism, the USFL held its third annual draft in New York on 4 January 1985, and once again pulled off a major coup in persuading the 1984 Heisman winning quarterback Doug Flutie to sign for the New Jersey Generals. It is hoped that this signature along with that of many other top draft choices will bring the fans through the turnstiles as Walker and Rozier did before. The 1985 season is undoubtedly the make or break year for the USFL. Talks of merger with the NFL have been strongly hinted although many owners deny them. Whether this will happen or not, or whether the league will roll on into the autumn of 1986, only time will tell.

The NFL publicly say No, the USFL say stubbornly Yes. 10 years ago the WFL failed, 20 years ago the AFL succeeded. In 1986 the USFL will . . . .

Did You Know
That the Birmingham Stallions led the USFL in rushing in 1983 with 3017 yards.

That the Tampa Bay Bandits called for only one fair catch in 64 punt receptions during the inaugural season. Chicago Blitz on the other hand, called for 16 fair catches whilst fielding 58 punts.

That tackle Ray Pinney of Michigan and linebacker John Bunting of Philadelphia both started in an NFL Superbowl and in the USFL's first championship game.

Did You know
That USFL coaches in their first year as professional head coaches compiled a record of 54–43 in 1983. Those with prior head football coaching experience had a 54–64 record.

That the Chicago Blitz and Arizona Wranglers franchises swapped cities on 30 September 1983, this being the first time in professional football history that two teams had swapped franchises and cities en bloc.

That the Arizona Wranglers managed only eight rushing touchdowns in 1983, this being the fewest in the United States Football League.

New Jersey Generals' multi-million dollar quarterback Doug Flutie shows his form. (All-Sport).

Final Positions: 1983

Atlantic Division	W	L	T	PCT	PTS	OPP
Philadelphia *	15	3	0	0.833	379	204
Boston	11	7	0	0.611	399	334
New Jersey	6	12	0	0.333	314	437
Washington	4	14	0	0.222	297	422
Central Division						
Michigan *	12	6	0	0.667	451	337
Chicago +	12	6	0	0.667	456	271
Tampa Bay	11	7	0	0.611	363	378
Birmingham	9	9	0	0.500	343	326
Pacific Division						
Oakland	9	9	0	0.500	319	317
Los Angeles	8	10	0	0.444	296	370
Denver	7	11	0	0.389	284	304
Arizona	4	14	0	0.222	261	442

* Divisional Champion
+ Wild-card team

Play-offs	Philadelphia	44 Chicago	38 (OT)
Semi-finals:	Michigan	37 Oakland	21

1st USFL Championship Game Sunday 17 July 1983
Michigan 24 Philadelphia 22
Played at Mile High Stadium, Denver, Colorado
Attendance: 50 906.

Final Positions: 1984

Western Conference	W	L	T	PCT	PTS	OPP
Central Division						
Houston *	13	5	0	0.723	618	400
Michigan +	10	8	0	0.555	400	382
San Antonio	7	11	0	0.389	309	325
Oklahoma	6	12	0	0.333	251	359
Chicago	5	13	0	0.278	340	466
Pacific Division						
Los Angeles *	10	8	0	0.555	338	373
Arizona +	10	8	0	0.555	502	284
Denver	9	9	0	0.500	356	413
Oakland	7	11	0	0.389	242	348

*Divisional Champion
+Wild-card team

Divisional Play-offs

Los Angeles	27 Michigan	21 (OT)
Arizona	17 Houston	16

Conference Final

Arizona 35   Los Angeles 23

Eastern Conference	W	L	T	PCT	PTS	OPP
Atlantic Division						
Philadelphia *	16	2	0	0.889	479	225
New Jersey **	14	4	0	0.779	430	312
Washington	3	15	0	0.168	270	492
Pittsburgh	3	15	0	0.168	259	379
Southern Division						
Birmingham *	14	4	0	0.779	539	316
Tampa Bay **	14	4	0	0.779	498	347
New Orleans	8	10	0	0.444	348	395
Memphis	7	11	0	0.389	320	455
Jacksonville	6	12	0	0.333	327	455

Divisional Play-offs

Philadelphia	28 New Jersey	7
Birmingham	36 Tampa Bay	17

Conference Final

Philadelphia	20 Birmingham	10

2nd USFL Championship Game Sunday July 15 1984
Philadelphia 23 Arizona 3
Played at Tampa Stadium, Tampa, Florida
Attendance: 52 662.

1985 Season Alignments

Eastern Conference
Baltimore Stars (formerly Philadelphia)
Birmingham Stallions
Jacksonville Bulls
Memphis Showboats
New Jersey Generals
Orlando Renegades (formerly Washington Federals)
Tampa Bay Bandits

Western Conference
Arizona Outlaws (formerly Wranglers who merged with
    Oklahoma Outlaws)
Denver Gold
Houston Gamblers
Los Angeles Express
Oakland Invaders (formed from merger with Michigan
    Panthers)
Portland Breakers (formerly New Orleans Breakers)
San Antonio Gunslingers

Gone but not forgotten
Pittsburgh Maulers
Chicago Blitz (will return for the 1986 autumn season)
Washington Federals (franchise switched to Orlando)
Oklahoma Outlaws (merged with Arizona)
Michigan Panthers (merged with Oakland)
Philadelphia Stars (moved franchise to Baltimore)
New Orleans Breakers (moved franchise to Portland,
    Oregon)

The United States Football League Facts and Feats

The Oldest Player
The oldest player in the USFL is Jacksonville Bulls' Lander McCoy Bacon. Bacon, a defensive end for the Bulls, was born on the 30 August 1942.

The Tallest and Heaviest Player
The record for the tallest and the heaviest player in the USFL goes to one man. Giant Texan Milton Buddy Hardaway Jr, offensive tackle for the San Antonio Gunslingers, stands 6ft 9ins tall and weighs in at a massive 305lbs, or 21st and 11lbs.

The Shortest Player
American football is usually a game for big men, but the shortest player currently playing in the USFL is Eddie Payton, a 5ft 6ins kick returner for Memphis Showboats.

101

The Lightest Player

Although most of the linemen weigh 250lbs and more, football still has a place for men of smaller size. Anthony Carter, match-winning wide receiver for Michigan Panthers in the inaugural championship game weighs in at only 156lbs (11st 2lbs). Carter, who now plays for the Oakland Invaders, is the lightest player in the USFL today.

Most Valuable Players

1983 Season MVP: Kelvin Bryant, running back, Philadelphia Stars
1984 Season MVP: Chuck Fusina, quarterback, Philadelphia Stars
1983 Championship Game MVP: Bobby Hebert, quarterback, Michigan Panthers
1984 Championship Game MVP: Chuck Fusina, quarterback, Philadelphia Stars

Interceptions

In 1983 Luther Bradley, Chicago's safety achieved a total of 12 interceptions, including 6 against Tampa Bay Bandits on 2 April.

The Longest Game

The divisional play-off game between Michigan and Los Angeles on Saturday 30 June 1984 went into the history books as the longest in professional football history. The game lasted a total of 93 minutes and 33 seconds, before Los Angeles Express's Mel Gray broke the deadlock in the third period of overtime. Gray ran in 24 yards to win the game for the Express 27–21. The match-winning running back then suffered the misfortune of breaking his arm, after being heavily tackled in the end-zone!

USFL Records

Tied Games

There has only been one tied game in the three-year history of the USFL.

The Oakland Invaders and the Baltimore Stars played a 17–17 tie in Oakland's Memorial Coliseum on Sunday 3 March 1985. The Stars had led 17–0 until the last seconds of the third quarter, but then the

The Denver Gold was the only USFL team to change coaches during the league's first season. Craig Morton replaced Red Miller on 5 May 1983.

The Houston Gamblers' record-breaking quarterback Jim Kelly.

Invaders, led superbly by quarterback Bobby Hebert, dragged themselves back from the dead to lock up the game and send it into overtime. In regular season games the USFL allow only one period of overtime, but as neither team was able to make any impact in the added period the game ended in a 17–17 tie.

Total Yardage Passing in One game

The Los Angeles Olympic stadium was once again the place where professional football's oldest standing record was broken on Sunday 24 February 1985.

It was in 1951 that Los Angeles Rams quarterback Norm Van Brocklin set an American football game passing record of 554 yards against the New York Yankees. 34 years later Houston Gamblers quarterback Jim Kelly chose the same city to write his name into the record books. Kelly threw for 574 yards and 5 touchdowns as the Gamblers beat the Los Angeles Express 34–33. His last touchdown pass, a record-breaking and match-winning 39-yard effort to Ricky Sanders, happened on the last play of the game with only 40 seconds left.

Kelly's 574 yards is the best single game passing record in all pro football.

USFL Career Leaders

Active coaches career records

	Yrs.	Regular season Won	Lost	Tied	Pct.	Post-season Won	Lost	Pct	Career Won	Lost	Tied	Pct
Jim Mora	2	31	5	0	0.861	4	1	0.800	35	6	0	0.854
Rollie Dotsch	2	23	13	0	0.639	1	1	0.500	24	14	0	0.632
Jack Pardee	1	13	5	0	0.772	0	1	0.000	13	6	0	0.684
NFL Total	6	44	46	0	0.489	0	1	0.000	44	47	0	0.484
WFL Total	1	14	6	0	0.700	2	1	0.667	16	7	0	0.696
Lindy Infante	1	6	12	0	0.333	0	0	0.000	6	12	0	0.333
John Hadl	1	10	8	0	0.556	1	1	0.500	11	9	0	0.550
Frank Kush	0	0	0	0	0.000	0	0	0.000	0	0	0	0.000
NFL Total	3	11	28	1	0.275	0	0	0.000	11	28	1	0.275
CFL Total	1	11	4	1	0.719	0	1	0.000	11	5	1	0.676
Pepper Rodgers	1	7	11	0	0.389	0	0	0.500	7	11	0	0.389
Walt Michaels	1	14	4	0	0.778	0	1	0.000	14	5	0	0.737
NFL Total	6	39	47	1	0.457	2	2	0.500	41	49	1	0.459
Dick Coury	2	19	17	0	0.528	0	0	0.000	19	17	0	0.528
WFL Total	1	7	12	1	0.350	0	0	0.000	7	12	1	0.350
Steve Spurrier	2	25	11	0	0.694	0	1	0.000	25	12	0	0.676

Other coaches career records

	Yrs.	Regular season Won	Lost	Tied	Pct	Post-season Won	Lost	Ptc	Career Won	Lost	Tied	Pct.
Jim Stanley	2	22	14	0	0.611	2	1	0.667	24	15	0	0.615
George Allen	2	22	14	0	0.611	2	2	0.500	24	16	0	0.600
Chuck Fairbanks	1	6	12	0	0.333	0	0	0.000	6	12	0	0.000
Ray Jauch	1	4	17	0	0.191	0	0	0.000	0	0	0	0.000
John Ralston	1	9	12	0	0.429	0	1	0.000	9	13	0	0.409
Hugh Campbell	1	8	10	0	0.444	0	0	0.000	8	10	0	0.444
Red Miller	*	4	7	0	0.364	0	0	0.000	4	7	0	0.364
Craig Morton	1	12	12	0	0.500	0	0	0.000	12	12	0	0.500
Joe Pendry	*	2	8	0	0.200	0	0	0.000	2	8	0	0.200
Ellis Rainsberger	*	1	7	0	0.125	0	0	0.000	1	7	0	0.125

* Miller coached Denver Gold for 7 games in 1983
* Pendry coached Pittsburgh Maulers for 10 games in 1984
* Rainsberger served as interim coach for Pittsburgh Maulers for 8 games in 1984

Leading career rushers

	Yrs.	Att.	Yds.	TDs.
Herschel Walker, N.J.	2	705	3151	33
Kelvin Bryant, Phila.	2	615	2848	29
Tim Spencer, Chi.-Ariz.	2	527	2369	23
Kevin Long, Chi.-Ariz.	2	487	2032	27
Harry Sydney, Den.	2	406	1762	19
Ken Lacy, Mich.	2	366	1728	8
Greg Boone, T.B.	2	367	1703	13
John Williams, Mich.	2	350	1608	20
Larry Canada, Den.-Chi.	2	311	1546	10
Gary Anderson, T.B.	2	365	1524	23
Joe Cribbs, Birm.	1	297	1467	8
Arthur Whittington, Oak.	2	397	1462	6

Leading career receivers

	Yrs.	No.	Yds.	TDs.
T. Johnson, Chi.-Ariz.	2	171	2590	23
Joey Walters, Wash.	2	161	2369	19
Eric Truvillion, T.B.	2	136	2124	24
Gordon Banks, Oak.	2	125	1792	7
Richard Johnson, Hou.	1	115	1455	15
Mike Cobb, Mich.	2	115	1319	10
Billy Taylor, Wash.	2	115	910	3
J. Flowers, Ar-Chi-Pit.	2	114	1773	19
Scott Fitzkee, Phila.	2	110	1626	12
Danny Buggs, T.B.-S.A.	2	109	1623	5
Derek Holloway, Mich.	2	101	2030	20
Ricky Sanders, Hou.	1	101	1378	11

Leading career passers

(Based on 500 attempts)	Yrs.	Att.	Comp.	Pct.	Yds.	Avg.Gain	TD	Pct.TD	Int.	Pct. Int.	Pts.
Jim Kelly, Houston	1	587	370	0.630	5219	8.89	44	0.075	26	0.044	98.2
Greg Landry, Chi.-Ariz.	2	783	471	0.602	5917	7.56	42	0.054	24	0.031	88.9
Chuck Fusina, Philadelphia	2	886	540	0.609	5555	6.27	46	0.052	19	0.021	87.6
Bobby Hebert, Michigan	2	951	529	0.556	7326	7.70	51	0.054	39	0.041	81.4
Fred Besana, Oakland	2	996	602	0.604	6772	6.80	35	0.035	28	0.028	80.8
John Reaves, Tampa Bay	2	803	452	0.563	5818	7.25	37	0.046	32	0.040	77.9
Johnnie Walton, Boston-N.O.	2	1101	610	0.554	7326	6.65	37	0.034	37	0.034	73.1
Mike Hohensee, Washington	2	590	323	0.548	4063	6.89	26	0.044	27	0.046	72.0

Leading career scorers

	Yrs.	TDs.	FG.	1XP.	2XP.	Pts.
David Trout, Philadelphia	2	0	54	86	0	249
Herschel Walker, New Jersey	2	39	0	0	2	238
Tim Mazzetti, Boston-New Orleans	2	0	48	73	0	217
Novo Bojovic, Michigan	2	0	40	95	0	215
Zenon Andrusyshun, Tampa Bay	2	0	40	87	0	207
Frank Corral, Chicago-Arizona	2	0	33	100	1	201
Kelvin Bryant, Philadelphia	2	32	0	0	0	192
Kevin Long, Chicago-Arizona	2	27	0	0	0	168
Tim Spencer, Chicago-Arizona	2	28	0	0	0	162
Brian Speelman, Denver	2	0	35	60	0	156

Leading career interceptors

	Yrs.	No.	yds.	TDs.
Marcus Quinn, Oak.	2	16	290	1
Mike Guess, Wash.	2	16	225	0
Luther Bradley, Chi.-Az.	2	16	205	1
Mike Lush, Phila.	2	13	149	0
David Martin, Den.	2	11	101	0
David Dumars, Den.	2	10	259	1

All-Time Individual USFL Records

Scoring

POINTS

Most Points, Career
248 David Trout, Philadelphia, 1983–84 (54 FG, 86 PAT)
238 Herschel Walker, New Jersey, 1983–84 (39 TD, 2 2-XP)

Most Points, Season
130 Toni Fritsch, Houston, 1984 (21 FG, 67 PAT)
128 Herschel Walker, New Jersey, 1984 (21 TD, 1 2-XP)

Most Points, Game
24 Sam Harrell, Houston at Chicago, 11 March 1984 (4 TD)
   Herschel Walker, New Jersey v. Washington, 25 March 1984 (4 TD)
   Leon Perry, Birmingham v. Washington, 10 June 1984 (4 TD)
19 David Trout, Philadelphia at Birmingham, 4 May 1984 (5 FG, 4 PAT)

TOUCHDOWNS

Most Seasons Leading League
2 Herschel Walker, New Jersey, 1983–84 (tied for lead in 1984)

Most Consecutive Seasons Leading League
2 Herschel Walker, New Jersey, 1983–84 (tied for lead in 1984)

Most Touchdowns, Career
39 Herschel Walker, New Jersey, 1983–84 (33-rush, 6-pass)
32 Kelvin Bryant, Philadelphia, 1983–84 (29-rush, 3-pass)

Most Touchdowns, Season
21 Herschel Walker, New Jersey, 1984 (16-rush, 5-pass)
   Gary Anderson, Tampa Bay, 1984 (19-rush, 2-pass)

Most Touchdowns, Game
4 Sam Harrell, Houston at Chicago, 11 March 1984 (3-rush, 1-pass)
   Herschel Walker, New Jersey v. Washington, 25 March 1984 (3-rush, 1-pass)
   Leon Perry, Birmingham v. Washington, 10 June 1984 (4-rush)
3 By nine players

Most Consecutive Games Scoring Touchdowns
8 Kelvin Bryant, Philadelphia, 1983
   Richard Crump, Boston, 1983
   Harry Sydney, Denver, 1984
7 Jackie Flowers, Arizona, 1983
   Eric Truvillion, Tampa Bay, 1983
   Gary Anderson, Tampa Bay, 1984

POINTS AFTER TOUCHDOWN

Most Points After Touchdown, Career
100 Frank Corral, Chicago-Arizona, 1983–84
95 Novo Bojovic, Michigan, 1983–84

Most Points After Touchdown, Season
69 Danny Miller, Jacksonville-Birmingham, 1984
67 Toni Fritsch, Houston, 1984

TWO POINT CONVERSIONS

Most Two-Point Conversions, Career
3 Maurice Carthon, New Jersey, 1983–84
   Steve Young, Los Angeles, 1984
2 By many players

Most Two-Point Conversions, Season
3 Maurice Carthon, New Jersey, 1983
   Steve Young, Los Angeles, 1984
2 By many players

Most Two-Point Conversions, Game
2 Steve Young, Los Angeles at Chicago, 20 April 1984
1 By many players

FIELD GOALS

Most Field Goals, Career
54 David Trout, Philadelphia, 1983–84
48 Tim Mazzetti, Boston-New Orleans, 1983–84

Most Field Goals, Season
28 David Trout, Philadelphia, 1983
7 Tim Mazzetti, Boston, 1983

Most Field Goals, Game
5 Scott Norwood, Birmingham at New Jersey, 9 May 1983
   David Trout, Philadelphia at Birmingham, 4 May 1984

Most Consecutive Field Goals
12 Tim Mazzetti, Boston, 1983
   Toni Fritsch, Houston, 1984
10 Novo Bojovic, Michigan, 1984
   Nick Mike-Mayer, San Antonio, 1984

Longest Field Goal
57 Jim Asmus, Arizona v. Los Angeles, 19 March 1983
   Brian Speelman, Denver v. Oakland, 22 June 1984
56 Novo Bojovic, Michigan v. Birmingham, 15 April 1984
   Eric Schubert, Pittsburgh at Philadelphia, 4 June 1984

Rushing

Most Attempts, Career
705 Herschel Walker, New Jersey, 1983–84
615 Kelvin Bryant, Philadelphia, 1983–84

Most Attempts, Season
412 Herschel Walker, New Jersey, 1983
318 Kelvin Bryant, Philadelphia, 1983

Most Attempts, Game
36 Herschel Walker, New Jersey at Chicago, 25 April 1983
33 Herschel Walker, New Jersey at Arizona, 3 April 1983
   Herschel Walker, New Jersey v. Chicago, 22 May 1983
   Joe Cribbs, Birmingham at Pittsburgh, 11 March 1984

YARDS GAINED

Most Yards Gained, Season
1812 Herschel Walker, New Jersey, 1983
1467 Joe Cribbs, Birmingham, 1984

Most Yards Gained, Game
208 Todd Fowler, Houston at Denver, June 3 1984
200 Sam Harrell, Houston at Chicago, 11 March 1984

TOUCHDOWNS

Most Seasons Leading League
1 Herschel Walker, New Jersey, 1983
  Gary Anderson, Tampa Bay, 1984

Most Touchdowns, Career
33 Herschel Walker, New Jersey, 1983–84
29 Kelvin Bryant, Philadelphia, 1983–84

Most Touchdowns, Season
19 Gray Anderson, Tampa Bay, 1984
17 Herschel Walker, New Jersey, 1983
  Tim Spencer, Arizona, 1984

Most Touchdowns, Game
4 Leon Perry, Birmingham v. Washington, 10 June 1984
3 Herschel Walker, New Jersey at Arizona, 3 April 1983
  John Williams, Michigan v. New Jersey, 16 May 1983
  Sam Harrell, Houston at Chicago, 11 March 1984
  Herschel Walker, New Jersey v. Washington, 25 March 1984

Passing

ATTEMPTS

Most Passes Attempted, Career
1101 Johnnie Walton, Boston-New Orleans, 1983–84
996 Fred Besana, Oakland, 1983–84

Most Passes Attempted, Season
589 Johnnie Walton, Boston 1983
587 Jim Kelly, Houston, 1984

Most Passes Attempted, Game
63 John Reaves, Tampa Bay at Denver, 9 April 1983
52 Johnnie Walton, Boston vs. Philadelphia, 29 May 1983

COMPLETIONS

Most Passes Completed, Career
610 Johnnie Walton, Boston-New Orleans, 1983–84
602 Fred Besana, Oakland, 1983–84

Most Passes Completed, Season
370 Jim Kelly, Houston, 1984
345 Fred Besana, Oakland, 1983

Most Passes Completed, Game
38 John Reaves, Tampa Bay at Denver, 9 April 1983
37 Johnnie Walton, Boston v. Michigan, 1 May 1983
  Jim Kelly, Houston v. Los Angeles, 30 April 1984

Most Consecutive Passes Completed
19 Fred Besana, Oakland, 1984
16 Greg Landry, Arizona, 1984

COMPLETION PERCENTAGE

Highest Completion Percentage, Career (500 attempts)
.630 Jim Kelly, Houston, 1984 (587–370)
.609 Chuck Fusina, Philadelphia, 1983–84 (886–540)

Highest Completion Percentage, Season (Qualifiers)
.649 Chuck Fusina, Philadelphia, 1984 (465–302)
.630 Jim Kelly, Houston, 1984 (587–370)
  Greg Landry, Arizona, 1984 (449–283)

YARDS GAINED

Most Yards Gained, Career
7326 Bobby Hebert, Michigan, 1983–84
  Johnnie Walton, Boston-New Orleans, 1983–84
6772 Fred Besana, Oakland, 1983–84

Most Yards Gained, Season
5219 Jim Kelly, Houston, 1984
4092 John Reaves, Tampa Bay, 1984

Most Yards Gained, Game
444 Bobby Hebert, Michigan at Houston, 26 March 1984
440 Johnnie Walton, New Orleans vs. Chicago, 25 March 1984

Longest Pass Completion
98 Alan Risher (to Jackie Flowers), Arizona at Washington, 11 April 1983 (TD)
86 Johnnie Walton (to Frank Lockett), Boston at Philadelphia, 24 April 1983 (TD)

AVERAGE GAIN

Highest Average Gain, Career (500 attempts)
8.89 Jim Kelly, Houston, 1984 (370–5219)
7.70 Bobby Hebert, Michigan, 1983–84 (529–7326)

Highest Average Gain, Season (Qualifiers)
8.89 Jim Kelly, Houston, 1984 (370–5219)
8.53 Cliff Stoudt, Birmingham, 1984 (212–3121)

TOUCHDOWNS

Most Touchdown Passes, Career
51 Bobby Hebert, Michigan, 1983–84
46 Chuck Fusina, Philadelphia, 1983–84

Most Touchdown Passes, Season
44 Jim Kelly, Houston, 1984
31 Chuck Fusina, Philadelphia, 1984

Most Touchdown Passes, Game
5 Bobby Hebert, Michigan at Chicago, 26 June 1983
  Cliff Stoudt, Birmingham v. Oklahoma, 20 April 1984
  Chuck Fusina, Philadelphia v. New Orleans, 27 April 1984
  Walter Lewis, Memphis v. San Antonio, 11 May 1984
  Jim Kelly, Houston at Pittsburgh, 12 May 1984

HAD INTERCEPTED

Most Passes Had Intercepted, Career
39 Bobby Hebert, Michigan, 1983–84
37 Johnnie Walton, Boston-New Orleans, 1983–84

Most Passes Had Intercepted, Season
26 Jim Kelly, Houston, 1984
22 Vince Evans, Chicago 1984
  Bobby Hebert, Michigan, 1984

Most Passes Had Intercepted, Game
5 Craig Penrose, Denver at Los Angeles, 2 July 1983
  Vince Evans, Chicago at Philadelphia, 15 April 1984
  Brian Sipe, New Jersey at Washington, 11 May 1984

Most Attempts, No Interceptions, Game
48 Johnnie Walton, Boston v. Michigan, 1 May 1983
44 Jim Kelly, Houston at San Antonio, 5 March 1983

Pass Receiving

Most Pass Receptions, Career
171 Trumaine Johnson, Chicago-Arizona, 1983–84
161 Joey Walters, Washington, 1983–84

Most Consecutive Games, Pass Receptions
36 Gordon Banks, Oakland, 1983–84
Trumaine Johnson, Chicago-Arizona, 1983–84
35 Mike Cobb, Michigan, 1983–84

YARDS GAINED

Most Yards Gained, Game
249 Jojo Townsell, Los Angeles v. Memphis, 14 April 1984
225 Frank Lockett, New Orleans at Jacksonville, 19 March 1984

Longest Pass Reception
98 Jackie Flowers (from Alan Risher), Arizona v. Washington, 11 April 1983 (TD)
86 Frank Lockett (from Johnnie Walton), Boston at Philadelphia, 24 April 1983 (TD)

TOUCHDOWNS

Most Touchdowns, Career
24 Eric Truvillion, Tampa Bay, 1983–84

Most Touchdowns, Game
3 Derek Holloway, Michigan v. Oakland, 19 March 1983
Jackie Flowers, Arizona v. New Jersey, 3 April 1983
Eric Truvillion, Tampa Bay at Washington, 24 April 1983
Trumaine Johnson, Chicago at Birmingham, 17 June 1983
Scott Fitzkee, Philadelphia at Pittsburgh, 24 March 1984
Jackie Flowers, Pittsburgh v. Oakland, 1 April 1984
Richard Johnson, Houston at Pittsburgh, 12 May 1984
Marvin Harvey, Tampa Bay v. Oklahoma. 14 May 1984

Most Consecutive Games, Touchdowns
7 Jackie Flowers, Arizona, 1983
Eric Truvillion, Tampa Bay, 1983
4 Scott Fitzkee, Philadelphia, 1984
Ricky Sanders, Houston, 1984
Jim Smith, Birmingham, 1984
Jojo Townsell, Los Angeles, 1984

Interceptions By

Most Interceptions By, Career
16 Luther Bradley, Chicago-Arizona, 1983–84
Mike Guess, Washington, 1983–84
Marcus Quinn, Oakland, 1983–84

Most Interceptions By, Season
12 Luther Bradley, Chicago, 1983
Marcus Quinn, Oakland, 1984
11 Mike Guess, Washington, 1984

Most Interceptions By, Game
6 Luther Bradley, Chicago at Tampa Bay, 2 April 1983
4 Marcus Quinn, Oakland v. Memphis, 19 May 1984

Punting

Most Punts, Game
11 Dario Casarino, Boston v. Chicago, 6 June 1983
9 Stan Talley, Oakland at Arizona, 26 February 1984
Stan Talley, Oakland v. New Orleans, 4 March 1984
Stan Talley, Oakland at Tampa Bay, 7 April 1984
Case deBruijn, Oklahoma v. Michigan, 7 April 1984
Stan Talley, Oakland v. Houston, 16 April 1984
Jeff Partridge, Los Angeles at Arizona, 23 June 1984

Longest Punt (In Yards)
89 Stan Talley, Oakland at Denver, 22 June 1984
75 Stan Talley, Oakland at Chicago, 3 July 1983
Jeff Partridge, Los Angeles at Arizona, 26 May 1984

AVERAGE YARDAGE

Highest Average, Punting, Season (Qualifiers)
43.97 Stan Talley, Oakland, 1983 (87–3825)
42.45 Jeff Gossett, Chicago, 1984 (85–3608)

Highest Average, Punting, Game (4 attempts)
52.3 Sean Landeta, Philadelphia at Arizona, 8 April 1984
51.7 Stan Talley, Oakland at Chicago, 3 July 1983

Punt Returns

YARDS GAINED

Most Yards Gained, Game
126 David Dumars, Denver v. Los Angeles, 9 April 1984
74 Garcia Lane, Philadelphia v. Pittsburgh, 4 June 1984

Longest Punt Return (In Yards)
79 David Martin, Denver v. Los Angeles, 9 April 1984 (TD)
77 Duane Gunn, Los Angeles at Oklahoma, 10 June 1984 (TD)

Kick Off Returns

YARDS GAINED

Most Yards Gained, Game
152 Calvin Eason, Houston at Chicago, March 11 1984
148 Derrick Crawford, Memphis at New Orleans, March 11 1984
Glenn Ford, Denver at Arizona, 23 April 1983

Longest Kickoff Return
97 Derrick Crawford, Memphis at Oakland, 19 May 1984
94 Eric Robinson, Washington v. Tampa Bay, 24 April 1983 (TD)
Clarence Verdin, Houston at Jacksonville, 25 May 1984 (TD)

QB Sacks By

Most Quarterback Sacks By, Career
36 John Corker, Michigan, 1983–84
24 John Lee, Chicago-Arizona, 1983–84

Most Quarterback Sacks By, Season
28 John Corker, Michigan, 1983
20 John Lee, Arizona, 1984

Most Quarterback Sacks By, Game
6 John Corker, Michigan at New Jersey, 10 April 1983

CHAPTER FIVE

Canada

If you had not already been told, you wouldn't know whether you were watching Canadian football or the United States version.

One team is lined up against the other, one has a football, the other is trying to take it away. The crashing of players' heavy bodies contrasts with the quick dancing feet of others; the football is flung into the air by one player and caught by another; a heap of bodies, then an orderly line-up again.

Soon it dawns on you. Each team has 12 players on the field; the punter comes on to the field in a third down situation; an opponent catches the punted ball; he is tackled in the end-zone and the referee signals one point for the punting team.

This is Canadian football: 12 men on the field; 3 downs instead of four; 1 yard between the teams on the line of scrimmage instead of their being nose to nose; 25-yard end-zones instead of 10; backfielders in motion in any direction before the ball is snapped; each quarter ending with a play instead of running down the clock; no scrimmaging of the ball within a yard of either goal; a single point or rouge scorable on a punt, a missed field goal or a kick-off.

Tacklers may not go within five yards of a punt returner until he has touched the ball, and there is no such thing as a 'fair catch', except that a returner may ground the ball in his own end-zone to concede a single point.

One of the main differences between Canadian and American football is apparent at first glance. The Canadian field is huge by comparison, measuring 10 400sq. yds, compared to the 6400sq. yds that make up a field in the USA. About half of the 40 000 sq. yds difference is made up in the two end-zones. In Canada the end-zone is 25yds deep. Overall, a Canadian football field measures 110yds from goal line to goal line, whilst its American counterpart is only 100 yds long. The Canadian field is 65yds wide whilst the US version is 53yds 1ft wide.

Because players love to corner a larger area, speed and agility are the prerequisite of the Canadian game, particularly in defensive players who have an additional 11yds 2ft to cover on wide sweeps.

In Canadian football the hashmarkings are placed 24yds from each sideline, leaving a 17-yd gap down the middle of the field. In American football the hashmarks are placed directly in line with the goalposts.

For field goal kickers this means that in the USA the kicker has an almost straight kick, but in Canada the kicker could be up to five yards outside the goalposts.

Origins

The Canadian Football League, as it is today, broke loose from the amateur Canadian Rugby Union in 1958 to shape its own destiny. But the true history of the game in maple leaf country can be traced back as far as the American version. It could even be said that the American game derived from Canada.

On 15 May 1874 students from Montreal's McGill University travelled over the border to play a friendly game with the students of Harvard. Until then both colleges had been practising a version of rugby union, but because four members of the Canadian team were ill and didn't travel, the scheduled 15-a-side game became a match between teams

107

of 11 men. If those four Chinooks had travelled to Harvard, the game as we know it today might have been played with 15 men.

In 1891 the Canadian Rugby Union became the sport's first governing body and set about drawing up the rules of the game. Teams in Quebec and Ontario had been playing according to rules which were slightly different from those of other provinces, and the CRU had a tough time sorting the matter out. Ontario actually left the Union from 1886–1891 in protest.

In 1907 the first league was set up in the east of the country when Montreal, Ottawa, Toronto and Hamilton formed the Interprovincial Rugby Football Union. The Governor General of Canada, Earl Grey, donated a cup to the fledgling league in 1909. The Grey Cup was open to all amateur rugby clubs and the first to win it in that year was the University of Toronto.

In 1921 a major change in the rules radically altered the face of Canadian football. Until then 14 players had been used by both teams on the field of play, but the number was now reduced to 12, one more than in American football, the extra player being in the backfield. Until this date the ball had been heeled back to the quarterback in rugby league style, but in accordance with another new rule the center now had to snap the ball backwards in the style we know today.

The year 1921 also saw the emergence, albeit briefly, of the western teams. The Edmonton Eskimos became the first western team to compete in the Grey Cup final. The Eskimos lost 23–0 to the powerful Toronto Argonauts but the match was a clear indication that football, Canadian style, was spreading.

The forward pass was adopted in Western Canada in 1929 and throughout the nation in 1931.

With the growth of the American game south of the border, more and more teams began to import players. The limit to the numbers allowed at the end of the Second World War was five per team, although nowadays up to 15 are allowed in a total squad of 34.

Football in Canada was becoming more of a national game. The teams in the west, whose history can be traced back to the 1920s and 1930s, were beginning to catch up with their eastern giants. Winnipeg Blue Bombers became the first western team to win the Grey Cup in 1935.

By 1954 the members of the western division had risen to five with the inclusion of the British Columbia Lions from Vancouver.

In 1956 the Canadian Football Council was formed to amalgamate the three different leagues: the western, the eastern, and the pirate Ontario Rugby Football Union. Two years later the Canadian Football League was born and since then football north of the 49th parallel has grown into one of the top spectator sports with huge crowds and national TV coverage.

Canadian football begins its season in the first weekend in July and runs through to the end of November when the Grey Cup final is contested. Each team in the nine-club two-division league plays the others twice to find the four participants for the play-off semi-finals.

The CFL at last came of age in 1983 when football was rated the country's second most popular sport behind ice hockey, a total of 3 million people buying tickets for games.

Canadian football is certainly progressing. Already plans are well advanced to increase the eastern division by one team in 1986. After giving birth to the American version, the CFL's rather unique brand of football is at last catching up with the more universally acclaimed NFL game.

The Immigrants

In today's very professional Canadian Football League nearly half of every team's squad is made up of American players. The CFL allows 15 of a team's 34-man squad to be American players. The other 19 players must be of Canadian origin.

This level has fluctuated over the years, but Canada has seen many top players use their league as a launching pad to further success and stardom in the richer playgrounds of the NFL.

One such player who is now known throughout the football world, but began his pro career in the CFL, is Washington Redskins' quarterback Joe Theismann. Theismann graduated from Notre Dame in 1971 and moved north to play for the Toronto Argonauts. Other ex-Argonauts are Ohio State's Outland Trophy winner Jim Stillwagon, and quarterback Bernie Faloney

from Maryland.

The Edmonton Eskimos have in recent years been a force to be reckoned with, mainly because of a coach and a quarterback now making their mark in the NFL with Houston Oilers. The coach in question is Hugh Campbell, and the quarterback is Warren Moon. With their assistance the Eskimos won the coveted Grey Cup in 1978, 1979, 1980, 1981 and 1982.

Another American legend in the coaching field made his mark in Canada, and entered its folklore long before his theories were tried and tested in Minnesota. Bud Grant spent ten years in charge of the Winnipeg Blue Bombers before moving over the border. In those ten years he won them four Grey Cups and numerous other awards, as well as being inducted into the CFL Hall of Fame. Every year the CFL unearths a future star for the NFL of the USA.

What's the difference?

	America	Canada
No of players	11 men on the field, 45 kitted and ready to play	12 men on the field, 34 kitted and ready to play
Size of field	100yds × 53yds 1 ft plus two 10-yd end-zones	110yds × 65yds plus two 25-yd end-zones

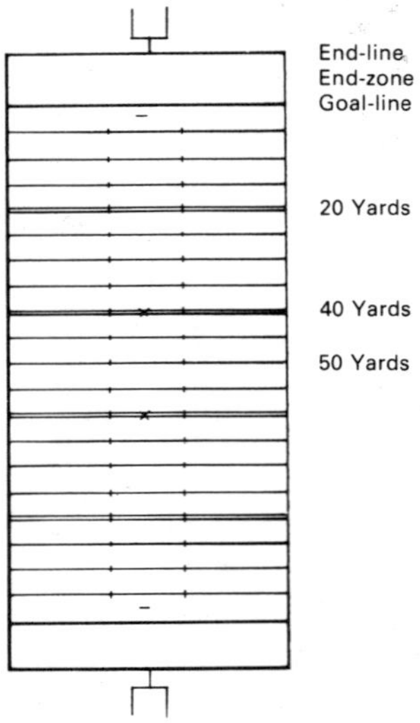

America field diagram labels:
End-line, End-zone, Goal-line
20 Yards
40 Yards
50 Yards

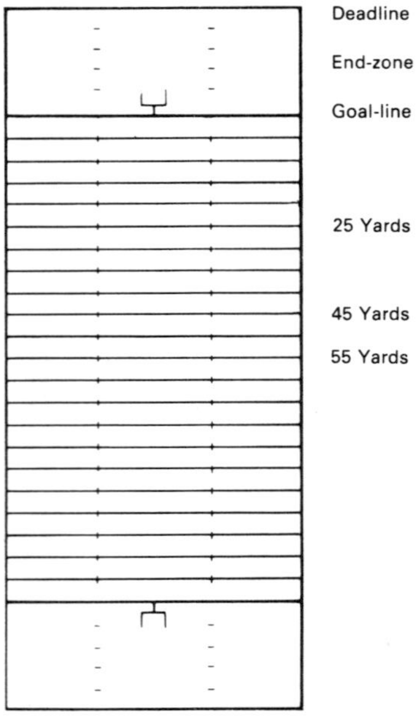

Canada field diagram labels:
Deadline
End-zone
Goal-line
25 Yards
45 Yards
55 Yards

	America	Canada
Downs	Four downs to make 10yds	Three downs to make 10yds
Scoring	Touchdown 6 pts, field goal 3 pts, safety 2 pts, conversion 1 pt	Touchdowns, safeties and field goals all the same. Conversions are one point but are worth two with a pass or run. A single scores one point
Single score	No such thing	One point score when a punt or missed field goal goes into the end-zone, is recovered by a defender who is tackled. Also when a punt or missed field goal goes out of bounds through the end-zone.
Timing	Four quarters of 15 minutes. Teams get 30 seconds to put ball back in play	Four quarters of 15 minutes. Teams given only 20 seconds between plays but officials allow for more time
Time outs	Each team has three per half	One only is permitted per team per half and must be taken in the last three minutes of that half
Backfield motion	At the snap only one back in the offense can move either backwards or sideways	All backfield players can move in any direction before the snap
Line of scrimmage	The lines should be separated by the length of the ball	The lines must be one yard apart
Kicks-offs	From the 35-yard line to start each half	From 45-yard line to start each half or after a TD. After conceding a field goal, a team can either kick off, scrimmage from their 35 or even receive.
Punt returning	Punts may roll dead or be received with a fair catch or returned. The ball can't be recovered by the kicking team unless touched by the receiving team. A punt through the end-zone is a touchback at the receiving team's 20–yard line	There is no fair catch, all punts must be run back. A returner tackled in the end-zone concedes a single. Tacklers must remain five yards away from the receiver until he touches the ball unless they are played 'onside' by the kicker
Penalties	Range from 5 to 15 yards	Start at 5 yards but rise to 25

The Canadian Football League

Western Division
British Columbia Lions
Edmonton Eskimos
Calgary Stampeders
Saskatchewan Roughriders
Winnipeg Blue Bombers

Eastern Division
Hamilton Tiger-Cats
Toronto Argonauts
Ottawa Rough Riders
Montreal Concordes

1984 Final Season Statistics

The Standings

EASTERN DIVISION

	W	L	T	F	A	Pts
Toronto Argonauts	9	6	1	461	361	19
Hamilton Tiger-Cats	6	9	1	353	439	13
Montreal Concordes	6	9	1	386	404	13
Ottawa Rough Riders	4	12	0	354	507	8

WESTERN DIVISION

	W	L	T	F	A	Pts
B.C. Lions	12	3	1	445	281	25
Winnipeg Blue Bombers	11	4	1	523	309	23
Edmonton Eskimos	9	7	0	464	443	18
Saskatchewan Roughriders	6	9	1	348	479	13
Calgary Stampeders	6	10	0	314	425	12

League Records Established – 1984 Season

Individual Career Records

SCORING

Most Points Scored	2237	Dave Cutler, Edmonton 1969–1984	
Most Converts	627	Dave Cutler, Edmonton 1969–1984	
Most Field Goals	464	Dave Cutler, Edmonton 1969–1984	
Most Singles	218	Dave Cutler, Edmonton 1969–1984	

PASS RECEIVING

Most Yards Gained	10837	Tom Scott, Winnipeg, Edmonton, Calgary 1974–1984	
Most Touchdowns	88	Tom Scott, Winnipeg, Edmonton, Calgary 1974–1984	

PUNT RETURNS

Most Yards Gained	4858	Paul Bennett, Toronto, Winnipeg, Hamilton 1977–1984	

KICK-OFFS

Most Singles Scored	30	Dave Cutler, Edmonton 1969–1984	

Individual Single Season Records

PASS RECEIVING

Most Touchdowns	18	Brian Kelly, Edmonton

PUNTING

Most Yards	7302	Bernd Ruoff, Hamilton

KICK-OFF RETURNS

Most Yards Returned	1040	Craig Ellis, Saskatchewan
Most Returns	42	Craig Ellis, Saskatchewan

INTERCEPTION RETURNS

Most Yards Returned	253	Harry Skipper, Montreal

FUMBLE RETURNS

Most Yards Returned	146	Alvin Washington, Ottawa (ties record set by Wayne Giardino of Ottawa in 1972)

Individual Single Game Records

SCORING

Most Field Goals	8	Dave Ridgway, Saskatchewan (at Ottawa, 29 July 1984)
Most Converts	9	Trevor Kennerd, Winnipeg (against Ottawa, 7 September 1984)

Individual Single Play Records

FUMBLED RETURNS

Longest Return	104	Alvin Washington, Ottawa (against Calgary, 7 July 1984)

Miscellaneous Records

Most Games With 100 Yards Gained Rushing in one season	10	Willard Reaves, Winnipeg
Most Consecutive Games With 100 Yards Gained Rushing	8	Willard Reaves, Winnipeg

SCORING

PLAYER		TD	CON	FG	S	TP
Passaglia	BC	0	46	35	16	167
Ilesic	TO	0	44	30	25	159
Kennerd	WP	0	61	26	13	152
Ruoff	HM	0	29	34	14	145
Hay	CG	0	25	33	11	135
Sweet	ML	0	27	33	5	131
Ridgway	SK	0	30	28	13	127
Cutler	ED	0	47	20	16	123
Dorsey	OT	0	37	26	7	122
Brown, Lester	TO	18	0	0	0	108

RUSHING

PLAYER		TC	NET	AVE	LG	TD
Reaves	WP	304	1733	5.7	68	14
Wilson, Dwaine	ML	226	1083	4.8	36	4
Cowan, Larry	ED	130	759	5.8	65	1
Dunigan	ED	89	732	8.2	69	9
Walker, Lewis	CG	139	732	5.3	87	2
McCray	OT	137	701	5.1	81	6
Ellis	SK	141	690	4.9	65	8
Brown, Lester	TO	140	594	4.2	24	10
White, J. H.	BC	102	523	5.1	42	3
Gill	ML	98	485	4.9	26	4

PASS RECEIVING

PLAYER		NO	YDS	AVE	LR	TD
Ellis	SK	91	871	9.6	37	4
Fernandez	BC	89	1486	16.7	78	17
DiPietro	HM	71	1063	15.0	80	5
Pearson	TO	71	910	12.8	42	5
Murphy	WP	70	1220	17.4	86	12
Greer	TO	70	1189	17.0	61	14
Arakgi	ML	67	1078	16.1	82	10
Poplawski	WP	67	998	14.9	62	3
Kelly	ED	66	1310	19.8	85	18
Crawford, Rufus	HM	66	864	13.1	47	3

PASSING

PLAYER		A	C	YDS	PCT	I/C	LG	TD
Brock	HM	561	320	3966	0.570	23	83	15
Clements	WP	446	279	3845	0.625	22	86	29
Dewalt	BC	437	258	3613	0.590	15	78	21
Dunigan	ED	412	220	3273	0.533	19	81	21
Paopao	SK	453	260	3270	0.573	19	94	12
Barnes	TO	378	231	3128	0.611	12	71	18
Watts	OT	360	189	3052	0.525	23	90	21
Gill	ML	375	199	2673	0.530	17	77	16
Holloway	TO	254	146	2231	0.574	8	63	16
Vavra	CG	324	161	1901	0.496	16	41	10

INTERCEPTION RETURNS

PLAYER		NO	YDS	LR	TD
Bess	HM	12	123	35	0
Hall, Darryl	ED	11	151	94	1
Irvin	SK	11	79	42	1
Hailey	WP	9	240	74	1
DesLauriers	ED	9	110	78	0

PUNTING

PLAYER		NO	YDS	AVE	LK	S
Ruoff	HM	156	7302	46.8	77	5
Clark	OT	150	7023	46.8	80	4
McTague	CG	153	6796	44.4	92	11
Ilesic	TO	140	6192	44.2	71	8
Passaglia	BC	125	5803	46.4	89	4

PUNT RETURNS

PLAYER		NO	YDS	AVE	LR	TD
Crawford, Rufus	HM	100	1108	11.1	63	0
McDermott	SK	81	724	8.9	28	0
Clash	BC	62	664	10.7	83	1
Carinci	TO	57	575	10.1	36	0
Hailey	WP	50	477	9.5	28	0

FIELD GOALS

PLAYER		TRIED	GOOD	YDS	AVE	LFG
Passaglia	BC	48	35	1111	31.7	54
Ruoff	HM	44	34	1068	31.4	57
Hay	CG	45	33	1075	32.6	57
Sweet	ML	43	33	1050	31.8	48
Ilesic	TO	46	30	931	31.0	53

CAREER COACHING RECORDS (REGULAR SEASON)

COACH		YEARS	WON	LOST	TIED	PCT.
Don Matthews	BC	2	23	8	1	0.734
Bob O'Billovich	TO	3	30	16	2	0.646
Cal Murphy	BC-WP	4	30	25	3	0.543
Jackie Parker	BC-ED	4	23	22	0	0.511
George Brancato	OT	11	82	90	4	0.477
Reuben Berry	SK	2	11	14	1	0.442
Al Bruno	HM	2	7	11	2	0.400
Steve Buratto	CG	1	6	10	0	0.375
Joe Galat	ML	3	13	33	2	0.292

DEFENSIVE SACKS

PLAYER		QB	OTHER	TOT
Parker	BC	26.5	4.5	31.0
Curry	TO	22.0	2.5	24.5
Jones, Tyrone	WP	20.5	1.0	21.5
Marshall	OT	16.5	4.5	21.0
Covington	HM	18.5	1.0	19.5

INDIVIDUAL SEASON HIGHLIGHTS

Longest Run from Scrimmage: 87yds, L. Walker, Cal. v. Ott., 14 September 1984

Longest Completed Pass: 94yds, Davis from Paopao, Sask. v. B.C., 5 August 1984

Longest Field Goal: 57yds, Ruoff, Ham., Hay, Cal.

Longest Punt: 92yds, McTague, Cal. v. Edm., 3 September 1984

Longest Punt Return: 96yds, Edwards, Ott. at Mtl., 21 July 1984

Longest Kick-off: 92yds, Ruoff, Ham. at B.C., 9 September 1984

Longest Kick-off Return: 100yds, Eckles (3), Baker (8), Edwards (89), Ott. v. Mtl. 28 October 1984

Longest Fumble Return: 104yds, A. Washington, Ott. v. Cal., 7 July 1984

Did You Know

That the Montreal Concordes were originally called the 'Alouettes' (Larks).

That it was Calgary's Jerry Sieberling who threw the first legal forward pass in Canadian football in 1929.

That Hamilton is the site of the Canadian Hall of Fame.

That the Montreal Concordes play in the magnificent Montreal Olympic Stadium.

That Canadian Football uses six officials compared to the seven used in the USA. Canada omits the side judge.

CHAPTER SIX

High School Football

High school football is the breeding ground for all football, it is the grass-roots level at which every star playing in the professional ranks today started. Every Autumn well over half a million kids between the ages of 16 and 18 play for their local high school, dreaming that one day they will aspire to the lofty heights of the NFL.

Every state in the Union has its own championships and all-star bowl games, and these annual championships can attract just as big an audience as the college and pro games. It is not uncommon for over 5000 fans to turn out on a Friday evening to cheer on their local school. Mums, Dads, brothers, sisters, even grandparents will join their local supporters' clubs, in an effort to provide their offspring and relatives with the best possible facilities and encouragement.

The various state and city championships are usually held in one of the local college or professional stadiums. These last all day as teams battle to the death in their efforts to become the local champions.

In some less populated states, where schools cannot find enough players to field full squads, football is played with eight men on each side. These games, with two linemen and a back omitted from the line-up, often produce some excellent play.

Each high school will have its own band and team of cheer-leaders at the games urging their heroes on, and rivalry between the local schools is very fierce.

The players, young though they are, will train for two or three hours every night after school, trying to get a place in the school team. To be included in the first squad brings overnight fame, not only in the eyes

Dickersen of L.A. Rams set High School records at Sealy High, Texas in 1978. (All-Sport).

of the fans but also those of the adoring girls who swoon over their macho he-men.

Some of the most famous names in the sport today are still mentioned in the current high school listings. Among these are Los Angeles Rams' running back Eric Dickersen who scored 84 touchdowns for Sealy High in Texas between 1975 and 1978, and the New Jersey Generals' Heisman-winning back Herschel Walker who ran for 45 touchdowns in 1979 whilst attending Wrightsville Johnson County High in Georgia.

Sadly, most of the current record holders in the High School ratings will never reach the dizzy heights of the professional game. For them, a mention as a record scorer or rusher or passer during their schooldays long ago will be all they remember of their fun on the gridiron.

High School Football Records

Team

All-Time

STATE CHAMPIONSHIPS

All-Time

26	Phoenix Union, Arizona (1913–54)
14	Fargo Shanley, N. Dakota (1952–77)
13	Limon, Colorado (1933–79)
13	Tucson, Arizona (1912–1971)

Consecutive

9	Phoenix Union, Arizona (1920–28)
6	Fargo Shanley, N. Dakota (1972–77)
6	Limon, Colorado (1963–68)
5	Stayton Regis, Oregon (1973–77)
5	Phoenix Union, Arizona (1913–17)

UNDEFEATED TEAMS (Includes Ties)

Seasons

28	Lawrence, Kansas (1891–1984)
19	Massillon Washington, Ohio (1909–77)
14	Muckegon Michigan (1904–1971)
12	Tuscaloosa, Alabama (1921–57)
11	Jefferson City, Montana (1957–78)
11	Caledonia-Mumford Central, New York (1928–80)
10	Montgomery Sidney Lanier, Alabama (1920–67)

Seasons – Consecutive

7	Jefferson City, Montana (1959–65)
7	Oklahoma City Douglass, Oklahoma (1949–55)
7	Shelbyville Bedford County Training, Tennessee (1943–49)
7	Tuscaloosa, Alabama (1925–31)
6	Hudson, Michigan (1969–74)

Games – Consecutive

82	Shelbyville Bedford County Training, Tennessee (78-0-4), (1943–50)
76	Oklahoma City Douglass, Oklahoma, (1949–56)
72	Hudson, Michigan (72-0-0), (1968–75)
71	Jefferson City, Montana (71-0-0), (1958–65)
64	Pittsfield, Illinois (64-0-0), (1966–73)

WINS

Consecutive

76	Oklahoma City Douglass, Oklahoma (1949–56)
72	Hudson, Michigan (1968–75)
71	Jefferson City, Montana (1958–66)
64	Pittsfield, Illinois (1966–73)
64	Picayune George Washington Carver, Mississippi (1958–65)

MOST TOUCHDOWNS

Season

130	Big Sandy, Texas, 1975 (14)

Game

38	Haven, Kansas v. Sylvia, Kansas, 16 Nov. 1927 (H 256-0)

Rushing

MOST YARDS

Season

7274	Sugar Land, Texas, 1953 (12)
4474	Thomson, Georgia, 1984 (15)
4280	Tucson, Arizona, 1970 (12)
4270	Covina South Hills, California, 1974
4251	Sealy, Texas, 1978 (15)

Game – One Team

734	Steubenville, Ohio v. Massillon Washington, Ohio, 1930 (S 68-0)
662	Elkins, Arkansas v. Winslow, Arkansas, 25 Oct. 1974 (E 74-0)
650	Lakewood, Colorado v. Golden Arvada, Colorado, 1963
641	Miami, Arizona v. Coolidge, Arizona, 1955
617	Canton McKinley, Ohio v. Alliance, Ohio, 1974 (CM 73-0)

MOST TOUCHDOWNS

Season

114	Big Sandy, Texas, 1975

Per Game – Season (Minimum 8 Games)

8.1	Big Sandy, Texas, 1975 (114/14)

Passing

MOST YARDS

Season

4120	Tallahassee Leon, Florida, 1975 (14)
3571	Tallahassee Leon, Florida, 1974
3463	Metairie Country Day, Louisiana, 1984
3352	La Mesa Helix, California, 1981 (13)

Game

638	Mogadore, Ohio v. Atwater, Ohio, 10 Nov. 1955 (98 att., 38 com.)
588	Houston Elmore, Texas v. Houston Aldine Carver, Texas, 1968 (HE 58-6)
546	Tamalpais, California, 1966
538	Virginia Beach Princess Anne, Virginia, 15 Nov. 1963
524	Barnesville Lamar County, Georgia v. LaGrange Troup Country, Georgia, 11 Nov. 1977 (BLC 48-28)

Per Game – Season (Minimum 8 Games)

309.4	Athena Weston-McEwan, Oregon, 1973 (2785/9)
294.3	Tallahassee Leon, Florida, 1975 (4120/14)
288.6	Metairie Country Day, Louisiana, 1984 (3463/12)
257.8	La Mesa Helix, California, 1981 (3352/13)

MOST TOUCHDOWNS

Season

42	Hamilton Southeastern, Indiana, 1981
42	La Puente Bishop Amat, California, 1970
40	Metairie Country Day, Louisiana, 1984
40	Fresno Bullard, California, 1981
40	Tallahassee Leon, Florida, 1975 (14)
40	Shreveport Woodlawn, Louisiana, 1968
39	Indianopolis Warren, Indiana, 1984
39	Barber Hills, Texas, 1963
36	Los Angeles Wilson, California, 1977
36	Granada Hills, California, 1970

High School Football in the United States is serious business. The annual State and City Championships attract large crowds and the play is always tough. (All-Sport).

Game – One Team

11	Smithfield, Virginia v. Smithfield Westside, Virginia, 1967 (S 124-0)
9	Seth Sherman, W. Virginia v. Chapmanville, W. Virginia, 1972 (SS 76-26)
8	Barbers Hill, Texas v. Deweyville, Texas, 1971 (BH 99-0)
8	Athena McEwan, Oregon v. Prairie City, Oregon, 1968 (AM 70-18)
7	Ottawa Marquetta, Illinois v. St. Charles Valley Lutheran, Illinois, 6 Oct. 1978 (OM 66-0)
7	Los Angeles Wilson, California, 4 Nov. 1977
7	Houston Elmore, Texas v. Cy-Fair, Texas, 1969 (HE 54-51)

Defense

Scoring

MOST SHUTOUTS

Consecutive

52	Shelbyville Bedford County Training, Tennessee (1942–49)
18	Portsmouth Woodrow Wilson, Virginia (1926–27)
16	Reese, Michigan (1958–59)
16	McLeod, Texas (1943–44)
14	Los Angeles, California (1897–99)

MOST INTERCEPTIONS

Game

18	Sandpoint, Idaho v. Bonners Ferry, Idaho, 1928 (S 31-0)
11	Denver Christian, Colorado v. Platte Canyon, Colorado, 23 Oct. 1982 (DC 48-13)
10	Woodruff, S. Carolina, 1983
9	Scottsdale Arcadia, Arizona v. Prescott, Arizona, 1962
9	Mesa, Arizona v. Yuma, Arizona, 1937

Individual

Offense

Scoring

MOST POINTS

Career

899	Ken Hall (Sugar Land, Texas), 1950–53 (127 TDs, 137 con.)
672	Mike Atkinson (Princeton, N. Carolina), 1977–80
664	Dick Todd (Cromwell, Texas), 1931–34
664	Dennis Mahan (Martinsville, Virginia), 1974–77
634	Scott Wright (Vian, Oklahoma), 1979–82

Season

395	Ken Hall (Sugar Land, Texas), 1953 (57 TDs, 53 con.)
364	David Overstreet (Big Sandy, Texas), 1975
351	Albert Glenn (Elkins, W. Virginia), 1922
333	Bert Grevitt (Denver City, Texas), 1960
323	Hupert Bobo (Dover Chauncey-Dover, Ohio), 1952

Game

90	Elvin McCoy (Haven, Kansas), 16 Nov. 1927
86	Don Wile (Salem, Illinois), 8 Oct. 1943
80	Frank Greene (San Diego Coronado, California) v. Chula Vista Sweetwater, California, 1929 (SDC 108-0, 11 TDs, 14 conversions)
78	Eddie Byrge (Huntsville, Tennessee), 26 Oct. 1968)
77	Ernie Perea (Los Lunas, New Mexico), 11 Nov. 1967

Per Game – Season (Minimum 8 Games)

32.9	Ken Hall (Sugar Land, Texas), 1953 (395/12)
31.9	Harold 'Red' Grange (Wheaton, Illinois), 1920 (255/8)
26.0	David Overstreet (Big Sandy, Texas), 1975 (364/14)

MOST TOUCHDOWNS

Career
127   Ken Hall (Sugar Land, Texas), 1950–53
98   Mike Atkinson (Princeton, N. Carolina), 1977–80
97   Dennis Mahan (Martinsville, Virginia), 1974–77
95   Scott Wright (Vian, Oklahoma), 1979–82
92   Robert Alexander (South Charleston, W. Virginia), 1974–76

Season
57   Ken Hall (Sugar Land, Texas), 1953
56   David Overstreet (Big Sandy, Texas), 1975
49   Albert Glenn (Elkins, W. Virginia), 1922
48   Curtis Warner (Pineville, W. Virginia), 1978
48   Arthur Owens (Stroudburg, Pennsylvania), 1971
48   Grant Burget (Stroud, Oklahoma), 1969
45   Herschel Walker (Wrightsville Johnson County, Georgia), 1979

Game
13   Elvin McCoy (Haven, Kansas) v. Sylvia, Kansas, 16 Nov. 1927 (H 256-0)
12   Ralph Colsen (Boston East Boston, Mass.) v. Boston South Boston, Mass., 1928
11   Frank Greene (San Diego Coronado, California) v. Chula Vista Sweetwater, California, 1929 (SDC 108-0)
10   George 'Swede' Anderson (Denver South, Colorado) v. Denver East, Colorado, 13 Oct. 1914
9   Frank Byrd (Mayo, S. Carolina), 1958

Per Game – Season (Minimum 8 Games)
4.8   Ken Hall (Sugar Land, Texas), 1953 (57/12)
4.5   Harold 'Red' Grange (Wheaton, Illinois), 1920 (36/8)
4.0   David Overstreet (Big Sandy, Texas), 1975 (56/14)

MOST FIELD GOALS

Career
33   Luis Zendejas (Chino Don Lugo, California), 1977–80
31   Kelly Ray Nemecek (Purcell, Oklahoma), 1981–83
29   Scott Webb (La Mesa Helix, California), 1980–82
28   Bruce Woods (Modesto Central, California), 1974–76
25   Mark Brasco (Jeannette, Pennsylvania), 1980–83

Game
5   Scott Webb (La Mesa Helix, California) v. El Cajon Granite Hills, California, 8 Oct. 1982
5   John Lee (Downey, California) v. Gahr, California, 7 Nov. 1980 (D 22-9, 31, 21, 41, 37, 25)
5   Jamie Clodfelter (McClave, Colorado), v. Arapahoe, Colorado 12 Oct. 1979 (Mc 36-2, 35, 25, 30, 40, 19)
5   Dave Dunwoodie (Huntington Park, California) v. Bell, Calfornia, 1970 (HP 22-6)
5   George Mousel (Cambridge, Nebraska) v. Farnham, Nebraska, 1928
4   Teemu Joustsi (Parchment, Michigan) v. Otsega, Michigan 9 July 1984 (P 18-13, 38, 28, 29, 35)

Longest
64   Erik Affholter (Agoura Oak Park, California) v. Carpinteria, California, 16 Oct. 1982 (C, 14-13)
62   Mike Kennon (Stanton Community, Iowa) v. Nishna Valley, Iowa, 29 Oct. 1982 (SC 65-0)
62   Russell Wheatley (Odessa Permian, Texas), 1975
62   Kelly Imhoff (Kent, Washington), 1929 (Dropkick)

Total Offence

MOST YARDS

Career
14 558   Ken Hall (Sugar Land, Texas), 1950–53 (11 232 rushing, 3326 passing)
11 451   Ron Cuccia (Los Angeles Wilson, California), 1975–77 (2647 rushing, 8804 passing)

Season
5146   Ken Hall (Sugar Land, Texas), 1953 (4045 rushing, 1101 passing)
4074   Jimmy Jordan (Tallahassee Leon, Florida), 1975 (24 rushing, 4098 passing)

Per Game – Season (Minimum 8 Games)
428.8   Ken Hall (Sugar Land, Texas), 1953 (5146/12)
291.0   Jimmy Jordan (Tallahassee Leon, Florida), 1975 (4074/14)

RUSHING TOUCHDOWNS

Season
43   Mike Atkinson (Princeton, N. Carolina), 1979
42   Herschel Walker (Wrightsville Johnson County, Georgia), 1979
41   Tony Goss (Randleman, N. Carolina), 1983
39   Bobby Wright (Vian, Oklahoma), 1980
36   Mickey Cureton (Compton Centennial, California), 1966
35   Steve Grady (Los Angeles Loyola, California), 1962
34   Steve Ampey (Gobles, Michigan), 1982
34   Scott Wright (Vian, Oklahoma), 1981
34   Jeff Womack (Warren County, Tennessee), 1980
33   Jerry Eckwood (Brinkley, Arkansas), 1973
32   Eric Dickerson (Sealy, Texas), 1978

100-YARD GAMES

Career
38   Ken Hall (Sugar Land, Texas), 1950–53
38   Steve Worster (Bridge City, Texas), 1964–66
38   Billy Sims (Hooks, Texas), 1972–75
34   Walter Moseley (Ellenville Central, New York), 1979–82
34   Scott Wright (Vian, Oklahoma), 1979–82
32   Jeff Womack (Warren County, Tennessee), 1979–81
32   Herschel Walker (Wrightsville Johnson County, Georgia), 1977–79
31   Eric Dickerson (Sealy, Texas), 1975–78

Consecutive
38   Billy Sims (Hooks, Texas), 1972–75
27   Walter Moseley (Ellenville Central, New York), 1980–82
21   Ken Hall (Sugar Land, Texas), 1952–53

Notre Dame's present head coach Gerry Faust ran up an impressive 174–17–2 record in 18 seasons at Moeller High School, Cincinnatti, Ohio from 1963 to 1980. (University of Notre Dame).

20	Steve Ampey (Gobles, Michigan), 1981–82
18	Jeff Womack (Warren County, Tennessee), 1979–80
17	Mike Armstrong (Barbers Hill, Texas), 1970–71
17	Archie White (Leonard, Texas), 1969–70
15	Herschel Walker (Wrightsville Johnson County, Georgia), 1979
14	Jeff Womack (Warren County, Tennessee), 1960–81
13	Dean Arcand (Forest Park, Michigan), 1982–83
13	Scott Wright (Vian, Oklahoma), 1979–82
13	Eric Dickerson (Sealy, Texas), 1978

Season

15	Billy Sims (Hooks, Texas), 1973

Passing

MOST YARDS

Career (6000 or more)

8804	Ron Cuccia (Los Angeles Wilson, California), 1975–77
8326	John White (Metairie Country Day, Louisiana), (1982–84)
7633	Pat Handen (La Puente Bishop Amat, California), 1968–70
6913	Jim Plum (La Mesa Helix, California), 1979–81
6726	Joe Ferguson (Shreveport Woodlawn, Louisiana), 1966–68

MOST TOUCHDOWN PASSES THROWN

Season

42	Pat Haden (La Puente Bishop Armat, California), 1970
41	Ron Moyer (Hamilton Southeastern, Indiana), 1981
40	John White (Metaire Country Day, Louisiana), 1984
40	Jimmy Jordan (Tallahassee Leon, Florida), 1975
40	Joe Ferguson (Shreveport Woodlawn, Louisiana), 1968
39	Jeff George (Indianapolis Warren, Indiana), 1984

Game

9	Randy Hendricks (Seth Sherman, W. Virginia), v. Chapmanville, W. Virginia, 1972 (SS 76.26)
8	Jabo Leonard (Barbers Hill, Texas), v. Deweyville, Texas, 1971 (BH 99–0)

Half

7	Ron Cuccia (Los Angeles Wilson, California), 4 Nov 1977

Receiving

MOST YARDS

Career

4477	Stan Rome (Valdosta, Georgia), 1970–73
3389	John McKay, Jr. (La Puente Bishop Amat, California), 1968–70
3220	Brian Streiffer Metaire Country Day, Louisiana), 1982–84
3024	Tyrone Vaughans (Marrero Ehret, Louisiana), 1980–82
3005	Mike Young (Mt. Whitney, California), 1977–79

Season

1846	Steve Martinez (Los Angeles Wilson, California), 1977
1741	John McKay, Jr. (La Puente Bishop Amat, California), 1970
1734	Jay McNabney (Carisbad, California), 1980
1665	Doug Stis (Hamilton Southeastern, Indiana), 1981

Game

323	John McKay, Jr. (La Puente Bishop Amat, California), v. Downey Plus X, California, 17 Oct. 1969
319	Steve Martinez (Los Angeles Wilson, California), 18 Nov 1977
316	Peter Demmerle (New Canaan, Connecticut) v. Stamford Rippowan, Connecticut, 7 Nov. 1970

MOST RECEPTIONS

Career

213	Bob Thomas (King of Prussia Upper Merion, Pennsylvania), 1970–72
207	John McKay, Jr. (La Puente Bishop Amat, California), 1968–70
204	Chad Finch (Sabine Pass, Texas), 1980–83
201	Stan Rome (Valdosta, Georgia), 1970–73

Season

121	Steve Martinez (Los Angeles Wilson, California), 1977
106	John McKay, Jr. (La Puente Bishop Amat, California), 1969
102	Pete Demmerle (New Canaan, Connecticut), 1970
97	Brian Streiffer (Metairie Country Day, Louisiana), 1984

Game

24   Steve Martinez (Los Angeles Wilson, California), 18 Nov. 1977

22   Frank Mobley (Live Oak Suwannee, Florida), 27 Oct. 1972

22   Bob Thomas (King of Prussia Upper Merion, Pennsylvania), 1972

21   Rex Hudler (Fresno Bullard, California), 1977

21   John Mistler (Tucson Sahuaro, Arizona) v. Tucson Sabino, Arizona, 11 Nov. 1976 (TSah 54-23, 296 yds).

Half

19   Steve Martinez (Los Angles Wilson California) v. Los Angeles Lincoln, California, 11–4, 1977

19   John Mistler (Tuscon Sahuaro, Arizona), v. Tucson Sabino, Arizona, 1976

Quarter

13   Bob Thomas (King of Prussia Upper Merion, Pennsylvania), 1975

MOST TOUCHDOWNS

Career

60   Tyrone Vaughans (Marrero Ehret, Louisiana), 1980–82

48   John McKay, Jr. (La Puente Bishop Amat, California), 1968–70

45   Stan Rome (Valdosta, Georgia), 1970–73

40   Robert Powell (Portsmouth Woodrow Wilson, Virginia), 1968–71

37   Brian Streiffer (Metairie Country Day, Louisiana), 1982–84

Season

29   John McKay, Jr. (La Puente Bishop Amat, California), 1970

27   Jerry Hamilton (Carpinteria, California), 1979

24   Tyrone Vaughans (Marrero Ehret, Louisiana), 1982

22   Brian Streiffer (Metairie Country Day, Louisiana), 1984

22   Doug Stis (Hamilton Southeastern, Indiana), 1981

Game

5   Tony Lopez (Dundee, Illinois) v. Cary-Grove, Illinois 25 Sept. 1982 (291/13)

Kickoff Returns

MOST TOUCHDOWNS

Game

4   Roger Maris (Fargo Shanley, N. Dakota), 1951

3   Brent Fullwood (St. Cloud, Florida) v. Leesburg, Florida, 29 Oct. 1982 (St. C, 47-28, ret.—96, 90, 89)

Punt Returns

MOST TOUCHDOWNS

Game

5   Al Colby (Wheaton, Illinois) v. Sycamore, Illinois, 3 Nov. 1923 (W 130-0, 315yds).

Defense

MOST INTERCEPTIONS

Career

59   Donald Moore (Splendora, Texas), 1976–80

47   Richard Bailey (Painter Central, Virginia), 1979–82

36   Reggie Ash (Pittsburgh Carrick, Pennsylvania), 1968–70

34   Paul Kinne (Paso Robles, California), 1969–71

33   Chip Caudill (Burch, Virginia), 1970–73

Season

23   Richard Bailey (Painter Central, Virginia), 1982

23   Kendall Barrow (High Island, Texas), 1979

22   Roy Deen (Willis Point, Texas), 1965

19   Steve Sumrow (Celeste, Texas), 1983

19   Tommy Kaiser (Klein, Texas), 1969

19   Jim Linstaeder (Brenham, Texas)

Game

8   Glenn Rogers (Sandpoint, Idaho) v. Bonner Ferry, Idaho, 1928 (S 31–0)

7   Donald Moore (Splendora, Texas), v. New Waverly, Texas, 1977

6   Robert Murski (Houston St. Thomas, Texas), v. Houston St. Plus, Texas, 1966

Coaching

MOST WINS

Career

391   Gordon L. Wood (Rule, Texas; Roscoe, Texas; Seminole, Texas; Winters, Texas; Stamford, Texas; Victoria, Texas; Brownwood, Texas), 1940–83, (391-81-11)

346   Julius 'Pinky' Babb (Duncan, Georgia; Gainesville, Georgia; Greenwood, S. Carolina), 1939–81 (346-86-24)

328   Pat Panek (Denver Machebeuf, Colorado; Denver East, Colorado; Norfolk, Nebraska; St. Paul, Nebraska; Fullerton, Nebraska), 1925–1977 (328-117-29)

324   E. B. Etter (Chattanooga Central, Tennessee and Chattanooga Baylor, Tennessee), 1943–83 (324-102-13)

313   Edward E. Buller (Bucklin, Kansas; Agenda, Kansas; Clyde, Kansas), 1940–83 (313-72-7)

'It's an immense game all right, but keep in mind that there are 600 million Chinese who don't give a damn whether we win or lose'. Former Tampa Bay head coach John McKay.

CHAPTER SEVEN

United Kingdom

Until the advent of Channel Four's television coverage of football in the autumn of 1982, the gridiron game had had a rather spasmodic history in Great Britain.

The first reported game took place in 1910 when two American warships, the *USS Rhode Island* and the *USS Georgia* played an exhibition game at the Stonebridge Road ground in Northfleet, Kent. A crowd of over 4000 turned out on a bitterly cold day to see the Georgia win 11—0. The date in the history books was Tuesday 14 December, 1910.

After the Second World War, American service teams played inter-divisional and inter-squadron games at their bases all over Britain, and it is thought that a game actually took place at Wembley Stadium in 1952 between two US Army teams. But, as a participation sport for the British, 1982 marked the real beginning of American football.

The new TV channel's weekly show, presented by co-author Miles Aiken, effectively lit the fuse, and from September to January Sunday tea-time in a traditionally conservative country was never the same again. Superbowl XVII, beamed live from California, was watched by over 3 million fans who staved off sleep and sat up until 3 a.m. to enjoy the excitement.

Once the first season was over it soon became apparent that there were groups of sportsmen all over Britain who wanted not only to watch but to play this exciting new game. In Birmingham and Manchester groups had formed, and in October 1983 the very first all British game was staged in London when the Ravens swamped the inexperienced Northwich Spartans 48-0. A return game in Cheshire resulted in the Ravens gaining another large victory, and thus 'British' American football was born.

Hyde Park, more remembered for Speaker's Corner and the bangs of ceremonial guns, was awakening to bangs of a different kind as the press and the public rushed to see Britain's newest sport in action, for the Ravens had chosen the park as a practice field and photos of their sessions were flashed all over the world.

Various attempts to form a national association foundered at this early stage, largely because most teams were more interested in their own individual birth and survival. But finally a February weekend in Bedford brought together some 35 teams. A further meeting in London on 3 March 1984 resulted in the forming of not one but two leagues: 19 clubs decided to form the American Football League of the United Kingdom, and 7 to form the British American Football Federation. The remaining 9 decided to remain independent. Headed by a 42-year-old Birmingham-based American named Gerry Hartman the AFL had its first meeting at USAF Chicksands in Bedfordshire on 17 March 1984, and set about putting some life into its new offspring.

The month until the first game between two AFL members was a trying time. Little did anyone at that first meeting realize how much time, effort and money would be required to launch the new project. However, Sunday, 8 April arrived and 3000 fans turned up to witness the baptism of the Poole Sharks and the Northampton Stormbringers. For the Sharks it turned out to be

119

Miles Aiken and Nicky Horne, the presenters on British television's N.F.L. game of the week, share a ball with Gerald Marks, Commercial Attaché of the American Embassy in London.

a baptism of fire as the Stormbringers, with three experienced Americans in their squad, walloped them 48–0.

Teams were now sprouting at the rate of four or five a week and within a month the membership of the AFL had increased to 28 clubs. Meanwhile, BAFF, the other league under the leadership of Mike Lytton, began organizing games between their own teams and kicked off eventually on 21 July when Ealing Eagles beat Crawley Raiders 20–0.

At varying dates clubs opened their seasons with a series of exhibition games designed to launch a new 'family spectator' sport on an unsuspecting British public, with marching bands, cheerleaders, clowns and all the razzmatazz of the imported American scene.

There were the inevitable teething problems. Teams couldn't find enough officials for their games; the national press, after an initial burst of coverage, did not then give the exposure that had been anticipated; and the enormous financial outlay needed just to get players into equipment was beginning to hit hard. In April 1984 there were just four teams who had spent over £7000 to buy equipment to play the game. Within a month that number had risen to ten, and when Milton Keynes Bucks opened their home programme with a match against the

unbeaten Northampton Stormbringers in June, it had increased to fourteen. Nearly 7000 attended the Bucks' inaugural game at the aptly named Milton Keynes Bowl, and witnessed one of the closest games to be played under the British banner as the Bucks outwitted the colourfully named Stormbringers 20–18.

American football was beginning to be appreciated. Nearly 4000 fans attended the Birmingham Bulls' first game with the Bucks in July 1984; a crowd of 3000 watched the Heathrow Jets go down to the Poole Sharks, and some 2500 witnessed the Glasgow Lions host the Manchester (formerly Northwich) Spartans in the nation's first venture on to astroturf.

That first season had no official end. Most clubs wanted to keep on playing throughout the winter, trying to gain as much experience as possible before the first championship schedule for both AFL and BAFF Leagues in 1985. During the winter months teams all over the UK played games, and controlled scrimmages; a series of meetings was held with the aim of bringing the two leagues together, and a referees association was set up in July 1984. The British American Football Referees Association was the brainchild of soccer official Dave Norton and by the end of the year the association had over 100 budding refs. At the beginning of the new 1985 season there were more than enough well trained officials to supervise every game.

At the beginning of the 1985 season the AFL had 40 members all fully equipped and ready to play a 16-week programme of games. Since the previous autumn BAFF had picked up nicely and its membership stood at 20 clubs, although only 6 of these were equipped for tackle football.

American football in Britain is played under amateur status to National Collegiate Athletic Association (NCAA) rules. The AFL has adopted a few of the NFL rules, because professional football is the staple diet of the armchair fan, but 95 per cent of the rules are governed by the NCAA.

The two main leagues (AFL and BAFF) have been joined by two other smaller leagues, both consisting of about six clubs each, The United Kingdom American Football Association, based in Birmingham, being the other major influence.

The London Ravens train under the watchful eye of the English bobby. (All-Sport).

An estimated audience of 9 million watched Superbowl XIX live on British TV and the growth rate of the game has yet to reach its peak. New teams are still sprouting at an astonishing rate, and there are now over 80 teams in the UK, about 50 of which actively play the game of American football.

There is no question that the game has arrived in Britain; whether it survives and prospers depends on the availability of finance and on the further education of the British public. A public sickened by soccer violence could make or break the sport. As there is a genuine demand for a 'family spectator sport' in Britain today gridiron football American-style could supply the answer.

Did You Know

That the first and only 0–0 tie on the British gridiron took place on Sunday 7 April 1985. The opening day of the new AFL (UK) season saw the Crawley Raiders and the Ealing Eagles matched up for a classic confrontation. But the only winner on the day was the weather, as the game became a mud-splattered battle that ended with no score.

That Richard Slaney, former British Olympic discus star, and recently married to American track idol Mary Decker, plays football as defensive nose guard for the Crawley Raiders.

That the Manchester Spartans were originally called the Northwich Spartans.

That Greenwich Rams' head coach Tony McKinnon once played professional football in Canada for Saskatchewan Roughriders.

That the London Ravens were the only unbeaten team in Britain in 1984.

That the first team to play on foreign soil were the now defunct Poole Sharks who played the European Champions Düsseldorf Panthers on 15 April 1984, and lost 69–0.

That the first magazine about American football played in Britain was published on 14 June 1984. Called **Gridiron UK**, *it now has a healthy following.*

AFL Membership

Capital Division

Crawley Raiders
Croydon Coyotes
Ealing Eagles
Greenwich Rams
Harlow Warlords
London Ravens
Stock Exchange Stags

Northern Division

Edinburgh Blue Eagles
Blackpool Falcons
Glasgow Diamonds
Glasgow Lions
Leeds Cougars
Manchester Spartans
Tyneside Trojans

Southern Division

Colchester Gladiators
Rockingham Rebels
Southampton Wolverines
Southend Sabres
Streatham Olympians

Midlands Division

Birmingham Bulls
Kings Lynn Patriots
Milton Keynes Bucks
Northampton Stormbringers
Nottingham Hoods
Walsall Titans
Warwickshire Bears

North Central Division

Leicester Panthers
*Locomotive Derby
Manchester Allstars
Mansfield Express
Newcastle Browns
*Luton Flyers
Staffordshire Stampeders

South Western Division

Dorset Broncos
Heathrow Jets
Oxford Bulldogs
Portsmouth Warriors
Southampton Seahawks
Taunton Wyverns
Thames Valley Chargers

* AFL members not competing in 1985 schedule

London Ravens
Milton Keynes, Bucks
Glasgow Lions

1984 Record

Team	W	L	T	Pct.
London Ravens	10	0	0	100
Brighton B52's	5	0	0	100
Oxford Bulldogs	3	0	0	100
Thames Valley Chargers	3	0	0	100
Walsall Titans	3	0	0	100
Northampton Stormbringers	9	2	0	81.8
Milton Keynes Bucks	10	2	1	76.9
Ealing Eagles	5	1	1	71.4
Birmingham Bulls	4	3	0	57.1
Windsor Monarchs	2	2	1	50.0
Tyneside Trojans	1	1	1	50.0
Harlow Warlords	1	2	1	37.5
Manchester Spartans	4	7	0	36.3
Leeds Cougars	2	4	0	33.3
Streatham Olympians	1	2	0	33.3
Glasgow Lions	1	3	1	30.0
Crawley Raiders	1	4	0	20.0
Poole Sharks	1	8	0	11.1
Croydon Coyotes	0	7	1	6.25

The first all British game took place in October 1983 when the London Ravens defeated the Northwich Spartans 48–0.

BAFF Membership

Abingdon Pharoes
*Brighton B52's
*Cambridge County Cats
Chingford Centurians
Fulham Cardinals
*Ilford Blackhawks
Kent Saxons

*London Mets
North Herts Raiders
Thames Barriers
*Walthamstow Warriors
Witney Wildcats
Swindon Steelers
*Leamington Royals

* teams playing tackle football.

Non-Affiliated Clubs

Addlestone Thunderbolts
Andover Cougars
Basildon Colts
Basingstoke Cavaliers
Bath Gladiators
Black Country Nails
Bolton Braves
Boston Blitz
Bristol Bombers
Burton Bruins
Camberley Falcons
Chelmsford Cheetahs
Colorado 86ers
Crewe Railroaders
Dunstable Cowboys
Eastbourne Crusaders
Gloucester Boars
Halton Demons
Hereward Rams
Horsham Predators
Johnstone Crusaders
Kingston Liberators
Leigh Razorbacks
London Capitals
Macclesfield Cobras
Margate Mammoths
Manchester MPs
Cardiff Tigers

Minehead Maulers
Newark Vulcans
Newcastle Knights
Norwich AFC
Orpington Owls
Plymouth Admirals
Rutherglen Ironhogs
St Helens Glasscutters
Scunthorpe Steelers
Sheffield Steelers
Shetland Redeyes
Slough Silverbacks
Stoke Sentinels
Thanet Vikings
Welling Warriors
Weston Stars
Wight Rhinos
Windsor Monarchs
Wirral Wolves
Worthing Gladiators
Dublin AFC

UKAFA

Huskies of Birmingham
Penwith Dragons
Reading Renegades
Torbay Trojans
Hereford Chargers

Teams without a win

Heathrow Jets 0–6
Stock Exchange Stage 0–4
Fylde Falcons 0–3
Southampton Seahawks 0–3
Walthamstow Warriors 0–3
Ilford Blackhawks 0–2
Leamington Royals 0–2
London Raiders 0–2
Taunton Wyverns 0–1
Kings Lynn Patriots 0–1

Other Teams' Records

Dorset Broncos 2–0–0
Portsmouth Warriors 1–1–0
Nottingham Hoods 1–0–0
Staffordshire Stampeders 1–1–0
RAF Wyton 0–0–1
Torbay Trojans 0–1–0

Gone but not forgotten

Poole Sharks, Devon Generals, Medina Mustangs, Tenbury Crusaders, Harrogate Bulldozers, Keighley Panthers, London Raiders.

Name Changes

After using a town name or a nickname in 1984 the following teams changed their names for 1985:
Fylde Falcons are now Blackpool Falcons.
Greenwich Bay Mariners have now merged with Kent Mustangs to form the Greenwich Rams.
RAF Wyton are now the Cambridge County Cats.

Britain's John Smith spent ten years in the NFL and scored 1000 points. (*Touchdown Magazine*).

Germany

There are over 500 000 resident American servicemen and their families in Germany, and it therefore seems difficult to understand why football *blitzkrieg*-style did not get off the ground properly until 1980. Until then teams had played the game, but no official leagues or championships had been arranged. However, in 1980, at a meeting in Frankfurt, the 20 or so teams that were then in operation in Germany decided to form the AFVD: American Football Verband Deutschland.

In their first season there were two leagues: northern and southern, but the two divisions did not find the national association to their liking and in 1981 they formed two separate leagues. Fortunately this dispute did not last long and the two factions combined again to put football in Germany back on an even keel.

Although superficial differences have been sorted out, underneath there is still an overwhelming degree of regional feeling. The northern teams, who over the past few years have been more successful than the southern, have been accused by many Bavarian and Württemburg clubs of professionalism and of recruiting players illegally. This criticism might be construed as sour grapes, because the northern teams include the Düsseldorf Panthers and the Cologne Crocodiles, two of the best teams not just in Germany but in the whole of Europe.

The Panthers came into being in 1979, and after losing the first nine games of their opening season they emerged as German champions in 1980. The Panthers have since dominated the German league, winning the league again in 1981, 1983 and 1984. Their close rivals in Cologne came into being at roughly the same time, and although their play is of much the same standard they have only won the title once, in 1982.

The game has become well established in the industrial cities of the north where over 4000 fans watch the top teams each week. As the majority of American servicemen are based in the south, this is a great achievement.

The German league today is a well organized association of some 50 clubs. The first division is divided into four regions: Bayern, Hessen, Sudwest, and Nord Rhein–Westphalian. The second division is again divided into regions, with promotion and relegation, and the third division is primarily made up of many of the top first division teams' junior squads. Germany is one of only a few countries that demand a junior team from its top league. As in most

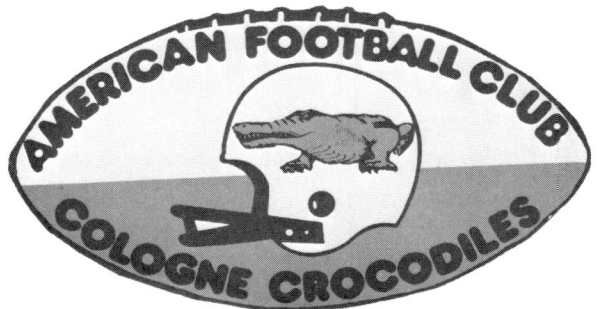

of Europe, the AFVD starts playing in April and runs the regular season until the end of July. August is traditionally a holiday month for most Germans, so the league accepts this and takes a break until the play-offs begin in September. The 'Endspiel' or Superbowl Final between the top northern and southern teams usually takes place during the second weekend in October. The location is usually decided on a geographical basis. In 1983 the Endspiel took place in Nuremburg, whilst in 1984 the event was staged in Essen, some 20 miles from Düsseldorf.

The 1984 final was a battle between the two 1983 contenders—the Düsseldorf Panthers and the Ansbach Grizzlies. As in 1983, the title went north to Westphalia as the Panthers, superbly led by quarterback Melvin Crandall, came from behind to win the game 27–13.

After five short years American-style football has certainly established a foothold in this traditional soccer-strong country. Its continued success seems assured as the AFVD prepares to host the 1986 European club championships.

German Champions

1980 Düsseldorf Panthers
1981 Düsseldorf Panthers
1982 Cologne Crocodiles
1983 Düsseldorf Panthers
1984 Düsseldorf Panthers

Divisional Alignments

First Division

North

Bonn Jets
Düsseldorf Bulldozer
Düsseldorf Panthers
Köln Red Barons
Cologne Crocodiles
Hamburg Dolphins
Berlin Adler

South and Southwest
Ansbach Grizzlies
Munich Cowboys
Nürnberg Rams
Mannheim Redskins
Stuttgart Stallions
Starnberg Argonauts

Central
Hanau Hawks
Frankfurt Lowen
Bad Homburg Falcons
Mainz Golden Eagles

Second Division

North
Hilden Hurricane
Castrop Bengals
Monheim Sharks
Bremerhaven Seahawks
Essen Eagles
Hamm Generals
Russelheim Crusaders

South
Munich Rangers
Erding Bulls
Kempten Comets
Stuttgart Scorpions
Karlsruhe Griefs
Saarlouis Hurricanes
Primasens Wildcats

Third Division
Düsseldorf Panther youth
Wuppertal Greyhounds
Mönchen-Gladbach Mustangs
Essen Cardinals
Solingen Steelers
Schlieden Warriors
Dortmund Giants
Cologne Crocodiles youth
Amsterdam Rams*

* Only Dutch team to play in German league. Until 1984 the Rams were the only team in Holland.

Italy

Since it is a Latin country steeped in the traditions of soccer, it is quite surprising to learn that American football is now the third most popular spectator sport in Italy.

Based largely in the north of the country, America football began in a modest way in 1980 with only a few teams. At that time the game was played mainly in Milan, Torino and the surrounding towns. Five seasons later, football has spread its wings and even has teams in Sicily in the boot of the country.

The major teams though, still come from the industrial north, Milan Rhinos being probably one of the best known and best supported teams. Under the auspices of the AIFA (Associazione Italiana Football Americano), the league in Italy now has a first division (known as Serie A) and a second division (Serie B). The first division in split into four regional conferences: Western, Eastern, Northern and Central, with six teams in each of them. Serie B, which began during the autumn of 1984, is, like the Serie A, divided into regions with four divisions of six teams.

At the end of the 1984 Serie B campaign the four top teams were promoted to Serie A to make up the six-team, four-division league we see today. Until 1984 there was no relegation to Serie B, but from 1986 there will be.

Each season the teams play ten games (five home and five away) within their own divisions plus two inter-divisional games (one at home and one away). The four divisional champions are automatically seeded into the quarter-finals, whilst the four runners-up have to do battle with the four third place teams to join them in the play-offs.

The 1984 season came to a climax on 6 July in Padua, with Superbowl V, the fifth Italian championship final.

The 1984 Superbowl was won by the Busto Frogs who beat off the challenge from Bologna Warriors, who were also runners-up in 1983.

One of the greatest teams in Italy, the Milan Rhinos, are being rebuilt after winning the first three titles, whilst across the city the Milan Rams are also strong contenders for each year's honours with ex-Cleveland Browns' head coach Sam Rutigliano now assisting them in their drive to the top.

As elsewhere in Europe, Italian football is strictly amateur, but transfer fees are paid and the record fee paid by the 1984 champs Busto Frogs for Milan Rams' linebacker Luca Saguatti before the 1985 season got underway was 40 million lira (about £15 000).

In line with their European neighbours, the Italians are strict about the number of American nationals allowed in teams. But in this respect their rules are much harsher than many other countries, in that they only permit two Americans per team, while the quarterback *has* to be of Italian origin.

American football is probably better established in Italy than anywhere else in Europe. Teams are sponsored by many multinational companies and, despite the lack of wages, the game is played and organized in a very professional fashion.

Every week from March to July crowds of 5000 and more flock to small municipal stadiums to watch their heroes in action. While it is in third place behind soccer and basketball at the moment, there are strong possibilities that sooner rather than later 'American' football may well overtake at least one of them in the popularity stakes in Italy.

The Italian League

Serie A

Eastern	Northern
Bologna Warriors	Bologna Doves
Ferrara Aquile	Milan Seamen
Bolzano Jets	Milan Rhinos
Varese Skorpions	Modena Falchi
Verona Redskins	Bergamo Lions
Trieste Muli	Rovereto Climbers

Central	Western
Pesaro Angels	Busto Frogs
Parma Panthers	Torino Giaguara
Milan Rams	Grosseto Condors
Rome Grizzlies	Torino Tauri
Milan Riders	Genoa Squali
Bologna Towers	Rho Black Knights

Japan

The most popular team sport in the land of the rising sun is baseball, so the emergence of another Americanized game in 'Sumo wrestling' country is really no surprise.

In 1934 a group of American university professors visisted Japan to study the educational system there, and left behind a legacy of their own football. The game soon began to flourish, and by the end of the decade was becoming an accepted part of student life for many young Japanese studying at the country's major universities.

However, during the Second World War, because of the anti-American feeling in Japan, epitomized by the events at Pearl Habor, football became one of the first 'yankee' traditions to be banned. As soon as the war was over football and baseball began to pick up the pieces but the original enthusiasm for American sports was lost, and would not be regained for at least 20 years.

During that period, whilst baseball began to recover its popularity as a leading imported Japanese sport, football was only played by a few collegians in the major cities.

In 1970, a Japanese journalist who was hooked on the gridiron game decided to publish a magazine about the sport. Within a year *Touchdown* as it was called had begun to get the proverbial football rolling again.

Before the publication of Sadao Goto's magazine there were only 19 colleges playing the game, but today there are over 170 college teams, 500 high school teams and more than 50 clubs organized mainly by large Japanese manufacturing companies. The total number of players participating in football in Japan today is estimated at about 10 000.

The NCAA and the NFL have not been slow to realize the potential of football in the Orient. In 1975 the St Louis Cardinals and the San Diego Chargers played one of their pre-season games in Tokyo before a crowd of about 38 000. Every year since then top college teams have played an exhibition game in Japan which is known as either the Japan Bowl or the Mirage Bowl, and this particular game draws huge crowds of up to 70 000.

Most of the clubs in Japan are based around the industrial cities of Tokyo and Osaka, although teams have even been known to have started in some of the smaller islands off the southern mainland.

In 1984 it was decided to pit the best of the college teams against the best the works teams and, in what was unofficially described as Superbowl I, Tokyo's Nihon University beat Renown Rovers 50–30.

The Japanese have even tried to produce players who are good enough for the NFL.

The last player to have a trial for an NFL team was Kyoji Matsui, a place-kicker who attempted to break into the San Diego Chargers roster in 1981. However Matsui, an all-Japan league player, did not make the grade, and as yet the Japanese American Football Association has no representative in American professional football.

But the game is Japan is well established and has good sponsorship, and there is no real reason to doubt that sooner rather than later the game in America will acquire an oriental connection.

The Rest of the World

American football is one of the fastest growing sports in the world today. It is widely played throughout Europe and is already acquiring a firm stronghold in Australia and New Zealand.

After Germany and Italy, one of the predominant nations in Europe is without doubt Finland. Today there are over 30 teams in Finland, the top team being the Helsinki Roosters. Football began modestly in 1979 with several university teams competing in a national tournament. The game caught the imagination of the Finns and soon teams were sprouting up all over this sparsely-populated land. The East City Giants from Helsinki took on and beat the PUS Espoo club in the first championship that year, and by 1982 the SAJL (Suomen Amerikalaisen Jalkappallon Liitto) had organized itself into two divisions. The 1983 final was won for the first time by the Helsinki Roosters who beat PUS Espoo, a grammar school team from the town of Espoo, some 50 miles west of the capital, 28–17.

In 1984 the Finns travelled to Castel Giorgio in Italy for the first European Championships, and, after beating Austria 87–0, narrowly lost the final to the Italians by 18 to 6.

Despite their massive defeat in the 1984 Euro-championships, the Austrians, with a dozen or so established teams, are confident that football in the Tyrol is here to stay. As in many other European countries, their game first got off the ground in the late 1970s and early 1980s, when teams were formed in the major cities of Innsbruck, Stürm and Vienna whose Ramblers are one of the top teams.

Next door in Switzerland, the game is still in its infancy, although there are clubs in the southern cities of Lugano and Lausanne.

For many years Holland relied heavily on only one or two teams to maintain their interest in gridiron. For three years the Amsterdam Rams have played their football in the German Second division as have the Den Hague Raiders. Now that there are 10 teams in the Netherlands, there is a strong possibility that the first Dutch National League will be formed for the 1986 season.

Football in France has in recent years suffered a terrible difference of opinion. At the end of the 1984 season there were 17 teams, of which the Paris Blue Angels were the champions. But after heated arguments five teams decided to break away and form their own league. Lyon, St Etienne, Montpellier, Antibes and the Blue Angels had not been happy for a while about the state of French football, and the resulting break was only healed by the intervention of the French Minister of Sport himself. Fortunately the 1985 season began with little problem. France is one country that does not allow any American players in its teams.

Throughout Europe all countries play to the NCAA rules (as used by the colleges in the USA), and all are strictly amateur. The EFA (European Football Association) holds a European Championship of nations every two years. The first was held in Italy and was won by the host nation when they beat Finland 18–6, while Germany finished third and Austria fourth. The 1985 championships will be held in July of that year in Milan. The 1987 contests will be held in Finland and the 1989 finals are to be staged in Germany. During the even years between the EFA are planning a European Team cup for the respective winners of each member country's leagues, the first of which will be played in 1986.

Football is already taking a foothold in many other European countries: Norway, Sweden and Spain have applied for membership of the EFA and Portugal is expected to apply soon. Football in Europe, the soccer-mad capital of the world, is at last on the up.

CHAPTER EIGHT

Equipment

The sight of a 280lb lineman standing bare-foot in nothing but his athletic support is awesome. With his rippling muscles, thighs and biceps like tree trunks, he is the epitome of athletic prowess.

But, before entering the arena to participate in the day's gladiatorial battle, a player must first don some 18 pieces of protective equipment. This will add a further 15lbs or so to his weight, and will instantly turn him into a fearsome beast of enormous magnitude.

Some say that an American footballer is more protected than an astronaut, but, considering the very violent nature of his profession, every piece of equipment is necessary.

After donning a thick cotton T-shirt and a pair of elasticated ankle socks the player will undergo a process that is almost unique to American sports. Nearly all college and professional teams insist that their players' ankles are taped by the training staff. Taping, when done properly, can eliminate sprains and decrease the severity of other injuries, thus cutting down the period a player might be out of action.

It is said that up to 130 miles of tape are used every season by each NFL team. The NFL is rated as the world's largest consumer of elastic tape. Up to 10 yards of tape may be used just to wrap two ankles, these being parts of the body where the most work is done. Years ago players would first shave their legs so that the adhesive would not stick, but nowadays with the invention of various types of pre-wrapping this is not necessary. Each team will employ a squad of trainers specifically to do this job.

First a spray of undercoat is administered over the ankles to prevent them from itching and to make the post-game removal process easier. Then special heel and lace pads are fitted to the foot. A light rubbery 'pre-wrap' comes next followed by the tape itself.

Shoes are often taped to the foot as well, with the aim of further decreasing the likelihood of silly knocks and sprains. The taping of ankles and feet is done an hour or so before the kick-off. After the players have returned from their pre-game warm-up the trainers will then get to work on other parts of the body: hands, shoulders, elbows, etc. The amount of tape used on the arms and hands depends entirely on the player's position. An offensive lineman will tape just his thumbs. Guards and tackles will often tape their entire forearms forming a rigid battering ram. Centers, who need more flexibility because of the snap of the ball will tape their forearms, but not as rigidly as other linemen.

Quarterbacks use the least tape of all. Because of their position, they need more mobility and flexibility than anyone else, so they only tape their ankles and wrists.

A running back will tape his wrists and forearm to a point just below the elbow, as will wide receivers and defensive backs. This gives the latter a certain amount of stickiness, which is an obvious advantage in pass receiving. The use of a substance known as 'stickum' (a sticky adhesive in which a receiver's hands and arms could be smothered) has long since been banned.

Knee injuries account for c 25 per cent of all serious football knocks. Players with a history of knee injuries are specially adorned

127

with knee braces and supports. Special team players also have their own taping processes. Kickers are often taped in a manner that will lock the toes in an upright position, which helps to increase the height at which the football can be kicked and is especially used if the opposition employ a quick rushing blitz against the kick.

After the taping process the next piece of equipment to be placed upon the body is the pants. Made of nylon they are designed to be close-fitting and are made with special pockets so that foam thigh and knee pads can be inserted. It is now a mandatory requirement that players also wear a girdle under their pants which is fitted with foam cushioning hip and spine pads. Back in football's pioneering days when man-made fibres like nylon and plastic were unheard of, the players' equipment would be manu-factured from cotton and wool.

Taping, while used in some areas, was certainly not as common and thorough as it is today, so injuries happened more often and were invariably of a far more serious nature.

The players' pants were made originally from either cotton or thick wool. It was not until the 1920s that the Notre Dame head coach Knute Rockne designed a pair made from silk. These were cut very tight and less baggy-looking than the older designs. Shoulder pads, too, were made of more traditional materials, most commonly leather, which was often soaked and tough-ened in such a way as to become rock hard. The cumbersome padding built into the shoulder pads was made of horse hair, and such was their weight and awkwardness that players found it virtually impossible to throw long passes, or indeed even to catch them, so the game remained a mainly rushing affair.

After the Second World War came the invention of nylons and plastics. As with everything else, football changed much because of these new materials. Various

Did You Know

That moulded, impact-resistant shoulder pads replaced the last of the leather pads in the 1967 season.

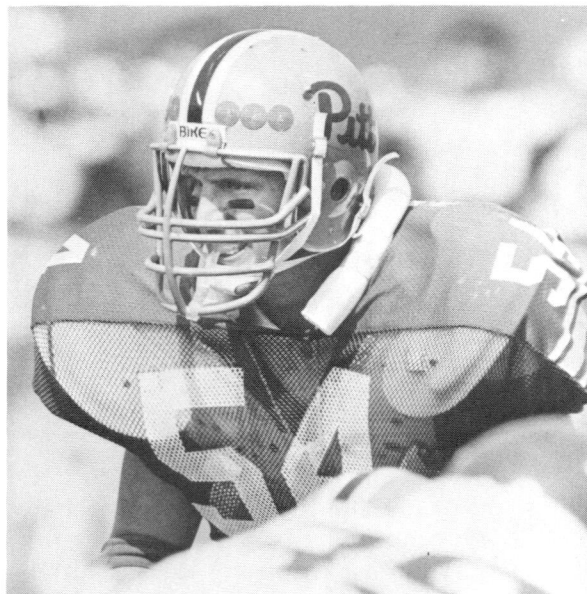

Pittsburgh University's Troy Benson, a modern day warrior ready for battle — warpaint and all! (University of Pittsburgh).

designs of shoulder pads were made to suit the needs of players in each position. Those of a quarterback would be slim to enable him to move his arms freely and effect the pass of the ball. Linemen on the other hand would wear enormous shoulder pads, with huge epaulettes over the shoulders and deltoids. The weight of a modern pair of shoulder pads varies, but the average pair weighs around 6 lbs. Nowadays they are made from nylon, plastics, rubber and other man-made fibres and afford the maximum protection to a player's upper body and shoulder area.

For injured players various pieces of equipment have been used over the years, but the best design dates from 1978 when Byron Donzis invented an inflatable flak jacket to protect the injured ribs of Houston quarterback Dan Pastorini. The Donzis jacket weighed only 7 ounces and soon other quarterbacks were copying it. The original design has since been further modified and very light-weight rib protectors that will enable even the most maimed and aching player to continue in the game are often used today. Attached to the main-frame of the shoulder pads are bicep pads, worn by some players, notably linemen, to protect the upper part of the arm, where so much of the hard hitting by the opposition line will be absorbed. Players who wish further to

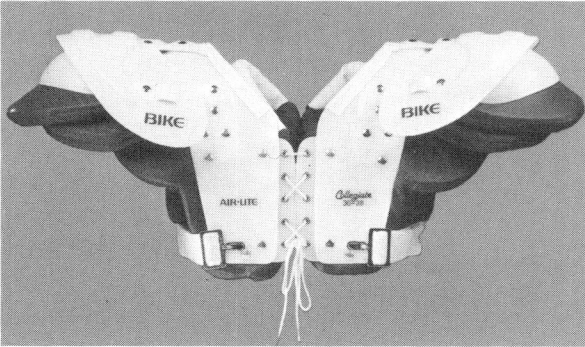

Shoulder pads.

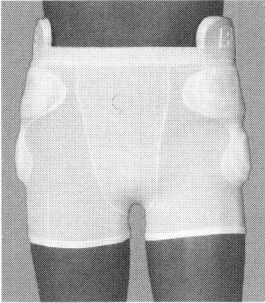

Girdle worn underneath pants.

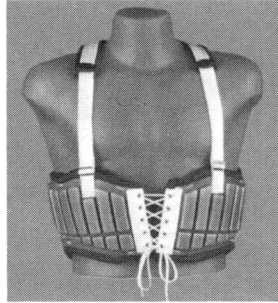

Rib protector.

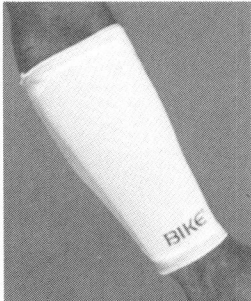

Arm and hand pads.

tification came in 1926 when the Duluth Eskimos wore jerseys with a black and white igloo on the front. Until the 1930s numbers were not to be seen. They were then first worn on the front of the jerseys only, but the difficulty of recognizing players from only one angle resulted in their being placed on the back as well. Players' names were not placed on their jerseys until the AFL and the NFL merged in the season of 1970.

A player's footwear was probably the first piece of standard equipment used when football became a dominant force at the turn of the century. Originally the first shoes used were modified baseball shoes. They were high-topped boots, whose metal heels and sole plates were removed because they were considered too dangerous for a contact sport. In the 1890s shoes were developed with permanent cleats or studs and by 1921 the interchangeable cone-shaped stud was in use. Shoes of the 1920s and 1930s were very like those worn by European soccer players, large, heavy 'pit-type' boots made of leather. Over the years, as in most other sports, these shoes have become slim-lined

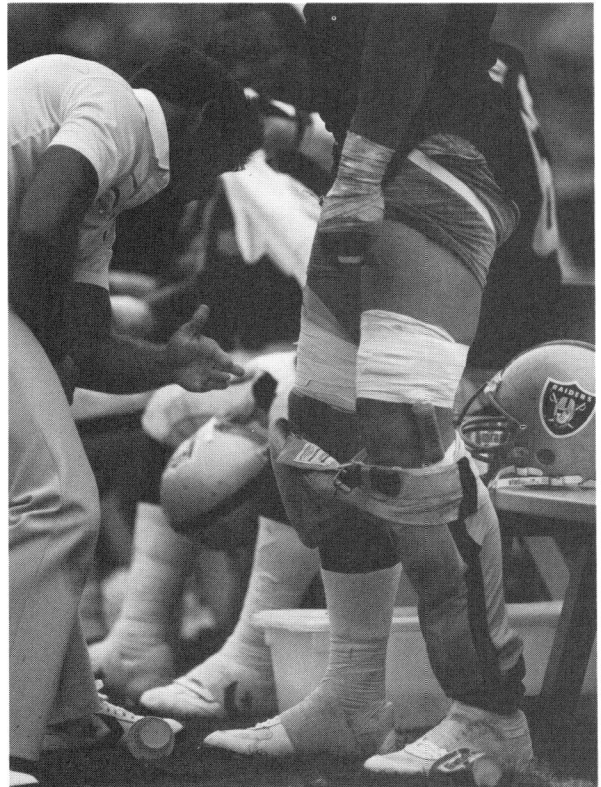

protect their necks (or those with a history of neck injuries) wear a neck roll, a soft piece of foam padding, which attaches quite easily to the top of the shoulder pad.

The player's jersey identifies him by his number, and is made from tough nylon with overstitched seams.

In the early days of football, however, jerseys were made from wool and carried none of the striped and numbered patterns seen today.

It was not until 1921 that the Green Bay club became the first team to wear a distinctive marking on their game tops. The Indian packing company which owned the team paid $500 to purchase jerseys with the words 'Acme Packers' boldly emblazoned on them.

The first uniform bearing a team's iden-

Injuries to players are treated as soon as possible, even on the sidelines. Note the knee brace. (All-Sport).

129

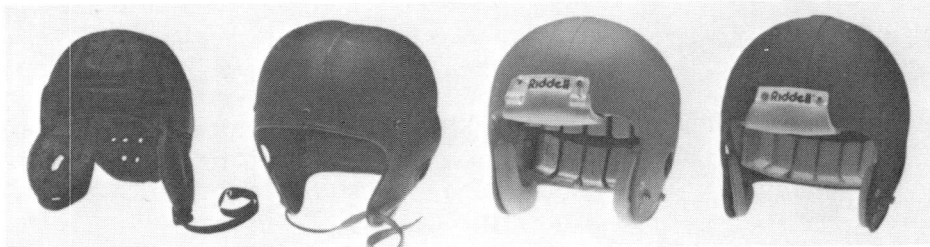

and are now almost 'slipper' like. Until the mid sixties the colour of a player's shoes was always black. In 1966 New York Jets' quarterback Joe Namath sported a dashing pair of white ones, and a new trend was born. Players were quick to follow Namath's lead and nowadays almost all footballers wear what has become the traditional white. However, Baltimore's Alvin Haymond, quick to see the publicity gained by the Jets' player with his white shoes, decided to go one better and wore green ones!

A professional player today can have as many as four or five different types of shoes in his locker. The traditional grass shoe has seven rubberized cleats (two in the heel and five in the front); whilst the artificial turf shoe can have as many as 100 cleats which are shorter, and smaller than for grass and give more grip on an unnatural surface. A shoe known as the Canadian Broomhall has become very popular in recent seasons. When stadiums switch from natural turf to a synthetic surface teams can have many problems, and the Broomhall with four rubber cleats on the heel and up to a dozen on the front can be a great help.

A running back may use a spiked shoe, similar to that of an athlete, which improves his grip when running at high speed. Kickers also need special shoes. Some use a square-toed shoe to help give the football a better flight-path. Many others, like high jumpers, for instance, will use one type of shoe for the non-kicking foot, to get a good grip and balance from a sound footing, and a different shoe often of another colour, for kicking.

Other useful pieces of equipment used by players are thermal underwear, shin guards, wrist and elbow braces, and of course socks, which were made a mandatory item in 1945.

To a non-American the most distinguishing piece of equipment is without doubt the helmet. Because of the ferocity of the sport the helmet is probably the most important item in a player's kit. However, the helmet of today with its air-powered cushioning is a far cry from that used some 50 years ago.

As late as 1937 helmets were little more than flimsy pieces of leather, much like those used by Second World War fighter pilots. Many players found them distasteful, preferring to use a bushy head of hair as protection. It was felt by most that the use of a helmet was a slur on a player's manhood. Broken noses and disfigured faces were seen as noble battle scars with which to woo girlfriends. One famous battle-scarred face is that of actor Charlton Heston, who broke his nose twice whilst playing football at college.

After the war players were required to wear headgear and, as with other pieces of equipment, helmets became more sophisticated.

The John T. Riddell Company which had manufactured pilots' helmets during the war years developed a plastic shell that became standard equipment in the league. It was initially rather weird in shape, but after more than a decade's development the modern style teardrop shaped helmet evolved. Face guards and cages, like helmets were first shunned by the players. These too were considered a slight to a player's masculinity. The Cleveland Browns' coach Paul Brown introduced the first cages in the early 1950s. Face guards had been around in various primitive forms as early as the 1930s, but as players suffered more and more facial

Did You Know

That the New York Titans, of the old AFL, were the last team to use leather helmets in 1960.

Cleveland coach Paul Brown introduced the first cages for helmets in 1950.

injuries varying types of guards and cages were used. One and two bar masks became standard issue for backs and receivers whilst the linemen began wearing a multiple crossed bar version known as the birdcage. Nowadays there are about eight or nine different types of guard, which can be screwed to the helmet itself.

All clubs playing professional football today, with the exception of the Cleveland Browns, have their own distinctive logo emblazoned on the sides of the helmet. The tradition originated in 1948, when Fred Gehrke, the Los Angeles Rams' running back, took his helmet home and painted two yellow rams horns on it.

In later years Gehrke used to say that he had been scared of getting the sack when he took his helmet into the club. But much to his amazement the management like his design, and soon all the Los Angeles Rams' helmets were laid out in Gehrke's garage being similarly decorated.

It was not long before the rest of the football world took up the idea and now, of course, every team except for Cleveland have their own logo painted on their headgear. Attempts to put bull-eyes on helmets have foundered, however, as the NFL regards them as too obvious a target, and therefore potentially dangerous. The helmet of today is a far cry from that used during the Gehrke era. What we now see is a highly sophisticated piece of equipment. The modern helmet weighs about 3lbs and is made up of polycarbonate vinyl-foam, styrene and leather with an ingenious interior. Until recently helmets were fitted with a honeycomb of pockets filled with liquid to fit a certain head size, but most of today's players wear helmets with air-filled pockets which are inflated to their full when placed on a player's head. Because all players' heads are of differing sizes this development has been extremely useful.

Twenty years ago when O. J. Simpson began playing college football these air-powered toppers had not even been invented. As Simpson's head was the oddest of shapes, when he joined the Buffalo Bills in 1969 he put the Bills' equipment manager into something of a spin. He told the Bills that he was unable to wear the conventional suspension types of helmet because of his unusually elongated face. A quick phone call was put through to his old college, U.S.C. in Los Angles and his hydraulic helmet was flown to Buffalo for him to use until a new one could be made.

A football helmet is not designed for use as a weapon. Each helmet bears the words: *WARNING—Do not use this helmet to butt, ram, or spear an opposing player. This is in violation of football rules and can cause paralysis or death.*

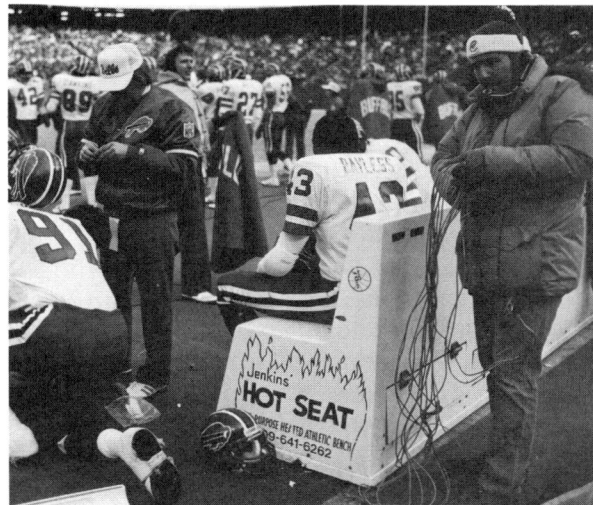

A 'hot-seat' bench warmer sited in New York's Giants Stadium during the Jets-Bills fixture on a cold day in the big apple. (All-Sport).

A football helmet is worn as a protective measure, and the amount of battering it has to endure whilst protecting a player's cranium throughout a season is truly phenomenal. In 1962 a University professor sent Detroit linebacker Joe Schmidt out to play in the Pro Bowl with a specially wired up helmet designed to measure the amount of stress the player was subjected to during a game. The test revealed some staggering facts. During the game Schmidt's helmet had had to withstand blows many times the force of gravity. To put this into perspective, an astronaut at blast-off is only subjected to 6Gs, and a fighter pilot, faced with a force of 20Gs will often black out.

Other pieces of equipment used in conjunction with the helmet are mouth-guards and chin-straps. Mouth-guards were originally modelled on those used by boxers, but at most clubs today a wax impression of a player's mouth is taken and a perfectly fitting guard is made for him. Quarterbacks usually dislike wearing mouth-guards because they cause speech problems when a player is trying to call plays, but as most have found to their cost it is better to put up with this than to lose three or four teeth.

The chin-strap usually has a four-point hook up and keeps the helmet firmly in place on the player's head. It is illegal for a player to go on to the field of play without having his chin-strap hooked up, and the penalty for doing so is the loss of a time-out, which, in an extremely tight game could be very costly indeed.

Odds and Ends

There are various bits and pieces that players can and sometimes cannot use. The National Football League requires all teams to have oxygen equipment and instant x-ray sets available within the confines of their stadiums. Oxygen is normally placed on the sidelines and often a TV viewer can see a player with the mask placed firmly over his face regaining some lost air after a long run.

During the winter months, and especially in the cold northern states, many teams wear women's tights for warmth. The Minnesota Vikings had theirs specially tested by a party of Everest mountaineers. Other little warming devices commonly in use are chemical bag hand warmers; battery-powered heaters which are taken onto the field during time-outs to warm up frozen fingers; electric blankets installed under the benches on the sidelines to keep feet warm; and pouch pockets, which are specially sewn-in pockets on game uniforms to enable the quarterbacks and also the receivers to keep their hands warm during play.

On rainy days ladies' hair spray can be seen on the sidelines for this is a good water repellant and can be used on shoes to keep players' feet dry. The St Louis Cardinals have a special ball dryer, a heated drum which keeps up to seven balls dry on wet days.

On days of sweltering hot weather, many teams use air-conditioning units on the sidelines to keep players cool. The first team to use such a device was the University of Southern California in 1977 whilst playing a game in steamy Alabama.

The Cost

The cost of kitting out an entire squad of 50 or so players and their coaches is colossal. Including such odds and ends as belts, shoe-laces, practice pants and jerseys, sideline jackets, a bill for a professional team can be as high as $250 000. A major college team can expect to pay almost as much, whilst the newer developing teams in Europe do not have such a high price to pay. They still have to conform to standards governing the quality of their equipment, but they do without many of the extras used by the American professional teams. A typical British team would be faced with a bill in the region of £20 000 per annum.

The Name Game

Like any sport, football has its fair share of oddly-named characters. One of the funniest named players ever must be former pro quarterback Yelberton Abraham Tittle. Other names from the past that stick in one's mind are Buzz Nutter, Elmer Bighead, Fair Hooker, Vitamin T. Smith and T. Truxton Hare.

Not to be outdone by the old timers modern players also have an assortment of amusing names. The USFL's Orlando Renegades offensive tackle Chuck Slaughter must have one of football's most apt surnames, whilst the Renegades, whose home is arguably the 'playground of America' (with Disneyland and the futuristic Epcot centre on its doorstep), are owned by a certain Donald R. Dizney!

In terms of family networks the Zendejas boys must rate highly. Tony Zendejas is the place-kicker for Los Angeles Express, cousin Luis is currently kicking for Arizona Outlaws after a record-breaking career at Arizona State University; Luis's brother Max is the current kicker for the nearby University of Arizona; another brother, Joaquin, is the place-kicker for the NFL's New England Patriots, and Martin Zendejas, brother of Tony and cousin of Luis, Max and Joaquin is the kicker for the University of Nevada at Reno.

Another kicker with a claim to fame is Obed Chuckwuma Ariri. Ariri was on Tampa Bay Buccaneers' books in 1984, and must have the most apt name of all-time for a kicker. His middle name of Chuckwuma translated literally from his native Nigerian tongue means, 'God Only Knows!'

CHAPTER NINE

A Basic Guide To The Rules

American football has been described as scrappy, competitive, physical, pragmatic, yet in its own unique way it is very much like a game of chess played with human beings.

Often referred to as the 'gridiron', the 100 yards by 53 yards 1 foot playing area is further divided by chalk stripes marked horizontally across the field at 5-yard intervals. At either end are the end-zones or scoring areas which are a further 10 yards deep.

At the back of the end-zones are the goal-posts, one upright with a crossbar 18 feet wide, 10 feet above the ground. At either end of the cross-bar are two uprights extending some 30 feet into the air. Rugby type goal-posts are still used in college football and here in the UK, but the new Y-shaped posts were adopted by the NFL in 1967.

Marked on the pitch itself are broken lines known as hashmarkings. These are placed 70 feet inside the sidelines and show the central playing area where all plays begin from. No matter where the play stops, the ball will always be re-sited within these lines.

The object of the game is to advance the ball by a series of plays, or 'downs' as they are called, into the opposition's end-zone for which one is awarded a touchdown worth six points.

The team in possession of the ball will have four attempts or downs to advance the ball a minimum of 10 yards. After each attempt the game will stop, the officials will measure the distance gained or lost, and spot the football parallel to the yardage advanced.

The two teams will go into a group, or 'huddle' as it is known in football, and the next play will be planned.

With this information we can see that the phrase 'second and seven' means the team has moved three yards forward and is making its second attempt with seven yards to go.

'Third and long' or 'third and short' mean exactly what it sounds like—the former means that the yardage needed to gain a first down is more that 10 yards, and the latter means that there is under 3 yards to go to reach the required distance and get another first down, and four more attempts.

If the attacking team, known in American football as the offense, reaches the 10 yards mark within the four downs allowed to them, they will then be allotted another four downs to advance further. If they fail, the opposition gains possession of the ball and attempts to do the same thing towards the other end-zone.

Unlike soccer, where both the offense and defense are on the field at all times, American football has 11 men on the field to attack, and another 11 to defend, and a further squad of specialist players who are interchanged at various times throughout the game as tactics are altered either to gain or to stop the progress of the ball.

If a team's offensive unit loses possession they will leave the field and be replaced by their defensive team. Similarly a team gaining possession of the football on defense will swap their defensive unit for their offensive team.

A 'touchdown' does *not* have to be touched down in the end-zone. As long as any part of the ball-carrier's body breaks the

First Down. L.A. Rams v. Detroit Lions. (All-Sport).

plane of the goal line six points will be awarded. The forward pass is legal so a player can position himself actually in the end-zone and receive a pass to score a 'TD' as the American commentators call it.

When a touchdown has been scored the offensive team will have a chance to score another point by kicking the ball between the uprights of the goal posts. In college football the team will also have the chance to score two points if they can return the football by rushing or passing back into the end-zone. This two-point rule also applies in the USFL and the British game.

Apart from the touchdown and the extra points that can be derived from it, there are two other ways that points can be scored. A field goal, which is similar to a penalty kick in rugby, can be attempted at any time by the offensive team. A specialist kicker will come on to the field and if he can kick the ball between the uprights three points will be awarded. The other score is called a safety. If a player is caught inside his own end-zone by a player from the opposing team, and brought to the ground, two points will be awarded to the opposition.

The playing time in American football is divided into four quarters of 15 minutes.

Unlike soccer, however, when the ball is not in play the clock is stopped. This is the reason why a game can last anything up to three hours.

As in basketball each team is permitted six time-outs (three per half). After the first and third quarters the teams will immediately change ends, and only at half-time do they leave the field for a break.

The continual changing of ends is designed to give neither team any distinct advantage from any adverse weather conditions.

In cases where the score is level at full time, a 15-minute period of overtime is played and the first team to score is declared the winner. In regular season games in the NFL a tie or draw is declared if after this extra time the scores are still level. In the championship games at the end of the season further periods of extra time are played until a winner is found.

The offense or attacking team consists of five linemen: the center, who passes the ball between his legs to the quarterback; two guards either side of the center; and on either side of the guards, two tackles. This is the engine room of the team, pushing and blocking to protect their quarterback from marauding defensive players, or creating openings for running backs to run through.

Also on the offensive line is a tight end, whose position is close to the other linemen at the end of the line of scrimmage, and a split end, who, as his name suggests, is split further out.

Behind the offensive line are four backs. They can be positioned in many ways, the most favoured one in today's game being the 'pro-set'. The no. 1 back is the quarterback, who is the most important player on the field, for it is his job to set up a play that will gain yards. By passing the ball to a

Did You Know

That Houston Gamblers quarterback Jim Kelly was voted the USFL's most valuable player of the year in 1984, after he had thrown 44 touchdown passes and his 5219 yards had taken the Gamblers to the Central Division title.

powerful running back or throwing a long pass to a receiver he will orchestrate the attack of the team.

Depending on the play there will be a variety of formations used by the running backs. Fullbacks, tailbacks, flankerbacks and receivers make up the backfield along with the field general, the quarterback. On one play the quarterback may use two running backs and one wide receiver, in another only one running back and two wide receivers who will sprint down the field expecting to receive a pass.

The specialist men such as the kickers and the punters will be positioned on the sidelines awaiting their chance of glory. They will only come on to the field if required. A punter will be brought into the game if after three attempts a team has not made their required ten yards, and still has a long way to go. Instead of simply giving the ball to the opposition at that spot, the punter will kick the ball as far away from his own goals as possible, thus giving the opposition that much more ground to cover when their offensive drive begins.

On the defensive unit the first line of defense is made up of the linemen. The defensive tackles and defensive ends form the front line troops. The number of these players on a team can vary. Some teams will employ a four-man front with two tackles and two ends, whilst others might use only three men: two tackles flanking a nose-tackle.

The number of interior linemen also depends on how many linebackers are used. If four linemen are used, then only three linebackers will be employed. But if three linemen are positioned then four linebackers, two inside linebackers and two outside linebackers, will be in the formation. The linebackers are the roughest and toughest of all players; it is said to be a bad idea to allow your daughter to be dated by a linebacker! They are strong, fleet-footed players, whose main job is to stop the rush; they have to be mobile, agile and very, very hostile. It is usually the task of one of the middle linebackers to be the defensive team captain. He will be able to tell in an instant what the offense is doing and direct his troops to the danger zones.

Behind the linebackers, the last line of defense is made up of the cornerbacks and safeties, often called the secondary or umbrella. The secondary consists normally of four men: a strong safety, a free safety and two cornerbacks. The strong safety will line up on the opposition's tight end and will attempt to tackle him should he receive a pass. If the ball goes elsewhere then the strong safety will act as a back-up to the other defensive players. The free safety, who is often called a rover, acts as a sweeper and

A huddle. (All-Sport).

will move to wherever the action is. The job of the two cornerbacks is to mark the wide receivers. They will try to intercept the ball and create a 'turnover'; or, if the intended receiver completes the pass, to halt his path towards the end-zone immediately.

Each player's number denotes the position he plays, for only the tight ends, split ends, wide receivers, quarterbacks and running-backs can receive a pass, in the right conditions. The only time one of the giant linemen can legally carry the ball is if the ball has been dropped by the opposition, and then the term 'fumble' is used. The substitution of players is allowed at any time, when the ball is not in play, and teams will have at least three players for every

Did You Know

That Arizona State and Florida State combined in the 1971 Fiesta Bowl to amass the highest modern Bowl score. A total of 83 points were scored as the Sun Devils beat the Seminoles 45–38.

New Orleans quarterback Richard Todd executes the perfect hand-off to Saints running back George Rogers. (All-Sport).

position on the bench ready to go into action should a tactical change be necessary. Only 11 players are allowed on the field at any one time, but clubs are allowed to have a maximum of 45 kitted players ready on the sideline.

The main rule as the players prepare to make the play is that, once in the down position on the line of scrimmage, offensive linemen are not allowed to move until the ball has been passed from the center to the quarterback. As soon as the center moves the football, all sorts of things happen as linemen on both sides of the field hit each other with ferocious speed, each trying to outdo the other.

Although the offensive players cannot move once they are in a 'set' position, defensive players are allowed to move around, provided that they do not cross the line of scrimmage. The defense will try and make the offense jittery and cause them to move too soon, thus giving away a penalty.

The offensive players will block, using their forearms, and can only use their hands when forming a pocket to protect the quarterback while he is attempting to pass the ball. Then they cannot grab at an opponent, they will just use their hands to fend off

attacking defenders as they retreat into their pocket.

The defense on the other hand can make greater use of their forearms and hands. They can use their hands in an attempt to get past offensive linemen, pulling or pushing them out of their path. For this reason, it is often said that defense come naturally, whilst the finer points of offense have to be taught.

At various times during a game, a foul may be called by one of the seven officials on the field. If a foul is spotted, a yellow weighted duster will be thrown to the ground. As soon as the play comes to an end, the officials will meet and decide if the foul call should stand, or if an advantage has been gained already by the team against whom the foul was committed. A small discussion will take place between the referee (distinguishable in the NFL by a black hat) and his other officials (in white headgear), and a ruling will be made. The captains of the teams will then be called forward and they will be told the options that are open to them. Sometimes there can be many options open to a captain, but it is a general rule that a referee will give the best option first.

The penalties for fouls are either the loss of yards, which the referee will mark by moving the ball forward or backwards to the new starting spot, or the loss of a down. Thus a penalty committed on a first down might result in the play having to begin again as a second down from exactly the same position. Sometimes, as a penalty for serious fouls, a loss of yards and the loss of a down will be imposed together.

American Football is a territorial game played with finely-tuned athletic bodies. It is without doubt one of the toughest games in the world, where players literally go through the pain barrier to ensure victory. The players' protective padding is often inadequate when two 20 stone 6ft 6in Goliaths collide at breakneck speed. However, despite what is sometimes said, gridiron is one of the most strictly-controlled games in existence, as a result of rules that have evolved over a century of play. In recent years they have been modified to increase the excitement of the spectator, thus keeping the fans on the edge of their seats for the entire game.

Did You Know
That the Oakland Invaders led the USFL in fumbles in 1983 with 51.

Common Offensive Formations

1 Pro-set

Line of scrimmage

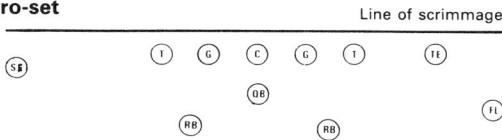

2 I-Formation

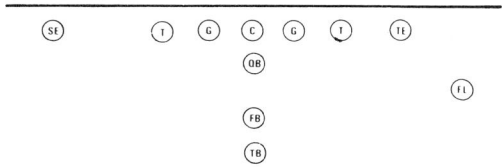

3 T-Formation

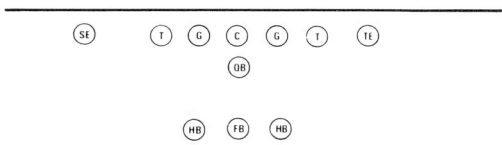

4 Shotgun Formation

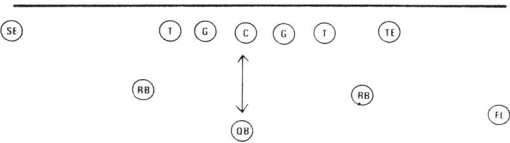

5 Short yardage formation (Used when only one or two yards are needed to gain a touchdown or a first down)

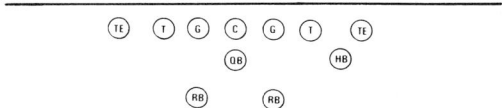

Note: Two tight ends used and no split end.

6 One Back Formation

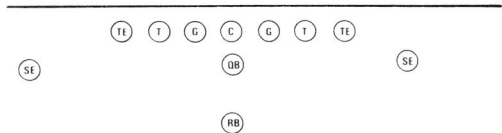

Note: Two tight ends and split ends used giving four possible receivers in a pass-orientated offense.

7 Man-in-motion

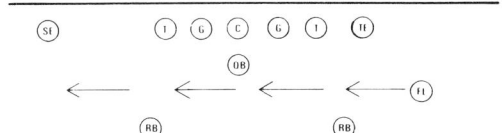

Note: The offensive unit may change formation at the line of scrimmage. The flanker can run laterally but cannot turn upfield until after the snap of the football.

The Pitch

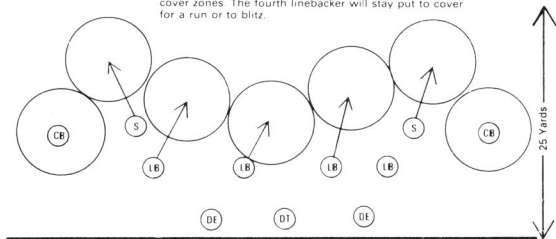

Common Defensive Formations

1 3–4 Defense

Line of scrimmage

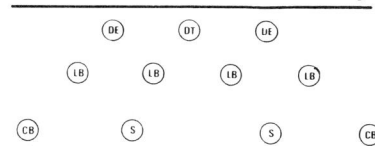

Key to Abbreviations

Offense
C – Center
G – Guard
T – Tackle
TE – Tight End
SE – Split End
QB – Quarterback
FL – Flankerback
FB – Fullback
TB – Tailback
HB – Halfback

Defense
DT – Defensive tackle
DE – Defensive End
LB – Linebacker
S – Safety
FS – Free Safety
CB – Cornerback

2 4–3 Defense

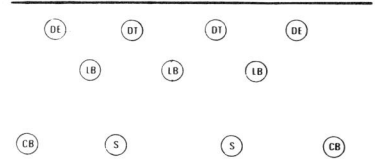

3 7–1 Defense used in short yardage defense

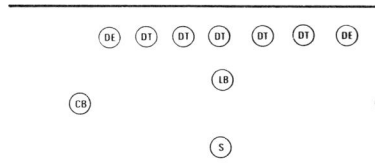

The use of a free safety

This man is positioned just outside and behind the defensive end, and may drop back in anticipation of a pass as illustrated:

Zone Defense

The cornerbacks cover the areas they are in at the snap of the ball. The wide receivers are likely to run into these zones or the zones covered by the safeties further upfield. On a 3–4 defense three linebackers will drop back to cover zones. The fourth linebacker will stay put to cover for a run or to blitz.

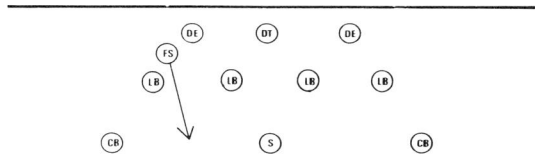

Official Signals

Time Out

Touchdown, Field Goal, or Successful Try

Personal Foul

Illegal Use of Hands

Illegal Contact

Delay of Game

Crawling, Interlocking, Interference, Pushing, or Helping Runner

Holding

Illegal Motion at Snap

First Down

Interference With Forward Pass or Fair Catch

Penalty Refused, Incomplete Pass, Play Over, or Missed Field Goal

137

CHAPTER TEN

Glossary

Audible The name of the signals called by the quarterback at the line of scrimmage which designates the play his team will use on offense.

Backfield The area behind the offense's line of scrimmage in which the quarterback and the running backs stand.

Blindside As its name suggests, a tackle on the quarterback from behind as he is attempting to pass the ball.

Blitz A defensive play in which the linebackers and safeties rush the offensive line in order to tackle the quarterback on a passing play. (If the quarterback can evade the blitz large open areas in the defense could be available for the quarterback to pass into).

Blocking Deliberately and legally obstructing an opponent who is not in possession of the ball. Blocking and tackling are quite distinct: a tackle can only be used on a player carrying the ball, whereas blocking is used by all players to stop an opponent from getting to the ball-carrier. Blocking is mostly done by offensive linemen, and their use of hands and arms is strictly governed by the rules of the game. A blocker is not allowed to use his hands to grab or hold a player. He is not allowed to wrap his arms around a player or trip him, and the block must be made from in front of the player.

Bomb A long downfield pass by the quarterback.

Bootleg Where the quarterback fakes a hand-off to a running back, and then runs the ball around the line of scrimmage and upfield himself.

Bump and Run Where a defensive back, whose job it is to guard against the pass, bumps the receiver as he comes off the line of scrimmage. To be legal, this action must take place within five yards of the line of scrimmage. If this happens beyond the scrimmage line a five-yard penalty will be called.

Chain Crew The officials who stand on the sidelines and measure the yardage gained or lost by the offensive team. They operate a ten-yard chain, between two brightly coloured poles, and if there is any doubt as to the amount of ground gained they will be called on to the field to measure it.

Chuck A quick push by a defensive player in the back of a player awaiting a pass. This is a very dangerous ploy, and can often result in a pass interference call which carries very severe penalties.

Clipping An illegal block involving the blocking of a player from either behind or below the waist.

Completion As it sounds, a successfully-caught pass.

Coverage Used to describe how a defensive player is marking a potentially dangerous offensive receiver. Also used in the terms double coverage (where two men cover one player); triple coverage (using three defenders); man-to-man coverage (where a defender will follow an offensive player wherever he goes); or zone coverage (where a defender will have a specific zone of the field to cover).

Cross Block Two offensive linemen swap their blocking assignments. One will block the other's opponent and vice versa. This is also known as a scissors block.

Cut A change of direction used by a ball-carrier when running at high speed.

Dead Ball A ball which is out of play. A ball becomes dead when it crosses the sidelines, when the clock is stopped or when the referee signals a dead ball.

Defense The team not in possession of the ball.

Defensive Backs These are the cornerbacks and safeties who play on the defensive unit.

Delay of Game When a play is not initiated by the quarterback within the allowed 30 seconds between the stop of one play and the start of another.

Direct Snap As well as a normal snap of the ball by a center to a quarterback, a direct snap or long snap is a ball played back by the center some seven yards to either a quarterback (as used in the Shotgun offense), or to a punter or kicker attempting an extra point or field goal.

Dogging A different name used for describing a blitz.

Double Teaming When two offensive players block out one defensive player.

Down An attempt by the offensive team to gain ten yards. A team is allowed four downs in which

Northampton Stormbringers' quarterback Bill Green shouts his 'audibles' in a game against Croydon Coyotes. (Northampton Stormbringers).

to advance the ball the required ten yards. In Canadian football a team gets three downs to get ten yards.

Draw Play The quarterback will drop back, as if to pass, and will then hand the ball to a running back who will run through the gap that the advancing defensive linemen have left open. This play is often used to foil a blitz.

Dropback The movement of a quarterback as he drops back into the backfield to pass. It can also be used to describe the backward movement of a linebacker as he covers a pass.

Encroachment Firing off the line of scrimmage and making contact with an opposing player before the ball has been snapped to the quarterback.

End Around A basic running play in which either the tight end or the wide receivers become rushers, running with the ball around the end of the line of scrimmage before heading upfield.

End Line The line at the back of the end-zone which, like the sidelines, indicates where a ball becomes dead.

End Zone The areas at each end of the playing field, measuring ten yards deep into which the ball has to travel for a touchdown to be awarded.

Extra Point After a touchdown has been scored, a team will have the chance to score an extra point by kicking the ball between the posts and over the bar of the goals. In college football as well as the extra kick for one point, teams have the chance to run or pass the ball back into the end-zone for two extra points.

Fair Catch When receiving a kick, the intended receiver may signal that he wishes to catch the

ball without defensive interference by holding up one arm prior to catching the ball. Upon taking the catch cleanly the player is not allowed to advance upfield with the ball. His team's offensive drive will begin from the point where the ball was caught.

Fake A quarterback will pretend to do something to confuse the defense. He might pretend to pass when in fact he will hand off the ball to a running back.

Field Goal A three point score, used by the offense. A kicker will come on to the field and attempt to kick the ball between the posts and over the bar of the goals. This can be attempted from anywhere on the field, although it is normally tried from within 35 yards of the opposition's posts.

Flag on Play When an official throws down a yellow weighted handkerchief during a play to indicate an infringement. When the play is over the officials will meet to decide whether to allow the play or to penalize the offending team.

Flanker A wide receiver who stands on the same side of the line of scrimmage as the tight end. He must stand at least one yard behind the line of scrimmage.

Flare Pass a short backfield pass thrown by the quarterback to a running back.

Flex Defense Shortened version of expression 'flexible defense'. Two defensive linemen will stand just a yard or two off the line of scrimmage. When the play offensive begins they will stand still for a couple of seconds to read the play before making their move.

The L.A. Raiders' defenders *blitz* the Kansas City quarterback. (All-Sport).

Flood To put a lot of receivers into an area of the field so that they outnumber the defenders.

Fly Pattern A pattern to which a wide receiver will run. He will take a direct route down-field without cutting in-field. Sometimes also referred to as a 'go' pattern.

Formation The positions taken up by both offensive and defensive players at the beginning of a play.

Four Three Defense A formation which employs

four linemen on the line of scrimmage and three linebackers. The four three and the opposite version, three four, are the most commonly used defensive formations in football today.

Fumble When a ball-carrier drops the ball while it is still in play. The ball can then be legally recovered by either side who will then have possession. This is one of the few times a lineman can handle the football.

Gadget Play Seen more often in college football, a gadget play is quite simply a trick play.

Game Plan Before each game, a coach will devise a strategy to use on each and every play. He will have plays designed for any eventuality.

Gap The space between two offensive linemen.

Goal Line The line separating the end-zone from the field of play. In order to score a touchdown the ball-carrier must touch or cross this line.

Hang-time The time that a punted ball is in the air.

Hashmarks The lines on the field marking the central strip of playing area and marking every yard of the field. After a play has finished the ball is always repositioned within these lines.

Hike Another word for snap. The action of passing the ball backwards between the center's legs to the quarterback.

Hole A space opened up by offensive linemen for a runner to run through. The holes are very small and will only stay open for a few seconds.

Huddle Both the defensive and the offensive players hold a meeting between plays to plan strategy for the next play.

I-Formation An offensive formation where two running backs stand in line behind the quarterback before the snap of the ball. It is so-called because on paper the formation resembles an I.

Incompletion A pass that is neither caught nor intercepted. It just drops to the ground and the play returns to the last spot.

Ineligible Receiver In a passing play a player not allowed to act as a receiver, (a lineman for instance). A lineman is not permitted to travel down field from the line of scrimmage until the ball has been thrown. If he does he is an ineligible receiver. On a punting play only the two players on the ends of the offensive line may move beyond the line of scrimmage between the ball being snapped and the punt being effected. All other players who move down field will be ineligible receivers.

In Motion On the offensive line, one eligible pass receiver (i.e. a wide receiver, running back or tight ends) may be in motion between the time the ball is spotted and when it is snapped during the start count of the quarterback. The quarterback will call a sequence of numbers or colours or a mixture of both; this is the start count. The man-in-motion may run behind or parallel to the line of scrimmage but never in front. He can only turn up-field when the ball has been snapped. If he does move before then a penalty for illegal motion is given.

Interception When a defensive player catches the offensive pass. By doing so he immediately becomes an offensive player and will try and run as far up field as possible.

Intentional Grounding A pass deliberately thrown to the ground by the quarterback trying to avoid being tackled in possession of the ball for a loss of yards.

Interior Linemen The five players, a center, two tackles and two guards, who form the interior of the offensive line.

Keeper An offensive play in which the quarterback keeps the ball and advances with it.

Key Hints given by the defense or offense that can be read by their opponents.

Knuckle Ball A forward pass where the ball rolls end over end instead of spinning. It is an expression used by commentators to describe the flight of the football.

Lateral A pass which travels to the side or behind the line of scrimmage. A rugby pass would be described as a lateral pass.

Lead Block Where a running back without the ball will run in front of the ball-carrier and block a path for the ball-carrier to run in.

Line Play Call Signals given to offensive linemen to alert them to their individual blocking assignments.

Lineman Any player on the offense or the defense who stands on the line of scrimmage.

Line of Scrimmage The imaginary line across the field where the last play ended and where the next will begin. It is at this line that the two teams of linemen will line up facing each other and wait for another play to begin.

Man-to-Man A defensive play where each linebacker and defensive secondary (cornerbacks and safeties) will mark one potential pass receiver wherever he goes.

Measuring Chain The 10-yard chain used to measure whether a play has made the necessary 10 yards or not.

Midfield Stripe The 50-yard line.

Muff Where a player touches a free ball (i.e. after a fumble) but then loses possession of it.

Neutral Zone The space between the ball and the offensive and defensive linemen at the line of scrimmage.

Nickel Defense A defensive formation using five defensive backs which takes its name from the US five cents piece known as a nickel.

Offense The team in possession of the ball.

Offensive Holding The illegal use of hands by an offensive player who grabs or holds an opponent.

Offside A lineman on either the offense or the defense is offside if he is beyond the line of scrimmage when the ball is snapped.

Onside Kick A short kick-off, as opposed to the more common long kick, which carries the ball the minimum required 10 yards and gives the kicking team a good chance of recovering possession of the ball.

Overtime In a regular season game in the NFL, if the scores are tied at the end of normal time a 15-minute period of overtime is played. The first team to score within this period is the winner. If, however, there is still a tie, then a tied (drawn) game will be declared.

In the post season championship games, if there is still a tie after one period of overtime, then a further period will be played until one team scores. Further periods will be played until a winner is decided.

Pass Interference No player, offensive or defensive, may unfairly prevent an opponent from catching the ball by deliberately charging into him.

Pass Rush A drive forward by defensive linemen to prevent the pass by the quarterback. It is usually coupled with an attempted sack, or at least an attempt to place the quarterback under so much pressure that he miscues his pass.

Penalty Like most sports, a penalty is the price paid for an infringement of the rules of the game, in this instance, a loss of yardage or the loss of a down or both.

Penalty Marker The yellow flag thrown to the ground by an official if he spots an infringement of the rules.

Personal Foul A personal foul is a foul of a serious nature committed with intent. It may involve striking, kicking or kneeing an opponent; grasping the face mask of an opponent; roughing the kicker, roughing the runner or clipping an opponent.

Piling On Adding the weight of other players to a tackle once a player is clearly downed.

Pinch A charge in-field by defensive linesmen. The opposite would be a fan, where the lineman goes toward the sideline.

Pitchout Where the quarterback tosses the ball under-arm to a running back as an alternative to handing it to him.

Plane of the Goal The imaginary vertical plane that must be broken if a touchdown is to be awarded.

Play Action A quarterback will fake a hand-off to a running-back, and then pass.

Pocket The protected area from where the quarterback delivers his pass. The pocket is formed by linemen and sometimes runningbacks.

Post Pattern A route taken by a wide receiver who runs down-field then cuts in-field towards the goal posts to receive his pass.

Power Sweep A rushing play in which the running back will take the ball around the end of the line of scrimmage, protected by offensive linemen running in front of him and blocking a path.

Preventive Defense A defensive formation where extra defensive backs are put into the backfield to guard against a pass attack.

Pull Linked with the power sweep. The guard will pull away from his usual position to block a path for a ball-carrier.

Punt A kick taken from the kicker's hands, similar to a goalkeeper's kick in soccer. Usually employed when a team is on their fourth down and cannot make the 10 yards necessary for another first down. By giving up possession, the team will attempt to punt the ball as far away from their own goal as possible, thus giving the opposition that much more work to do.

Punt Return The distance that the player who catches the punt moves back up-field with the ball.

Quarter A 15-minute period of play. In a game there are four quarters, with a halftime break after two. In high school the quarters are of 12 minutes duration.

Quarterback Sneak A short yardage play in which the quarterback keeps the ball and attempts to rush through the line of scrimmage on his own.

Quick Count A play where an abbreviated signal call is used in an attempt to catch the defense off their guard.

Reverse A trick play basically, where the quarterback will hand-off to a running back moving laterally in one direction, who in turn will hand-off to another back moving in the opposite direction. A good play for dragging the defense all one way, before charging up field in the opposite direction.

Rollout A move the quarterback uses after dropping back to pass. He will make a lateral run across the backfield looking for an open receiver to whom he can deliver his pass.

Roughing the Kicker Deliberate contact with a kicker *after* he has kicked the ball.

Roughing the Passer Deliberate contact with a passer *after* he has thrown the ball.

Rushing Play Any play that involves running with the ball after a hand-off, pitch-out or lateral pass.

Sack When a quarterback in possession of the ball is tackled in his own backfield.

Safety This occurs when the player in possession of the ball runs into his own end-zone and is caught by a member of the opposition. If he is tackled or grounded a 'safety' worth two points is awarded to the opposition.

Screen Pass A delayed pass in which a hand-off to a running-back is first faked, then a pass is made to another player behind the line of scrimmage. Most teams use this to avoid a blitz, although it can be very dangerous.

Secondary The defensive backfield consisting of cornerbacks and safeties whose job it is to prevent the pass.

Shift The movement of offensive players before the snap of the ball to counter a change in the defensive formation.

Shotgun An offensive formation where the center will snap the ball back to the quarterback who is standing some seven yards behind him. It is in this formation that the quarterback, if required, can be used as another pass receiver, if the ball is snapped to another back.

Sideline The outside lines running the length of the field, like the touchline on a rugby field. When it is crossed by a ball-carrier the ball is immediately declared dead.

Signals The combination of words and numbers called out by the quarterback to his team mates prior to the ball being snapped. It is used to confirm the play to be used.

Slant A blocking charge by offensive linemen to the left or right to create a gap for the ball-carrier to run through.

Snap The pass between the legs by the center to the quarterback, punter or ball holder (in the case of a field goal attempt). Also known as a hike.

Sound A term used to describe a play that is put into motion without the use of audible signals. On the first sound that is used the center will snap the ball to the quarterbacks.

Spearing An illegal act which involves diving straight at a grounded player helmet first.

Spike When a player who has just scored a touchdown throws the ball to the ground in a celebratory manner. Under NCAA rules the spiking of the football is not permitted.

Spot Pass A pattern used where the quarterback will throw to a particular pre-ordained spot on the field, expecting his receiver to be in that position.

Squib Kick A kick-off designed to travel low over the ground, bouncing as it goes.

Stack A defensive formation where a linebacker will stand directly behind a lineman, as opposed to his more normal stance of being in the gaps between the linemen.

Strongside The side of the offense on which the tight end stands, before the snap of the ball. The tight end, whilst being a linemen, is also an eligible receiver.

Stunting A defensive ploy used by linebackers and linemen who loop around each other to try to penetrate the offensive line. A tactic aimed at confusing the offensive linemen, so that gaps are created for defenders to rush through.

Sweep A running option used by the offense where the running back takes the football from his quarterback and sweeps around the end of the line of scrimmage before making his move upfield.

Time-Out Time during which the game clock is stopped by an official at the request of one of the captains, or the referee. Each team is allowed three time-outs per half.

Touchback When a kick or punt has taken the ball right through the end-zone and out past the dead ball line, the game is re-started again from the receiving team's 20-yard line.

Touchdown Worth six points, a touchdown occurs when either a ball-carrier breaks the plane of the goal line, rushing into the end-zone, or a pass is completed to a receiver standing in the end-zone.

Two Minute Warning In the last two minutes of each half the officials will call an official time-out, and warn both sides that there are only two minutes of play remaining.

Two Minute Offense After the two-minute warning is sounded there are two options open to a team, depending upon whether they are in the lead or behind on points. If they need a score to win they will use a series of passing plays to try to advance up-field. Each pass will be directed to a receiver standing near the sidelines, who will automatically stop the game clock when he goes out of bounds. A team can thus advance up the field using the minimum amount of time. If the team is however in the lead, then they will use plays designed to use up as much of the clock as possible, such as rushing plays up the middle of the field.

Undershift A defensive formation where the linemen shift one place over towards the weak side of the offense. Their aim is to have one defensive lineman unmarked when the ball is snapped.

Unsportsmanlike Conduct As this suggests, the use of foul or abusive language, the persistent violation of the rules, or general 'conduct unbecoming'. In British sports the term 'ungentlemanly conduct' is used.

Weak side The opposite to the strong side. The end of the line without the tight end.

Yardage A distance on the field measured in yards.

Zone A defensive backfield formation where the players are assigned a specific zone or area to patrol. Any offensive player who comes into that zone is their responsibility.

Did You Know

That the Washington Federals' Eric Robinson had the only kick-off return for a touchdown in 1983. Robinson, who led the league in kick-off return averages, returned one for a 94-yard touchdown.

Index

Page numbers in *italics* refer to illustrations, insets or tables.
Players and teams mentioned only in the summary tables (NFL pp 64–70; NCAA pp 93–95; USFL pp 103–106; CFL pp 111–112; high school pp 114–118) will not be found in the index.